WHAT MORE COULD A SOLDIER ASK OF A WAR?

Memoirs Of A World War Two Soldier

Also by A.J. Lane:

It Wasn't Enemy Action, Odhams.

WHAT MORE COULD A SOLDIER ASK OF A WAR?

Memoirs Of A World War Two Soldier

A.J. Lane

The Book Guild Ltd
Sussex, England

The Book Guild Ltd
25 High Street
Lewes, Sussex

First published 1990
© A. J. Lane 1990

Set in Baskerville

Typesetting by Pulsecrown,
Saxmundham, Suffolk.

Printed in Great Britain by
Antony Rowe Ltd.,
Chippenham, Wiltshire.

British Library Cataloguing in Publication Data
Lane, A.J. (Alfred Joseph), 1921 —
What More could a Soldier ask of a War?
1. World War 2. Army operations during. Great Britain.
Army — Biographies
I. Title 940,548141
ISBN 0 86332 488 6

CONTENTS

CONTENTS *continued* ...

This book is dedicated to Queenie

"For me, as for those who have gone before me, the perplexity of the dual philosophy of logical explanation for the pattern of man's evolution and progression or that of phenomenal happenings caused by mysterious forces of the unknown."

A.J. Lane

Soldier RE (European Campaign Winter 1945)
The author aged 24

INTRODUCTION

We had made the most of our last evening together and we enjoyed each other's company greatly. We were three young men who were to be separated after a very close friendship of many years because we were due to obey the national call to serve in HM Forces for war service.

Our evening ended with a discussion about the war and what was likely to happen to us, with each of us contributing views, forecasts and predictions on the likely fate of each other. We parted with a great deal of speculation as to what stories and experiences we might talk about if ever we got together again at the end of it all.

Such was the evening, early in the year 1941, which long afterwards came to mind and served to remind me that perhaps I did, after all, have a story to tell . . .

Let me therefore start at the beginning of the beginning by explaining that somewhere along the south-west coastline of Wales there was — as it was so in my early days — a lonely and lovely stretch of sandy beach which had the descriptive Welsh name of Cefn Sidan. In the English translation it means 'Silk Back.'

It was, as I remember, a sandy strand and golden extension of several miles long; and when the tide was out it was a good half mile wide. The surface of the beach was as firm and flat as a billiard table and had, I believe, on earlier occasions been used for motor cycles etc., speed record attempts and trials. It was somewhere offshore in this area where the intrepid Miss Amelia Earhart descended to become the first woman to fly the Atlantic.

It was as a young teenager that I knew the Cefn Sidan as well as anyone could know it because of the regular beachcombing journeys I made with a bicycle. Over a few years I regularly searched for, and found, pieces of wooden flotsam and jetsam which would be put to good use in those not so prosperous days by my cabinet-maker Dad. Those rough pieces of mahogany and oak etc., which I often found, were quickly turned, moulded or carved into fine items of furniture. My father was one of the old school of cabinet-maker craftsmen who could produce, entirely by hand, some exquisite finished piece of furniture out of what might possibly be an old tree trunk washed up by the sea.

In those days stormy weather was no deterrent to beachcombing either; on the contrary, it was often the most productive time, provided, of course, that you were around to gather the flotsam before it was carried away again by the ebb of the tide.

It was all fine healthy stuff, particularly if you cycled for many miles, being driven along by a good strong wind at your back and then having to return, loaded up to the handlebars, with head down, pedalling or shoving the bike back along those same miles so carelessly covered when wind driven.

It was, I recall, at a point somewhere along this particular stretch of God's own peaceful coastline where I first became 'acquainted with the tainted' — by which I mean those deadly man-made devices associated with deadly man-made wars.

It was at a spot below tall sandbanks, eroded and washed by high spring tides, where I could often find empty shell boxes, shell cases and sometimes even a shell or two. They were relics of World War One that were suddenly exposed by rough seas and thrown up from an old dumping ground which was close to the ruins and overgrown site of a First World War munitions factory.

Brass shell cases could fetch a bob or two even for their scrap value and were worth rummaging around for and dismantling. For a lad who, in a few years' time, would be fighting in World War Two, it was, I suppose, a providential kind of exciting introduction to things warlike — as it was also a fateful preliminary to the mine-lifting, booby trap, etc., experiences of later life.

The ruins of the old munitions factory was also a place I visited quite often. The broken-down old buildings, magazine bunkers, etc., were scattered over a fairly large desolate and unrestricted area, deserted, mysterious and altogether fine rambling territory for a lad who was adventurous and imaginative, a place full of ghosts and echoes of World War One. It was a place in summertime overrun with wild strawberries, blackberries and dewberries. There were skylarks overhead and below the creepy-crawlies in the shape of grass snakes, lizards, mice, etc.

There was one roofless building, I remember, which had tall elderberry bush trees growing inside, and it was here in one afternoon I disturbed the peaceful roost of a golden owl which had a truly enormous wing-span — well-fed, no doubt, on an abundance of creepy-crawlies. I later often dreamed of capturing that feathered beauty and having it stuffed and put into a fine cabinet, made by my old Dad. It was not for the want of trying that I didn't get it that way, for many a trip and many a grab I made, which fortunately for that fine bird's future generations all ended in failure — although I was never to see another bird quite like it again. It was, I suppose, a golden eagle owl.

So, on the subject of birds, it was like the phoenix of Egyptian mythology that a year or two later a new munitions factory arose at the same site and out of the debris of the old.

I was hardly aware of the uneasy political scene in Europe in 1937-39, when it seemed that an ambitious German politician was mainly the cause and reason for it. A fellow named Adolph Hitler was getting too big for his soiled jackboots and was making neighbouring countries nervous. Britain, too, was forced to look to her shaky defences, and hastily began to try to make good the neglect, deficiency and imbalance in military matters. Because of this the new munitions factory was speedily completed. I was fortunate enough to have a short spell of youngster's employment in the construction and building work before it ended to make way for the production of high explosives.

Just a couple of miles away a new airfield was also under construction, and it was here I found new employment as the other ended.

War had already been declared for the start of World War Two, but it was as remote and unreal in our part of the country as it was in most other parts during the early 'phoney war' days.

I was seventeen years old at the outbreak of war, and I remember most clearly the occasion some time later when war, for the first time, became grim reality, suddenly and frighteningly very close at hand. It happened as I worked at the site of the airfield under construction, and it was on the occasion when I found myself idly observing a solitary aircraft circling the sky overhead before seeing it move but a short distance away to circle again the sky above the new Pembrey munitions factory. I heard the explosions and saw the smoke and dust arise as I witnessed what must have been the first — or very earliest — German bombing raid on British soil in World War Two.

The sky raider's stick of bombs, as I was to discover later, killed and injured a number of factory workers. I also discovered that the bombs were dropped around the spot where earlier grew the elderberry bush trees — the place where I had tried so often to capture the great golden owl during my ramblings among the ruins of the old factory.

It was also, in the minutes following the raid, that I heard for the very first time — of what was later to become a great many times — the wailing and chilling sound of an air raid warning siren. I remember on that occasion all the airfield workers were regimentally marched away to some place offering the shelter of high roadside banks and low ditches. I remember also feeling shaken, frightened and insecure in thinking that Jerry, having got away so easily with what I had just seen, could just as easily search us out with his machine-guns. I wanted somehow to strike back, yet knowing that we were nakedly defenceless.

World War Two was upon us, and for me anyway — as a witness to one of the first bombing raids by the Germans on the British Isles — already involved, mentally primed and committed!

I soon joined the local defence unit, 'LDV', 'Home Guard' or 'Dad's Army' as it was differently called, although the latter was something of a misnomer because there were as many youngsters as there were oldsters in those early days of the organization. I joined simply because I wanted a rifle, and to be less defenceless than I felt myself to be in those grim and dangerous times.

Those were days also when it was not at all difficult to be issued with a Lee Enfield type of rifle and cotton type bandolier loaded with plenty of rounds of ammo, with apparently little accountability for their use. For example, one could go shooting rabbits using .303 bullets which could be regarded as good training in the use of firearms. It was, after all, a time when Germans were really expected every day to drop from the skies, or invade from the beaches. But my own shooting sessions were as much a matter of sport as training, for many a weekend was spent on the sand dunes firing out to sea, in competition with two friends of mine. Our targets were bottles, cans, sticks, etc., except when occasionally we would make the long trek to seek the better game to be found on the low-tide sands of the Cefn Sidan. Far out to the seaward side we would find the hulks of old shipwrecks which, according to local folklore, were the result of attacks by a band of villains called 'the Pembrey Hatchetmen' who in the days long ago found profitable ways of luring unwary ships to their doom.

The incoming tide would sweep high over the wrecks, leaving great deep dark pools of sea water in the hulls as the tide receded. It was in such pools where huge sea conger-eels might be found and shot at.

It was a patient game of waiting and watching from the water's edge for the opportunity of a rifle snap-shot as the python-like fish appeared near the surface for sudden and brief moments. Some were monsters of several feet long and of thick girth. They were fearful looking creatures, and not at all the sort one would wish to swim or fish around for in a dark pool. A ferocious looking mouth and teeth, with a great fin-mane along its body made the sport a bit like dragon killing. It really was done for the adventure and rifle skill and not for the prize of succulent fish food which I now know it to be. We would never, in those days, consider eating eels of any kind because they were considered by us — or by me anyway — as sea snakes.

It was, as I then hoped, all good practice to make me a rifle crackshot and sharpshooter which I felt would undoubtedly put me in good stead for any war service I might be persuaded to render. But really my call-up for service in the war was inevitable; it was happening to people of different age groups all the time in 1941 and it would certainly happen to me.

When the time came for me to register and record my preference for one of the three fighting services, I indicated my choice for service in the RAF. It was not to be, however, because when my call-up papers arrived I learned that I was called upon to serve in the Corps of Royal Engineers. For me it might have been worse, as, for example, a call-up to the 'PBI' would have been. So I was not too disappointed at the prospect of being 'a gentleman of the Royal Engineers' — as the correct address was held to be for the British Army's Sappers.

My two pals were rather more disappointed, one being called up for service in the RAF although his preference was for the RN; the other whose preference was for the Royal Engineers had his call-up for the Royal Welsh Fusiliers. The three of us had grown up together and were the closest of friends. I well remember our last evening together before going our different ways, to different lands, to play our different parts in a ghastly war. We leg-pulled as usual and wisecracked about who was best able to survive the difficult days ahead. My taller friend according to my shorter friend 'was only fit to . . .' and would stand no chance. The other, however, claimed that he was the more crafty of the two and therefore more likely to survive than the other whom he considered too cocky and too much of a show off — in fact just the right sort of guy to cop it all too quickly. As for me, well, I was the in between to whom anything could happen . . .

1

In The Early Stage of Soldiering

It was an August day in 1941 when I set off in accordance with my joining instructions for compulsory military service under the War Conscriptions Act.

I was at that time a raw young Welshman who had never before been beyond the Welsh border — and for that matter had never lived away from home before.

It was therefore a significant day for at least one north-bound train passenger who sat alone with all the mixed feelings of bewilderment, excitement, apprehension, etc., of a nineteen-year-old on his way to be a soldier and to fight a war.

My instructions were that I was to report on that day by 23.59 hours to the barracks of 1st Training Regiment RE at Clitheroe in the county of Lancashire.

It was for me, of course, a journey involving several hours of travelling and different train connections along the way. It is true to say that up to that time the only real travelling I had done was no further than to Porthcawl and Barry Island for the occasional trip to the seaside. I was therefore not too wise in the ways of railways routes, timetables etc., added to which was the fact — so often confirmed in later life — that military orders and instructions were not always foolproof, sometimes difficult to obey and often impossible to comply with. Also, in such troubled times, trains and railways had their problems and disruptions, too.

So when I encountered the first snag at the earliest beginning of my military life, I was not to know whether it was the result of ignorance on my part, incompetence on the part of the military or disruption on the railway. What I was to know, much to my dismay and concern, was that I could not get a connecting train for the last leg of my journey which would get me to Clitheroe before the critical midnight hour.

15

It had become clear that having got as far as Accrington — a name and station totally unfamiliar to me then — in reasonably good time, I was unable to proceed further because for some reason there was not another train until well into the morning of the following day.

It should be pointed out that 1941 was a time of blackout, of food and petrol rationing; of harsh wartime restrictions and controls etc., and therefore being stranded in 'the middle of nowhere' at night-time was hardly the good start to service life I had been hoping for.

It was a dilemma which had me worried. I was, after all, a very inexperienced village lad from Wales to whom telephones and telephone numbers in those days were a secret, mysterious and remote kind of communication. I had also heard and read something about the disciplines of the last war concerning army deserters, absentees and the like, and I was disturbed to think that perhaps in this war, too, they could shoot people like me for not properly obeying orders to turn up on time. Maybe there was some fault on my part — although I couldn't see how.

In the circumstances there was little I could do except wander around and about the area of the railway station. It was a gloomy and deserted place and well into night-time as I pondered the problem of reporting a day late and having to prove that I was let down by the train service.

The time was a half hour before midnight when I thought about the possibility of corroboration, witness or proof of my situation, and the idea occurred to me that with luck I might find a policeman or police station to sort the problem out.

I was, I suppose, a little stupid in not thinking earlier about such a course of action, but policemen and police stations had for me always been people and places to avoid, as one would for trouble. Just then, though, I felt that perhaps there were more troublesome people and places than policemen and police stations.

I was soon explaining my situation at the Accrington Police Station to a sympathetic police sergeant whose friendliness made me feel quite at home in the place. A good hot cup of cocoa and a nice warm open-door cell for the night made me fell like an honoured guest — particularly when I was taken around the cells of the different prisoners to see them through the peep-holes in the doors.

My cell bed, I remember, was a wooden one having a fixed wooden pillow, but both were made less uncomfortable by the extra blankets given to me.

So, by courtesy of Accrington Police Constabulary, I was soon settled in 'comfortably' for the night. I was quickly to sleep, but not before thinking that it was altogether a darned peculiar start to my life of military service . . .

The barracks of the RE Training Regiment at Clitheroe, I soon discovered, were large, formerly disused cotton-mill and weaving-shed buildings, reminders of the past glorious, or inglorious, tradition of Lancashire's textile trade and industry. But the tradition, perhaps, had not entirely died out because during the months of recruit training at the place, I could see and hear many a pretty Lancashire lass, with her wooden clogs, clop-clopping her way to and from work along the narrow cobbled streets of Clitheroe. The war, perhaps, had got many of the locals weaving again in some of the smaller factories. They were the friendliest of people who, I remember, had the usual delightful accent and question — by way of opening up a conversation — 'Ar's in't RE's lad?'

Also the expression 'get weaving!' was a military command we young soldiers were to hear a good many times at ITRRE. Those early months of training were, by any standard, a period which made for a pretty hard time. Army pay amounted to ten shillings and sixpence per week, less two shillings and sixpence (an agreed deduction as an allowance for Mum back home, and considered a useful pension if her dear son was killed while on Active Service). Training and exercises, guard duties, spud-bashing duties, mobile column duties, fire duties, air raid precautions and passive air defence duties, escort duties etc., all ensured that free time, or off-duty hours, amounted to almost nil.

The basic training of a soldier of the Royal Engineers, in those days, was probably more comprehensive, tough and longer than that for most other regimental soldiers of the British Army. Besides the basics applicable to all soldiers — weapons, drill, PT, battle training etc. — sappers were generally also trained in most aspects of Military Field Engineering, mines, explosives/demolitions, bridges, roads, water supply etc. The demands of a critical war situation and the generally high casualty rate among operational sappers determined a concentrated basic training slog, which for many a poor RE recruit was more of a murderous hammering. But there were those of us who were privileged to suffer a little less of the regimental grind because of certain priorities given to competitive sport. It transpired that I became involved in a few of the sporting activities, and it is enough to say that I was considered pretty good at one of them. Also my earlier days in the LDV (Home Guard) had given me quite an advantage over the other recruits, especially when it came to rifle shooting. My 'Cefn Sidan' potshot days had certainly helped me with an enthusiasm and skill which, over a certain period of time, was to gain me a number of valuable prizes for regimental shooting. By valuable I mean the ten shilling or (exceptionally) the one pound NAAFI vouchers, which were, of course, more than a week's army pay and gave me luxuries — and a little popularity in the sharing of them — not possible otherwise.

But they were prizes well and truly earned considering some of the ridiculous shooting competitions, courses and programmes devised at ITRRE. The activity seemed more often to be directed towards endurance and obstacle-course training than shooting skills; as for example, having to run a hundred yards in quick time before firing at considerable range, in quick succession, in the standing position with a rifle having a bayonet fixed at the end — while all the time wearing a gas mask! I was never afterwards to find anything near so tough anywhere else. But generally my shooting won through and there were times when I felt a little guilty at being held up as a model recruit during shooting practice and instruction '. . . He's only had the same training, so why can't the rest of you guys do as well? etc. . . .' I had, of course, said nothing about my time and training with the LDV!

But being a rifle crackshot, however — particularly at that early and inexperienced stage of my military life — was something I was later to regret since it was to do me more harm than good. Being selected as one of the Battalion's top four marksmen for the task of zeroing the Battalion's rifles was an honour indeed, particularly as I was but a raw recruit along with the three others who were Senior NCO Instructors. The task was one that took me away from regimental training routines for a six day continuous shooting programme for the purpose of zeroing more than a thousand of the Battalion's rifles. It meant firing and refiring rifles to assist the regimental armourer to check and correct the gunsights for accuracy. For me it was a straightforward task of receiving continuous batches of four rifles, and firing four rounds into each of the target cards placed in front at good distance, in respective order 1-2-3-4. The appropriate target card would then be affixed to the correct rifle for 'reading' in due course by the armourer, who would note the grouping shots and make any adjustment necessary for the weapon's accuracy.

It was therefore an opportunity for me to fire away to my heart's content all the rounds I could ever have wished for — indeed much more so considering my waning enthusiasm after the first couple of days. It was then that I was beginning to make the painful discovery that my constant banging away was more than a little punishing to my ear and shoulder. The rifles of those 1941 days were mostly, if not all, the old Lee Enfield type, with each and every one of them having peculiarities all of their own — some having the kick of a mule and the bang of a cannon no matter how properly handled.

I was perhaps too proud, naïve, inexperienced and subordinate to think of complaining, or to think of sensibly protecting myself with cotton wool plugs for my ears and a pad for my shoulder. Instead I continued to do all that was required of me and suffered in silence that which was anything but quiet.

I returned from my 'zeroing outing' with what seemed to be more penalty than reward. I had completely lost all my enthusiasm for the shooting game, and besides having a sore and bruised shoulder I had become quite deaf. Indeed, my right eardrum had taken such a reverberatory bashing as to become useless and — since I was to do nothing about it in the way of treatment — embarrassing for some time afterwards.

And I think it was the deafness I sustained in this way that caused me the first bit of trouble that was to put me into the 'disciplinary black book', which was to linger for some time. It may well have been a primary cause for me not making the early promotion which had appeared to have been very much in the offing — which, had it happened, would no doubt subsequently have changed my war fate and this my record of it. Little incidents, we discover, can certainly change the course of one's life tremendously, and who is to say whether or not a broken leg today becomes a reason for not getting killed tomorrow?

My particular spot of bother had much to do with a certain bullying sergeant (as they generally all were in the Training Regiments of those days) whose antics were a bit more than I could stomach. Our differences started when I intervened to stop the sergeant's drastic punitive measure of forcing the face of a bed-wetting soldier into the bedside puddle of his own urine. I might have been wrong to do so since I had much less experience than the sergeant in knowing whether or not the soldier concerned was just another one 'trying to work his ticket.' But at the time I felt sorry for the pathetic little man who looked to be twice the sergeant's age.

The barrack rooms at ITRRE were tightly packed with recruits who, in the matter of living and sleeping space, had little option but to reach for the ceiling on the high three-tiered bunk-beds filling the place. Fortunately for me and the soldier just below me, the bed-wetter had the bottom section of the bunk; and in the circumstances it was good to know that water was heavier than air and that nature's gravitational pull was unlikely to change direction! The usual puddle on the floor, and the culprit's early morning activity in mopping it up, was something I found disgusting and hardly tolerable within the constricted bed area. But even so, I could not watch and stand idly by on one particular morning as the raging sergeant began forcing the unfortunate fellow's head to the floor with the expressed intention of 'rubbing the filthy little b---d's face in it'! The tip of the offending soldier's nose had just about made it when I felt compelled to move to apply a strong head lock and twist on the sergeant to prevent further maltreatment of the pathetic character who I believed suffered genuinely from a weak bladder. He had earlier confessed that it was a malady which had led to his two divorces.

I considered that my own rough handling of the sergeant was a necessary counter to prevent the sergeant 'going over the top' in his manhandling of a subordinate. But my restraining action, however, was hardly the kind to be appreciated by a Training Regiment NCO of the rank of sergeant. Such military people of such military establishments are gods who can do no wrong — as the sergeant seemed set on proving. He was, though, hardly in a position to bring a charge against me for that particular piece of action.

But it was soon obvious that he was all for getting his own back in other ways because early next morning I was awakened by violent blows to the stomach from the fist of the sergeant. It was reveille, and because of my hearing problem I had not heard the usual awakening cries of 'Wakey-wakey. Rise and shine!' It was obviously an excuse for the sergeant to put in his vicious thumps.

To be awakened in such a manner was not in the least acceptable, and after nursing an extremely painful midriff for some time, I resolved to see to it that he would not get away with anything like it again.

Reveille of the following day saw me prepared and waiting for my own bit of retaliation. With half-closed eyes and a pretence at still being asleep, I was horizontally poised and ready to meet the likely threat of a second dose of the bullying sergeant's 'belly treatment.'

The trap was set, and the sergeant was clearly intent on a repeat performance as he climbed, perched and delivered his first blow. His stance and face were perfectly positioned to receive the full impact of a beautifully timed kick with the instep of my right foot, which landed in the region of his big mouth. It was a full-blooded wallop which sent him somersaulting, as if from a catapult, to land with a heavy crash to the floor.

It was several minutes before he got to his feet, pale-faced and shaken as he then went off without a murmur. As I watched him painfully depart the scene I was sure that he was unlikely to chance his fist on my stomach ever again.

The incident, however, was one that was to do my budding promotion prospects no good at all, and this was made clear to me by my OC when I found myself 'on the carpet' soon afterwards. I was fortunate indeed when the OC very generously gave me the benefit of doubt when I defended myself by claiming that the collision between the sergeant's face and my foot was an accidental contact as I sprang out of bed half asleep, etc. Dismissing the case the OC remarked that although he was doing so his reservations were such as to put a serious question against the very good reports passed to him by my training party officer who had me scheduled for special cadre training. Such considerations would be scrapped, I was told, and instead I should have to watch my step in future. (Perhaps he meant my instep!)

Anyway, I was not the type with any great inclination or ambition to burst rapidly through the ranks to make Field Marshal; and I was, I suppose, more pleased than disappointed at not being considered for a possible permanent staff post at the Training Regiment. I was, too, more a philosopher than the ambitious type, and was not therefore unduly worried about falling out of favour for a while. It could be hard sometimes to please authoritative military minds.

But, of course, army disciplinarians of those days — as with most other days and places — were of a kind that could make life even harder if they were not pleased, and I was careful not to add to the hardships of my basic training by invoking any further displeasure of those in command and authority at ITRRE.

Life, therefore, was not very exciting as the months of basic sapper training passed slowly by, taking me into the North Country winter of 1941. But winter or no winter I was more than anxious to leave the place, such a military establishment could commend itself to the ordinary soldier only for its primary purpose of recruit training, in which it was most effective. It was clearly planned and ensured that the ordinary soldier's terror of such a military training depot was greater than that of serving elsewhere — even on battlefields. It was a matter of amazement to me that in such a comparatively short time so many men from different walks of life — the butcher, the baker and candlestick-maker etc. — could be received, trimmed, moulded or hammered into a well recognized and defined conformation generally known as 'Army Standard Requirement', being little more than obedient figures or numerals in a vast military war machine.

With the end of basic training at ITRRE, some soldiers were lucky in having postings from the place quickly, while others, like myself, were kept waiting for a couple of months or so. But it was not exactly a doldrum period, and I was to find myself regimentally employed in some peculiar duties which, I suppose, had some part to play in my development and history as a wartime soldier. One of the duties may have had something to do with finding an answer to a peculiar kind of dilemma on the part of somebody in command. It might have been that some form of revolt was threatened by a certain intake of new recruits, made up mainly of coloured personnel from Jamaica and other parts of the West Indies. The problem, as I was to gather later, was that, rightly or wrongly, they felt that they had been conned into the British Army, and were showing a tendency to violent resentment about it all. The story they were to give to me was that back in their own countries they had been policemen, farmers, technicians, etc., who had responded to a British recruitment campaign for personnel from the British Dominions to work in Britain's War Production Front, in factories and elsewhere (no doubt in some way to make up for her depleted manpower because of service in HM Forces). But apparently, after arriving in England, many individuals and groups of West Indians were considered unsuitable for the intended civilian employment because of the cultural differences in behaviour, language, literacy, etc., by the British authority who conveniently directed the rejects for military enlistment in the British Army. To what degree the situation had been misrepresented or unfairly enforced I was not to know, but I was soon to know that there was a great deal of unrest among the West Indians, who loved the sun and freedom too much to take kindly to the cold climate and disciplines at ITRRE.

Their resentment was apparent in the fact that many of them were constantly in and out of the guardroom punishment cells because of assaults on NCOs and refusal to obey orders. Most of them were of fine physique and, when they were not in detention, they would usually indulge themselves in the sporting activities of the gymnasium, where I befriended a few of them during boxing training and sparring sessions. Such sport was the only aspect of army life in which they seemed to have been interested, obviously because there were so many good boxers amongst them. One in particular was reported to have been an ex-contender for a world boxing championship. He was an ugly fellow with extraordinary long arms and was known to have a tendency from time to time to go berserk within the barracks — when it would take almost a regiment of armed guards to put him securely behind bars!

I could therefore understand the reluctance of officers and NCOs to have anything to do with the wild men of the West Indies, who in turn seemed to have their own justified reluctance in accepting orders from such alien authority. They could not be treated or handled in the same way as Britishers, and somebody, therefore, had the problem of how best to accommodate them in such a situation.

It must have been the RSM, or someone else of rank, who cottoned on to the fact that I was on good terms with the rebellious coloured soldiers (coloured being a matter of degree since it varied considerably from dark to light-skinned) and could therefore be useful as the one Britisher they would tolerate and hopefully work under — perhaps even be guided and advised by! Having regard to past experience, a non-ranker like myself would be the best answer to getting them away from the barracks and perhaps employed in some useful work?

It was a well considered scheme which resulted in my being instructed by the RSM. I was to be answerable to him for our 'working party' of twenty-five. Officially we were to move around the nearby countryside on local defence tasks: i.e. the maintenance and improvement of dugouts, trenches, weapon pits — some of which might be camouflaged, extended, re-vetted etc. Unofficially the main purpose of the assignment was to keep a party of 'misfits' happily away from the barracks, where they were considered dangerously troublesome.

Rations, transport and all the necessary gear were laid on daily and, for my part, I had little choice but to make the best of a situation which allowed me more freedom than regimental duty within the training area of the barracks would allow. The West Indians were also more disposed to be outside the barracks than within, despite the fact that it was well into wintertime.

It snowed on our very first outing together, and I remember the way they danced around like children to catch and examine the snowflakes as they fell and appeared for the very first time of their lives. But it was, however, a novelty that soon passed with the many more snowy and colder days to come. They were, of course, more naturally evolved for the sunny side of the world, and were prone to shivering miserably after an hour or two in the biting winter air of Lancashire. Fortunately that particular problem was solved when I found a large factory boiler room where we could all be sheltered and stretched out in a comfortable position above the great lagged boilers. The gift of our surplus rations was enough to keep the boilerman happy.

But as the days passed I was aware that despite my efforts to help out in every way I could, there remained among many of the West Indians a suspicion, resentment, discontent and even downright hatred towards anything and everything to do with the British Army. Although I got on rather well, as I thought, with most of them, there were a half dozen who were positively mean and moody, with two more in particular who could best be described as evil characters in no way to be trusted. The difficult ones were a group apart in the way they usually separated themselves from the main body as if to whisper and plot amongst themselves. Indeed, so suspicious was I of the way they carried on that I was fairly certain that they were planning somehow to do a bunk in order to try to get back to their own country.

For my part I was little concerned as to whether or not they would carry out such a plan, since I felt sure that the RSM and his like back in the Training Depot would be more relieved than displeased. But to some degree I was sympathetic to their cause after hearing them continually complain that they should not, by rights, be in the British Army. Who could blame them anyway for taking such action if what they complained of was true?

But the truth of the matter was that something more serious and alarming was brewing, and it was only a matter of luck that I got to know of it. Although I was suspicious that something was afoot, I would never have imagined what it was the ringleaders were really up to had it not been for the discovery I made of a hidden haversack containing about a hundred rounds of live .303 ammo. I was to learn later (from someone whose trust I had) that it was a cache, intended by the evil ones of the group, for use in a forthcoming 'demonstration' directed against the officers' mess and the NCOs' and Sergeants' mess at the Training Regiment.

The rounds could possibly have been stolen from the pouches of other soldiers or more likely whipped from ammo boxes at the firing ranges, all too carelessly left unguarded at times. But, for everybody's sake, it was a matter to be carefully dealt with, and I found the right tactic and opportunity for effectively getting rid of the ammo by tossing amounts of the stuff into the factory furnace. This I did secretly, although I was well aware that suspicion would fall upon myself soon enough. In my favour, of course, was the fact that nobody could make a song and dance about it all.

But I was not to get away with it completely unscathed, however, because a short time later, almost without warning, I was grabbed around the neck by the long powerful arms of the boxing 'gorilla' of the group, who clearly had every intention of dishing it up to me. Some West Indians were quite good-looking fellows, but not the fella who took hold of me. His was a primitive and primordial ugly face made more ugly by many a pugilistic battle, to exhibit a kind of facial billboard displaying a gluttony for punishment both in the receiving and giving of it. I had no wish to tangle with such a man, but as he drew back his reputably fearful fist the best I could do was to draw back my own much less reputable, but quite deadly, right steel-studded army boot capable of snapping his shinbone like a piece of candy stick. Fortunately, before the blood began to flow — mine almost certainly — the intervention of a few 'old faithfuls' shouting 'No, no! Him good fella!' saved the day. I was released by a vicious push which sent me flying and tumbling for several yards, but with nothing physically worse than a couple of bruises around my neck.

Soon afterwards, I found ways and means of getting different work to do, and it was a relief in the circumstances to part company with the West Indians, especially the nasties of the bunch. Pressed men to the fighting services they may have been, but then — as I was to reflect later — so were an awful lot of others of many nationalities, in the international crisis of such a war, my sympathy had somehow become much less than it had been.

I mentioned nothing to the RSM, or to anyone else, about finding the illegal hoard of ammo, the consequent destruction of which may, indeed, have prevented a blood bath within the

Training Regiment. I could only convey a view that such a malcontented lot should not have rifles and rounds made so easily available to them.

Thereafter I had little or no contact with the group, and consequently had no idea as to what became of them and their complaints.

But I was soon to learn that my new lines of duty had their own kinds of difficulties also, with that of sometimes escorting military prisoners being as hazardous as any. Army absentees, deserters, offenders, etc., were usually held in civilian police custody until handed over to a military authority and establishment secure enough to detain them as necessary for trial etc. Such incidents were never-ending, with individual cases varying from the good guy going AWOL to see a sick or dying mother to the criminally desperate bad guy always on the run from military service and punishment. It was a duty I was detailed for on many occasions, and although I remember each and every case as having an incident of some kind or other, it was the very last of my escort trips I remember best — as being the worst!

It was a dark winter's evening as 'the old corporal' and myself set off to collect a prisoner from the Burnley Police Station. As far as we were concerned it was just another escorting mission involving just another unknown prisoner. But rules and regulations governing the practice and procedures for escorting such prisoners (absentees, deserters, etc.) had recently been changed by army authority so that dress order was only belt and bayonet to be worn and carried with a soldier's battledress uniform. Hitherto it had been rifle, waistbelt with pouches supported by shoulder straps, with a clip of five rounds of ammo in one of the pouches. The change, so it was said, was because so many soldiers were getting shot trying to escape from custody and escorts. Such a disarming change hardly favoured the escorting guards in any awkward situations with tough and dangerous escortee prisoners, and on this particular occasion, despite a request to the RSM, we were off on our way without the set of handcuffs which normally would have made things easier and more secure (perhaps just then there was a shortage of handcuffs for some reason?). But we were not in a position to argue with the RSM, who pointed out that 'the two of us should be able to handle just one of them.'

The view was somewhat different, however, when we arrived at Burnley Police Station where a burly and surly police sergeant expressed grave doubts as to whether we could manage such a bad and slippery prisoner. The sergeant explained that the guy we had come to collect was a persistent army deserter who had escaped from custody on at least two earlier occasions, the last time breaking escort by jumping from a moving train. The fact that we had no firearms or handcuffs drew the pessimistic view from the sergeant that he could not, in the circumstances, see us getting back with the prisoner that night. My reply to the police officer was that if the matter was potentially as difficult as suggested then the best answer was for us to borrow a set of the police station handcuffs. But the request was one that was flatly refused on the grounds that station cuffs had been lent in similar circumstances before, never to be returned. The result was acute shortage, and consequently there was to be no more lending of such vital police equipment — to the army in particular! He could, said the sergeant, only offer advice on the best way of securely holding and restraining the prisoner, which was that I should take a tight grip with my right hand on the loosened sleeve cuff of his left arm, with the corporal having his left arm linked through the prisoner's right arm. After a quick demonstration of the gripping and grasping method to be used, the sergeant then instructed one of his constables to bring the prisoner from his cell for the handover.

I expected to see the usual weedy, inadequate, deserter type of young soldier, but instead I was surprised to find a big, beefy thirty-year-old who gave the impression of being a good-natured and good-humoured type of fellow as he grinned, shrugged his shoulders and behaved almost apologetically when standing in front of a bellowing and threatening police sergeant.

We left the police station with severe words of warning still issuing from the grim-faced sergeant to the prisoner about his behaviour for this occasion, and woe betide him if he should be brought back to the same place again, etc.

It was a cold frosty night as we set off with our man held firmly in the manner suggested by the police sergeant. Holding on to a fellow-being in such a way was for us a most unpleasant duty and, after travelling for some distance in silence along a dimly lit road that took us in the direction of Burnley Railway Station, I ventured to say a few friendly words by asking the prisoner how long he had been held at the police station. The response I got was hardly the kind I expected or appreciated. I remember vaguely that we were walking past a wall, railings or barrier of some sort to the right of us when it happened. The prisoner lunged viciously to the right to slam the corporal's head and body against the barrier and in doing so the nasty man in the middle pulled his right arm free to deliver a most savage punch to my face. It was a manoeuvre, timed and executed to perfection, that had the corporal and myself dazed, if not completely stunned for a few moments. For my part, I went down as if pole-axed — but remarkably I still held tight to the man's sleeve cuff with my right hand. But my desperate attempt to hold fast did me little good. On the contrary, as I was lying face upwards on the ground, he found it easy to break my grip by leaning over me to smash a downward blow to my face. It was a second vicious blow that left me spitting blood from a few loosened teeth. I struggled to my feet to see the 'ex-prisoner' galloping away at full pelt. I shouted instinctively, 'Stop or I'll fire!' without being fully acquainted with the fact that I no longer carried a rifle (a fact I was a great deal happier about later, for such was my anger at being the victim of such viciousness that undoubtedly I would have shot him there and then. I could understand afterwards much of the reason why rifles and rounds were no longer carried on such duties.). As it was, I unsheathed my bayonet and gave chase. The road was icy and, by the overhead dimmed and hooded corner street lighting, I saw him slip and fall as he tried to negotiate a side street turning. He got to his feet quickly, but not before I let fly with my bayonet from less than a dozen yards away. It missed him by the merest fraction of an inch, and I was as lucky as he was that I was not left with a 'stuck pig' on my hands and conscience. He got away in the darkness of the night, and I hastened back to find the corporal still badly shaken by the wallop received to his head when shoved so violently. We both recovered quickly to realize that we had little choice in the matter of our next course of action.

We had left the police station less than twenty minutes

earlier, and were both feeling something less than returning heroes as we made our way back to the place. The police sergeant took one look at us as we got through the doorway and shook his head. 'Yes I know. You don't have to tell me!' said he, communicating at the same time a tone mix of disgust, acceptance and expectancy for the occurrence. I felt sufficiently upset and injured to be somewhat bold and insubordinate to the sergeant by telling him that if he was that clever in knowing what would happen then why the Hell did he not provide us with handcuffs? It was a question he preferred not to answer, and instead adopted a more helpful attitude, in advising us as to what we should do to try to recover our lost prisoner.

The escapee was a person known by the police to have lived and lodged in the district during his marriage to a local girl, and after the marriage breakdown (a reason given in his defence, for his aberrant 'off the rails' behaviour, at his eventual court-martial held at Barnard Castle in Durham). The sergeant considered it likely that 'Big O' had gone to ground at one of his old haunts in the district, and he suggested that the corporal and myself accompany one of his standby plain-clothes officers to do the necessary rounds to search the likely premises. The police themselves would require search warrants — difficult to obtain at such short notice — for such an operation, whereas we, the army, as represented by the corporal and myself, required no such warrants under martial law to go in search of an army deserter into any building.

For my part, I was anxious to do all that was necessary to find the man and therefore satisfactorily to complete my duty. It has to be a blow to the pride of any self-respecting soldier escort to suffer and admit the loss of a prisoner in such circumstances; and to have to report back to the Depot RSM empty handed was a most negative something to be most positively avoided. One might say that excuses are not so readily given or taken in the best of disciplined military circles!

The plain-clothes policeman was soon on hand to direct us to possible locations in our search for the absconder. The man's wife still lived in the area and it was to her place of dingy residence where we first made our way. It was a terrace house in which she rented a couple of upstairs rooms. The door was opened for us by the landlady who, after being told quietly of our business, told us that she had not seen the man we were looking for, and that it was a different man who was upstairs in bed with the estranged wife at that moment. Her definite tone of voice was a good enough reason for us to doubt the matter and we dashed upstairs to find the woman and her considerably younger companion both asleep in bed. We woke them to question them about the runaway soldier, but it was soon apparent that they knew nothing. Indeed they were both quickly out of bed, being not so much concerned about their nudity in our presence than the fact that the husband was on the loose. They had thought him to be securely locked away, and they were obviously scared of being found together. In their state of agitation when we left them they could hardly be described as a loving couple.

Our next visit, as directed by our policeman guide, was to the house where the hunted man was known to have been at one time in digs. We knocked and waited impatiently as an elderly woman shuffled around at the window before opening the door to us. She appeared to be a friendly old dear who seemed sympathetic to our cause, willing and ready to cooperate with our demand to search the house although she had not, she said, had sight of her ex-lodger for quite some time.

Whilst my companions held watch to the front and back of the house I went inside to be shown around by the woman. I felt rather awkward and embarrassed at disturbing the old lady late at night, and, because she was so cooperative in every way, I regarded the matter as a formality and simply took a quick look into each of the rooms before apologizing for putting her out in such a way. But as I left the place I was not to know then (until later at his court-martial) that I had been completely fooled by the sweet-talking old lady who at the time of 'innocently' showing me an 'unoccupied' bedroom was well aware that her ex-lodger was hiding there in the wardrobe.

Our search for the rest of the night ended at the suggestion of the policeman who — since our return by train to our unit was by that time out of the question — kindly proposed to help us get fixed up in the way of bed and breakfast. He knew a couple of addresses where, he said, he was fairly sure the persons he had in mind would oblige. True to his word, we were duly fixed up with surprisingly little fuss and bother considering the imposition at such a late hour at night. With the corporal and myself being placed at separate addresses, it was agreed we would meet around nine in the morning at the police station before returning to unit. There could be fresh developments in the meantime perhaps?

And fresh developments there were indeed; rather over-fresh, and of a kind I least expected or would have wished for considering my tired mind and bruised body just at that particular time. The problem I soon faced after entering the house was that my host for the night was an elegant and cultured forty-year-old bachelor who from the start was much too nice to me. The accommodation was near perfect, with everything about the house being tasteful, neat and tidy. The only snag was that my host's personal attention to me was more than I would have wished for just then, and to avoid further embarrassment I soon made to get ready for bed.

But rest and sleep were not easy to come by. The moods of both of us were very much in contrast, with the man of the house being in good humour, fine fettle and with time to tease and talk. I on the other hand — after what for me had been a bad night — was worried, tired and still suffering the sore effects of some hefty blows to the region of my mouth and jaw. I was in no way receptive to his advances and overtures when he followed me to my bed, to sit on it and to rest or move his hand on the bedclothes above my thighs. It was perhaps politeness and some naïvety which prevented me from more bluntly showing my distaste and irritation with him when he proposed that we sleep together. Instead I successfully contrived an easier way to get him out of my bedroom by suggesting a drink of tea or cocoa. I had noticed a bolt on the bedroom door and this I quickly secured as soon as the 'queer' fellow was on the other side of it.

But it was apparent a few minutes later that his ardour and expectation were not so easily diminished by the barrier of a securely locked door between us, and behind which he was to spend much time demanding, coaxing and threatening to no avail. Eventually he could only give up, when I was allowed to sleep in peace. Before I did so I couldn't help thinking what a funny sort of person and place to be taken to on such a night.

When morning came my host was a rather more pleasant character who offered a simple but sincere apology before preparing a really smashing breakfast for us both. It was an occasion when I was better disposed to chuckle to myself as I watched him setting out the meal so meticulously and expertly, wearing a lace-trimmed apron (or pinafore) as he hummed and sang the while. No housewife could have done better, and he obviously was the true 'Bachelor Gay'!

Arriving as arranged back at the police station, I was to discover that the corporal and myself would not after all be returning to our depot 'empty handed.' Another soldier — a deserter from the Royal Inniskilling Fusiliers — had a short time earlier been brought in to the station, where conveniently we were available to escort him to the custody of the military establishment at Clitheroe.

And so it was not long afterwards that my time at Clitheroe came to an end with a posting to a Field Company RE at Maidstone in the county of Kent. ITRRE was a place I was more than happy to leave behind — but I was not to know then that ahead of me were worse places and nastier experiences! Perhaps a damaged ear, a cracked chin and a good bit of throttling were a sample taste of the nice little feasts to come?

2

There Are Those Who Have Guardian Angels

My posting away from the Training Regiment took me into my secondary stage of soldiering and if, so to speak, I had been just a little bit in the wars at Clitheroe, then I was to find myself progressively more so soon after my posting to the Field Unit, RE, in Kent. I would, though, still have some time to wait before getting into the big one — the real war — which, for those of us who were home-based soldiers at the time, was the distant conflict on a foreign battlefield. In the meantime I would have to endure and survive a few more preliminaries to the big one. There are, after all, the dangers of the great battles abroad and those of the little wars back home, with luck or misfortune having the usual part to play in those with which one is involved. In my case I was to be very lucky, or even in some way perhaps blessed!   Here then — in order to give a certain perspective and direction to the following chapters — it may be said that in war death is obviously a close companion of the battle-hardened and weary soldier. He who has sufficiently experienced the Hell of many close combats will have 'died' a few deaths. At the very least he would have anticipated death or dying often enough somehow mentally to anaesthetize himself as a preparation for the reality of death, or near death, if and when it comes. For most warriors we may suppose that fear in battle is not so much about if and when one dies, but rather about how and where one gets killed. My own experience makes me think not so much that soldiers die in battle, but rather how they die. Natural and certain it must be that on every battlefield a simple and silent philosophy prevails: 'if we have to go, then, please God, let us go as quickly and painlessly as possible.'

But military combatants know well enough that the fortunes of war are seldom, if ever, kind and that they are a great deal more cruel to some than to others. It would seem to be altogether a providential matter that there are those who have been chosen for the deadly fate while others are allowed to have the most amazingly charmed life.

I should, I suppose, put myself in the latter category since it is true to say that I was destined to have my own skirmishes with death, with some quite remarkable escapes. Indeed, there were to be early incidents in my military life — before my battlefield service began — that gave me reason to believe that I was being protected more by divine intervention than by mere chance. I was therefore to make my later arrival on the scene of battle with more confidence and reason than most in thinking that there are those who have Guardian Angels and that I was lucky enough to be one of them.

I should perhaps clarify what I mean by 'remarkable escapes' so as to make clear that my belief was a sincere one. There were, in particular, three incidents which happened within a comparatively short time before I embarked for overseas service. There were, of course, other incidents, minor scrapes, escapes etc., but I think that the particular three incidents are worth recalling as being good examples to show that I must surely have had some good angels taking care and watching over me.

The first happened during a particularly severe training exercise sometime early in the month of December. 'EX SPINACH' was aptly named for the very good reason that it was surely intended to test to the full the endurance limits of the Bailey Bridge — mine-lifting — demolition (etc.) teams of REs. The exercise was indeed tough in that for the seven days or so of the exercise period there was little food or sleep, with an overdose of work of the heaviest kind. (I find it difficult to imagine anything harder than humping heavy bridging equipment, often for long periods and distances, wallowing in mud.)

From my lowly view of military affairs as a young sapper, it was ordered that it was the active part of one unit to construct several kinds of Bailey Bridge (pontoon, pier, wet gap, dry gap etc.) and the part of another unit to follow behind dismantling the bridges and reloading the equipment — a task carried out mainly at night, and in the darkness of a Britain under enforced 'blackout' regulations.

For my part, I was detailed, together with a dozen of so other soldiers, to be detached from my own regular unit and attached for the duration of the exercise to some other similar, but unfamiliar, unit who were to be the 'dismantling' outfit. So it was that at the height of the exercise I found myself slithering around in mud and slush at the site of a Bailey pontoon bridge. The river, so far as I could tell, was either the River Thames or the River Wey. I recollect feeling at the time that I was not too far distant from Guildford, though the confusion of a night exercise can too easily distort direction and information. What I do remember most clearly is that the river appeared to be almost bursting its bank as if in flood, and dangerously fast-flowing. Conditions could hardly have been more severe. We were cold, hungry and weary — and the time was around midnight.

I had made a quick visit to the 'gents', the wheel of a nearby vehicle, and then returned to the water's edge to find a commotion being made by a couple of soldiers standing on a pontoon. I quickly understood that somebody's feet had been fouled by one of the many ropes lashing around, and that the somebody had just disappeared into the dark swirling waters.

Just then I thought of nothing except to try and save the unfortunate and unseen somebody, who might well be trapped by a rope. Impulsively I jumped into the water. I was heavily clad in winter clothing, with army boots, a cigarette in my mouth and a cap on my head. I shall refer to my forage cap later.

I remember striking the icy water with a spluttering, shivering gasp that almost shook the life out of me at the outset. I felt myself going down some considerable depth, being unable to rise to the surface because of the sodden weight of clothing, also because of the extra weight and struggles of a body which suddenly, frantically and quite miraculously attached itself to me in the murky depth of the water.

I was close to drowning myself at that point and it was fortunate indeed that the struggling body gave up much of the struggle and I was able to detach the right side of my own body. My left arm, however, was held fast in a drowning man's desperate grip. Somehow — perhaps by the kindness of the Almighty — I managed to reach the surface with an unconscious passenger in tow, held by his own frozen grip of the sleeve of my left arm.

I found myself swimming as best I could in the pitch blackness of night. We had been carried out to the mainstream of the river and I was totally lost for direction. I had always considered myself a fairly strong swimmer but at this point I was fast losing the battle for both of us. The Almighty was truly on our side that night because, when I was sure that my life was at an end, suddenly a light was beamed from the river bank to search us out. Someone had been struck with the glorious idea and sense to shine the headlight of a motor-cycle on to the water in the somewhat forlorn hope that we might somewhere be around. We were spotted by a group of four or five soldiers who moved with the motor-cycle on the bank downstream, keeping pace with us, ready to fish us out if and when we could make the bank.

The river was deep, and the bank slippery and treacherous, and I could gradually make out that the group had chain-linked themselves to the water's edge, with a boat-hook to the fore.

I remember the nightmare effort to get within striking distance of the boat-hook; of my near fatal failed attempt to grasp it at the first desperate moment, when I again came near to disappearing altogether. My second attempt to get to the boat-hook was the truly 'in the nick of time' lifesaver. I was hauled on to the river bank hardly aware that another body was locked on to my own. It could only be truly amazing if there was any spark of life left in the unfortunate passenger after being under water for so long.

There was a great deal of dither and panic around two prostrate bodies on the river bank, and I was dimly aware of figures all around pumping and slapping like mad in a frenzied effort to get some life back. They were obviously unaware of who was who in the confused situation. The resuscitation, the right way and the wrong way, activity continued for some time until someone had the sense to realize that in any case we would die of exposure if we were not moved quickly out of the wet and icy conditions. Someone remembered seeing a hotel somewhere in the neighbourhood, and we were duly transported — by what means I cannot recall — to better surroundings by far.

I awoke at around two or three o'clock in the afternoon, having little or no recollection of events in the meantime. I felt well and comfortable, for the hotel was a grand place indeed, considering the hardships of the exercise. I was later informed that I was visited by a medical doctor and two officers during the night. The doctor — so I was told — had spent the night fighting desperately for the life of the other guy, and 'pumping out buckets of water.' The fellow had been taken to hospital alive but critically ill. He was to remain in hospital for many weeks.

I was to learn that the person in question was a certain 'Tommy S' who, strangely enough, was a soldier from my own unit, on detachment like myself. I knew him only slightly, and then only because he had been a batman to our Major OC some time earlier. I learned also that he was a non-swimmer and that he came from Chichester.

(The rest of the story is hardly relevant to the present chapter's main theme. It should however be told as being hopefully of some further interest.)

During my stay at the hotel for a day or so, I was visited by an Army Padre whose main mission seemed to be to thank and praise me for what I had done. He was generous enough to tell me that he had gathered that 'Tommy S' would have undoubtedly drowned had it not been for my action.

The exercise ended within a day or two and I quickly rejoined my own unit. I remember being questioned briefly by my OC upon my return about the 'Tommy S' mishap. I must have been somewhat over-modest in making light of my own part in the matter because the discussion was mainly around questions such as 'why was no one issued with regulation kapok life-jackets (in accordance with Military Standing Orders for wet bridging operations, etc.)? Why was there no safety boat? Where was Captain X at the time? How could such a thing happen with so many people around?'

The OC was a good man and a fine officer, but he was obviously not particularly well-informed of the circumstances of the matter, which clearly had been completely out of his control.

Thereafter there was no further reference to the matter except for the occasion, a few days later, when I had to account to the SQMS for the loss of my forage cap, referred to earlier, which had disappeared when I jumped into the river for 'T.S.'. I tried quietly to explain the circumstances for the lost cap to the SQMS, a bald little man who was a long-serving regular soldier, but who would have none of it. He insisted on my paying for the lost item of kit through the usual procedure of AB64 (part II) debit entry. My protestations were to no avail — perhaps because there was no easy way of squaring his store account book with such dubious explanations — and to take the delicate matter further might well make me look a fool, particularly among people so remote from the incident.

So it was that I was forced to pay for a small item of kit lost in the struggle to save a man's life! I received no recognition or award of any kind by the military, other than that by the friendly Padre mentioned earlier. I could not but wonder whether the situation would be a great deal different had I been 'Major X' or 'Captain B.'

There was however a somewhat happier sequel when, many months later, I received two visitors to my dingy barrack room. 'T.S.' had come to see me with his newly-wed bride. Tommy — whom I had never personally met before — came to thank me for my part in saving him from drowning. He and his wife had brought as a gift for me, a very valuable pair of gold cuff-links, since lost in the bedlam conditions of war and battle. It seemed that they often talked of coming to see me earlier, but had decided on getting married first. The happy couple left me to start their honeymoon journey. I have never seen or heard of them since. I went overseas not long afterwards and we obviously went our different ways.

I found it hard to forget the injustice of paying for a lost item of kit in such circumstances, but I was more than happy to know that it was, after all, but little price to pay for helping to save the life of such a fine fellow who so very nearly had a very watery grave.

Above all I shall remember how, in my own moments of darkness, close to death — almost without hope — how a light arrived on the water mercifully to allow me to live.

The second incident concerned a tragic accident. It was one I was to remember for a long time, not only because of the sad consequence for someone I very much liked, but also because it made me feel that I was somehow fatefully privileged, and that from that time onwards I should be grateful to 'somebody up there' for again saving my life, very much against the odds.

It happened in the lovely, peaceful country of Kent. We were getting ready to move out of our more permanent camp of Nissen huts to set up a bridging camp for a fortnight's 'Wet bridge' training at a river near a small place called Pangbourne. Kits were packed and soldiers were waiting for the arrival of vehicles which were to travel in convoy over a distance of many miles.

A few last minute jobs and details included receiving a Bren (machine) gun together with a box of magazines from the platoon storeman. Instructions were that as our section vehicle was to be the tail-end vehicle in the convoy, the gun would be alert and ready for protection against possible air raid attack. German aircraft in Britain's skies were not then so uncommon that we could afford to take chances by travelling unprotected.

The storeman explained that the magazines in the carrier box were loaded each with twenty-eight rounds of live .303 bullets, and that an extra live loaded magazine was readily available for the possibility of immediate action. The storeman then placed the Bren gun and magazine box under the bed nearest to the door at the end of the hut. The loose magazine was placed on top of the bed.

A shout from outside the hut indicated that the kit, bedding, tools, etc., truck had arrived, and that the kit etc., could be loaded. As always, it was a signal for the mad scramble, by the Section's twelve men, to see who could obtain and best and most secure spots for their personal kit etc., on the vehicle. It was all too often the case that the last items of kit to be placed on top of the pile were anything but safe since there was a tendency sometimes for it to be 'bumped off' as it travelled separately and unaccompanied.

With equipment and kit safely loaded, it was then again a case for some of us to wait around inside the hut for the arrival of the truck which was to carry the section troops.

A Nissen hut was anything but a spacious and comfortable building for the living accommodation of twelve soldiers. In size, at most, it was about six paces wide and perhaps double that in length. There were entrance doors at both ends with a bed placed crossways on either side of the doors, more beds on both sides down the middle, making a total of twelve beds in all. Two wooden tables, one at each end, were placed a few yards or so from the entrances.

In the few moments remaining before our final departure, I found myself in leg-pulling conversation with a close friend of mine. He had, on the evening of the previous day, been on a drinking binge, and it was I who had got him safely back to barracks and comfortably put to bed. I joked with him about the matter as I stood facing him, with my hands gripping the edge of the table behind me. Also behind me, a yard or two from the table, was the bed under which was the Bren gun — as yet only handled by the storeman who had placed it there.

The fellow I laughed and joked with was merely a couple of feet away from me. He was in a sideways position whilst stooping slightly to strap together his small pack.

A jovial light-hearted moment was suddenly transformed into a time of Hellish terror and deadly tragedy. It was without warning that I was suddenly struck the most violent blow to the back of my head. I was aware of explosions and flashes of fire passing around my head as I was viciously struck to the ground as if by a giant sledgehammer. As I fell I was aware that the person I had been joking with had been hit by whatever it was that doled out such awful violence. Although considerably stunned and dazed I found myself trying to get away from the terrible flashes and explosions by crawling flat on the floor towards the furthest and opposite door exit. I managed to move a few yards when the explosions, flashes and firing suddenly stopped. I turned to see what the Hell had been the cause of it all when, with horror, I saw a young soldier, near the table I had just left, holding and loosely swinging the Bren gun which had earlier been under the bed. I could hear him crying out in great shock and dismay, 'Oh God, what have I done?' I dashed across with some anger and threw him down while snatching the Bren gun away from him. I then went across to see the damage done to my friend. He was slowly sliding along the inside of the hut when I caught him. I spoke and asked him if he was all right, but I saw that his eyes said it all. As I lowered him to the floor his head fell to one side and blood poured from his mouth. I checked for heartbeats, also to see where he had been struck. He was dead, having been shot through the heart.

Heads were nervously appearing at the doors of the hut to know what all the firing was about. I remember shouting or yelling for someone quickly to get an ambulance and doctor, although I was certain that my friend was beyond help.

It was then only a matter of time for the police, photographers, doctor, etc., to make their appearances. The doctor examined the body, the photographers took photographs, the police made their investigations and took statements from the three or four of us who could be regarded as witnesses.

I was soon to know the circumstances that led to the soldier's tragic death and my own miraculous escape from what should have been a similar fate.

What happened was that the young soldier — from whom I had snatched the Bren gun — had only recently rejoined the section after a lengthy trade training course at another military establishment. He was not at all familiar with the Bren gun, having had but little training using dummy rounds of ammo. His course had been training as a surveyor, and he was therefore somewhat lacking in his weapon training. He had come into the hut, spotted the Bren gun under the bed and had taken it up to familiarize himself with it. With little knowledge of the gun and a good deal of ignorance about the live magazine, he had moved the safety-catch to 'Rapid fire', with the magazine also placed in the firing position. He then pointed the gun towards myself and the person I conversed with — both of us with our backs to him. At less than two yards range he pulled the trigger! Some of the shots — as I was to discover from the bullet holes drilled through the side of the hut — had passed on either side of my neck. I did in fact suffer scorch marks on both sides of my neck, as well as having a fair old headache for several days because of the blow received from close range blast. Other bullet holes were also evident in the side of the hut, including the one that passed through the body of the stricken soldier. They were truly puzzling and inexplicable in that they were in direct line to where I had been standing from the firing gun position. It appeared that even the killer bullet should have struck me first since my own body seemed to have covered the other.

I did — believe me — many times later measure myself against the bullet holes, clearly visible in the side of the hut, to find some explanation as to why some of the bullets had not passed through my body also. It was all very strange indeed that I could plainly see that really and truly I should have died.

At the inquest held later the coroner was at first sharp and critical of the poor lad responsible for the shooting; but his early harsh comments were followed later by more sympathetic ones when he urged the unfortunate fellow to try to forget the matter which, he said, was just another regrettable but inevitable wartime incident. Young soldiers, he pointed out, all over the country were daily handling what were often strange and complicated weapons of war and death. Such incidents and accidents were sadly a common enough occurrence in wartime.

Fate again took a strange turn in that the soldier with the sad conscience was himself killed when the ammo vehicle he was driving was blown up by enemy action on the D-day assault landings.

For myself, I was sure that I could only be a very privileged person. To be standing less than two yards away from the blazing barrel of a machine-gun — and to be still around to tell the story. Indeed to get away without a scratch was a matter which perplexed me long afterwards, so much so in fact that I have since even felt that a possibility existed that if I had made a close examination of my body at that time I might well have found a puncture or two. Who knows? Perhaps it was after all a painless kind of acupuncture experience — a bullet or two at very close range that somehow penetrated my flesh and passed unnoticed! No one ever thought of looking during a time which was obviously one of panic and tragedy.

Another incident, not long afterwards, was again one to clearly show that my Guardian Angel was still around, and was not the fleeting or deserting kind.

It was, I remember, a time when there was plenty of talk, even preparation, for the opening of a 'Second Front', by which — early in 1944 — was meant the invasion of the Continent by Allied Forces.

The German threat of invading our own British Isles had been dead for some time, with the situation now being somewhat reversed. It was they, on the opposite shores, who were now laying the mines and anti-invasion obstacles, while we on our side were making arrangements to free our shores of such unnecessary, dangerous and spoiling clutter — no longer considered defensive!

Within our own Regiment there was talk that one Field Company RE — perhaps ours — would be given the task of clearing mines along stretches of British coastline so as to free certain beaches for D-day training and rehearsal operations. Within the unit it was rumoured that the task was one to be done by one of our company platoons. After more speculation about who was to be clobbered for such dangerous work, the reality of the matter became the worst possible eventuality. Not only was it our particular section who was chosen to do the nasty work, but it was I who, above all, was to lead the way into the minefields, and to start the 'ball' rolling.

As far as the Company was concerned there was no one who had experience of lifting the live 'Beach-mines', most of which had been planted and laid five years or so earlier. We knew enough of the design of the mine, and the theory of mine-lifting procedures, but none of us had any real experience.

What we certainly were unaware of at the time — which was fortunate perhaps — was that men of some other regiment had already been put to work on this kind of operation with rather unfortunate results. They had, it seemed, suffered too many casualties, were disheartened and duly relieved of the task.

We spent a few days settling in at our seaside location, and I was able to see the minefields which were clearly marked and well-fenced by rolls of barbed wire. The minefields were well above the high water mark on high ground and in fields of high dense grass.

I had been warned that the condition of the mines was not known, but that it was likely, because of deterioration caused by the number of years buried in the ground, that they would be highly dangerous because of the volatile state of the explosive. It is a fact that deteriorating HE becomes sweaty with highly sensitive nitro-glycerine. It was believed also that the original protective rubber covering of the mines would be perished, after the long burial period, allowing damp to rust up the works and interfere with the 'make-safe' mechanisms.

The British 'Beach-mine' was a well-designed device and

most effective as a weapon of defence. It was circular in shape and deep enough to hold sufficient explosive to blow men or vehicles to pieces. The detonating mechanism consisted of a bowspring device, below which was a firing or striker pin. The tension of the bowspring could be screw-adjusted so as to regulate the pressure in setting the mine. A reasonable downward pressure on the arched bowspring would cause the firing pin to strike the fuse detonator of the armed mine to initiate the explosive charge. To arm or disarm the mine, a small locking bar could be could be pushed forward or pulled back, to or from a position below the bowspring, which in this way would allow or disallow the bowspring mechanism to function. Obviously when the mines were set in the ground some five years earlier, the bars were in the withdrawn 'unsafe' position to meet the threat of invasion by the Germans.

The mines had been laid in the panic period 1939, with the result that no maps, charts or sketches were available. In normal circumstances this would have been done in order properly to indicate positions, datum points, spacing etc., all of which would certainly make the job of mine clearance a good deal easier.

So it was that on one damp and misty morning I found myself cutting a gap in the barbed wire fence of the minefield, to let myself on to the 'not-so-hot' trail of my first live mine. I anticipated that the most difficult part of my operation would indeed be to find the first mine, in unknown territory where there could be many or few mines, where there might be rows of properly spaced or irregularly spaced mines. They could perhaps be randomly scattered and difficult to find. Obviously it would take the lifting of a number of mines before any laying pattern would emerge — if such existed.

To assist with my pioneering efforts into unknown territory was another soldier. He was the fellow with the marking tape and I was the chap with the mine-detector.

I know not when the metal mine-detector was invented or first put to use by the military (REs), but I could well believe that the one I was using for the immediate task ahead was the earliest of early models — if not the actual prototype. It was big, heavy and very clumsy to use. It was a rather complicated gadget which involved carrying a box of tricks in the form of a large pack strapped to my back — altogether a bundle of equipment far removed from the metal-detector types that followed in later times. With the earphones, the buzz pitch — the variation of which was the 'reading' by which the detection of metal objects could be made — was also more of a noise than a tune, having too much interference for reliability.

Our minesweeping drill was fairly simple and straight-forward. I would move forward with the detector, making semi-circular sweeps, the edges of which would be well-defined and marked by good stiff white marking tape. In this way cleared and uncleared areas in the minefield would not be confused because of the method of working in 'lanes.' My job was to detect the mine, push the safety bar inwards to disarm the mine, then to lift it and place it on the left inside the cleared lane, and to continue doing so. Others in the team would follow up, defusing and carrying the mines away.

Because of the greater dangers involved in the first stages of the operation, there were only the two of us, from our section of twelve soldiers, to seek out the first mines. The others, together with a young and inexperienced sub-lieutenant, watched anxiously from behind a good mound of earth or sand at some safe distance away. The danger to personnel would therefore be minimized at the dangerous early groping stage.

Entering this minefield was a bit like entering a cornfield, with grass and scrub wild and overgrown. I covered about twenty or thirty yards — a few bits of metallic rubbish causing early false alarms — before locating the very first of the live beach-mines. Using the bricklayers trowel I carried for the purpose, I gently removed the topsoil to expose the rubber covering of the mine. Surprisingly it was not as perished as I expected it to be. Gingerly clearing a bit more soil revealed the all-important bar projecting from the side of the mine. This I would have to push inwards to neutralize the danger of the bowspring striking the detonator. I tried hard to force the bar forward by hand but had little success until I tried a method of trowel leverage, using the point of the trowel in the ground. I was relieved to see the bar go forward with a comforting click.

I stood up and gave the thumbs up sign to the anxious and apprehensive watchers behind the mound in the distance.

The second mine was then located, neutralized and

excavated in the same way. For the third mine, however, I experienced difficulty in finding it, and this was due in some measure to the fact that I was not yet able, with only two mines as yet lifted, to determine the line or spacing of the mines.

The first two mines were about a couple of yards apart, but I had no guarantee that the others would be similarly spaced out. I leaned, reached and inched forward as far as I dared, without getting the expected response through my earphones. I had flattened the foliage with my steps for a good couple of yards without having the success I sought, and I worried about proceeding beyond the point where I felt the mine might logically and sensibly be. I retreated and reswept the ground already covered from where I had lifted the second mine. I again inched and leaned forward, with the full weight of the extended heavy detector bearing mostly on my foremost leg. Again there was no response, and again I decided to try another search over the old ground. This time I was slow and deliberate, pressing the detector panel tight to the ground and covering every square inch. It was when I covered the spot pressed flat by my weight at the outermost limit of my pacing that I detected what I thought was the slightest of slight change in the hum or buzz through my earphones. It was here unbelievably where I found the third mine. I had, in God's truth, been standing on it on at least two occasions whilst bearing the heavy detonator in an extended forward position.

Because of my amazing luck, I made a thorough examination of the duly uplifted mine to find an explanation for its failure to explode, given the weight it had directly borne, which certainly exceeded the critical twenty pounds or so. I found that the mine was in every way in perfect working order. The mine should really have gone off killing two (expendable?) soldiers.

The trouble of course was in the detector I used which had somehow become affected by wet grass and had malfunctioned. We live (perhaps?) and we learn!!

However, clearing the minefield of several hundreds of mines was thereafter a simple enough task since the six foot spacing, along good straight lines, between mines was all very clear and predictable.

My Guardian Angel had seen to it that I was baptized in the only way possible in the matter of mine warfare. Only the very privileged can be baptized in this way!!

3

The Normandy Assault Landings

We all knew that there would come a day quite soon when we should find ourselves sailing away towards and into that which for most of us soldiers we could only welcome and dread at the same time — the Second Front.

We welcomed it because it was necessary and certain to bring the end of the war a good deal closer, which was what we all wanted; but we also dreaded it because we knew that in the mighty clash and battles that were inevitable, a great many soldiers would die — maybe oneself.

For many of us the Second Front was already planned and well-advanced. We were for some time already involved in intensive training and extensive exercise preliminaries for the sapper role we were to play in the invasion of the continent of Europe. It was also by now obvious and evident that we were to be in the vanguard of the attacking forces for the initial assault — H-hour on D-day as it would be known.

That critical time was approaching fast, with our briefings, training etc., becoming more specific, concentrated and specialized. We were now encountering for the first time exact replicas of the beach obstacles we would have to remove or destroy in order to make the necessary gaps in the stout coastal defences of the enemy.

Hedgehogs, Tetrahedrons, Element 'C' barriers, poles, mined ramps, grounds mines and barbed wire entanglements, etc., were some of the anti-tank, anti-vehicle, anti-seacraft and anti-personnel obstacles likely to be met with by assault engineers in early attacks — and we worked hard on these in training.

Our formidable enemy had already done much to deter and prevent the landing of allied troops, and it was certain that besides the kinds of obstacles already mentioned, he would also have his fortifications, ditches, bullets, shells, bombs, etc., to make it altogether a Hellish cocktail to greet us with. In preparation for the great day, we were for a few weeks placed into special security areas which we called 'concentration camps' because of our confinement and lack of communication with the outside world. Because of the tight security required for such a major operation, where surprise was all important, the spearhead troops with their dangerous knowledge had to be constrained within well-defined limits, orders and regulations. We were confined to allocated camp areas with communication restricted to military members of our group units.

Inside the camp we REs had little time for worrying about what lay ahead. Much work had to be done in preparing ourselves, our equipment and weapons for the big test, which was sure to prove fatal to any weakness, failure or unreadiness on our part.

It was expected that for the real task, our first efforts would have to be directed towards blasting obstacles above and below sea water. A good deal of our time in the camp was therefore spent in making up neat packages and parcels of explosives into ready-made waterproof charges. These were designed so as to be rapidly placed on the various obstacles for equally rapid demolition. It may be of some interest to know that many boxes of good old-fashioned Durex rubber goods were used — or misused — for the purpose of waterproofing igniter switches — the safety pins of which could be extracted within the stretched outer skin of the Durex covering. They were also used for the protection of wrist-watches and other personal items. There was also no doubt that many were hopefully secreted away in reserve for purposes and moments more for love than war.

No. 4 Commando Group were with us at the same camp enclosure, and it was, I remember, interesting to see how they also trained and prepared for their part in the forthcoming assault. I was most impressed with many demonstrations of their fighting skills, particularly in close combat encounters etc.

On one fine morning we received the order to move out in 'marching order' to a small country lane not far from the camp. I remember that we had to wait in file in the country

lane for some time without any idea of what was to happen
next. What eventually did happen was that a black limousine
drew up at the end of the line and out stepped King George
VI accompanied by a couple of high-ranking officers. He
looked as if his own call-out on parade at this desolate spot was
as much of a sudden call to him as it was to us. He came down
the ranks stopping, it seemed, to look directly into the eyes
and face of each man in turn. He certainly paused and looked
at me as I looked at him. His inspection of what obviously were
to be the spearhead troops was quickly over. No word seemed
to have been spoken by anyone and it was what it appeared
to be — altogether a speedy and hush-hush occasion.

The visit of King George was significant indeed, because in
the evening of the same day we found ourselves embarking on
a very large ship. We were at this time unable to tell whether
our move was another kind of rehearsal exercise or whether
this time it was for real.

We were to find out at a certain specified time later after
sailing away in extremely rough seas and weather.

Months of rumour, speculation and anticipation were at an
end with the distribution aboard the ship of an official
announcement in the form of a leaflet about the opening of
the Second Front. It was a gravely worded piece of paper
which began with something like, 'You are about to embark
on the greatest crusade . . .' etc. This was later followed by
statements by the ship's captain over loudspeakers. We were
also given progress reports by the captain, who at one time
informed us that the only thing in front of us, between us and
the enemy, was a minesweeper. He also told us we had a
British destroyer as our escort.

Because of the very bumpy passage in the rough sea, many
troops on board our ship suffered badly from seasickness. It
was even rumoured that a few soldiers had died. I myself was
as violently ill and sick as it was possible to be, and I remember
having my knees up tightly to my stomach to try to counter the
huge rolls, swells and crashing of the ship.

I also remember that it was around the break of dawn when
a marvellously good breakfast was served. It was good and
plentiful because, I suppose, there were but few of us who
could appreciate it. There were some tough old soldiers
amongst us pointed out as ex 'Wingate Chindits' who had no

such reservation or hesitation in tucking into platefuls of ham and eggs, etc. For those who could manage it — even for those who couldn't — it was a fitting last meal for such condemned men!

A few minutes of watching those able to scoff sent me hurrying up to the top deck for fresh air and more heaving space.

I saw, in the first breaking light of dawn, the huge outline of our escort destroyer close on our starboard side. Her great hulk loomed large in great silhouette against the faint skyline. My sickness and misery was suddenly added to by shock and dismay because I was aware of an explosion that seemed to lift the destroyer out of the water and smash somewhere around her midship area. I watched, giddy and disbelieving, as her middle went down, leaving her two ends upturned and floating visibly. She had struck a mine just as I had, for those few sad precise moments, watched her. A strange experience indeed, which had me rubbing my eyes as if it had been a kind of illusion or hallucination caused by seasickness.

The reality, however, became all too evident when I could see over the side the pieces of wreckage floating in the water — some with human figures clinging to them. Our ship must have been a bit near to the destroyer when she was hit because it appeared to me that we actually sailed into and over the drifting wreckage. I remember my horror at seeing some of the wreckage and human figures disappearing directly under our ship; also my furious astonishment that nothing was being done to save the poor devils in the sea. They were obviously doomed to die. I was shocked and frantic without realizing just then that the war and invasion were now on with a vengeance; that the fleet was now on its way and could not be stopped or turned back; and that there was little or nothing we could do in the way of rescue.

It was my first sight and experience of what war and battle were all about.

Back on the lower decks troops were getting ready for the final fifteen minutes of the sea journey which was to be made in a smaller assault craft. These we understood would land us in reasonably shallow water on the early ingoing tide.

The captain of our larger craft called us together for a short service of worship and prayer, which for many on board ship was an occasion for praying as they never prayed before. For others like myself it was a bit like 'For what we are about to receive, Oh Lord . . .'!

As assault engineers we were well weighed down with heavy personal loads to carry, with myself suffering even worse than most. Besides other kit I also carried a Bren gun with two heavy boxes of magazines, some of them being heavy 100 round mags.

Even without such cumbersome gear, it would have been difficult getting aboard the assault craft which was now alongside and ready to take us. It really did turn out to be a near impossible task which led to injury to a few, and caused ill afforded delay. Because of the violence of the sea, the assault craft could not be steadied or controlled sufficiently for all men to get aboard quickly and orderly. Instead, the craft swung madly and wildly to and from the large ship's side so that men were forced to jump and tumble into the smaller boat as it came crashing alongside on vicious waves.

I doubt whether there was anyone who was not feeling the worse for a great deal of wear and tear already as we crouched low in the assault craft which was now speeding away towards land. The French coast was clearly visible, as was the shellburst on the land and the intervening stretch of sea before us.

We could see that we were in for a pretty hot reception ourselves for already exploding spouts of water were appearing all around us. We received one hit on the stern of the craft which wounded a few of the troops before we got ashore. Perhaps it was that first hit which altered the RN craft commander's intention and promise to land us in shallow water. When the ramp of the craft went down so did we — in very deep water indeed! I know that when I dropped off the ramp, my Bren gun etc., took me down like a stone leaving me with several feet of water above my head. It was only by underwater walking towards shore that I saved myself from a watery end, almost before having a chance to begin anything. I could see that some people were either drowned or drowning already, some I could see were screaming and waving their arms while going backwards and seawards. Many were wounded whilst in the water and were unable to move in the advancing tide. The whole area was under fire with casualties already high and rising.

Some teams of engineers were landed just before us, because of our delay earlier in boarding the assault craft, and it was all too evident that they had suffered badly. To describe the scene before us as we landed, might best be done by quoting OC unit who later wrote in an official journal 'The scene on the beach was indescribable — an absolute inferno, burning tanks, broken down vehicles, and very many dead and wounded lying about in a narrow strip between the sea and the barbed wire at the back of the beach. There were shells, mortars and the occasional bomb falling, and a considerable amount of small arms fire. For a few moments I thought none of the things we had planned had come to pass. We were late and the tide was almost high. We were all on one beach instead of spread along the whole divisional front. Our task of clearing beach obstacles was obviously hopeless so I organized four sections into parties for clearing beach exits and laying track to try to clear some of the congestion.'

Here I have to explain that our principal tasks as assault engineers were obstacle clearance; construction of exits from the beaches to assist in getting troops ashore and off the beach; to provide engineer assistance to respective formations for advance inland. Some of the RE teams were using AVRE (armoured vehicles RE) and flail tanks (CRABs), some of which carried attachments and equipment suited to the clearing or crossing of obstacles (facines, bridges for crossing ditches or sea walls, 'bobbins' and 'Sommerfield Track' for covering mud and sand, 'Petard' for breaching concrete obstacles, pillboxes, etc.).

The time of 'H' hour had been fixed so that in most places the obstacle clearance teams would be able to work when the depth of water on and around the sea-most obstacles would be no more than a foot or two. But delays and strong inshore winds meant that by the time we arrived the water was considerably higher.

It should be noted that the clearance of obstacles both above and below high water mark was to be carried out by army engineers, some of whom were trained specially as divers. Normally in combined operations, the Royal Navy undertake all work seaward of the high water mark. In this case, however, the navy could not undertake the responsibility, so that the whole duty fell upon RE teams.

We were part of 3rd British Division, which in turn was part of 1 Corps plan to attack along a twelve mile or so stretch of Normandy coast on a two divisional front. 3rd Canadian Division on the right sector with two brigades leading, and 3rd British Division on the left, with one brigade leading.

Our particular stretch of beach was near to the mouth of the River Orne, which was on the extreme left of the sector and of the entire landing operation. The landing here was from the outset expected to be one of the most difficult of all because it was within range of the heavy guns at Le Havre and elsewhere, with our flank exposed to the high ground to the left of the River Orne. It turned out that our right flank was also exposed because of a two or three mile gap, between the two divisions, that was to remain for some time.

When I landed I could see that the gapping and obstacle clearance teams were suffering heavy casualties. Much of the work had to be done in the open, in three out of four lanes, owing to the heavy loss of covering armour. Six out of eight Crabs and many if not most of the AVRE were out of action. Local resistance was heavy, with shot and shell coming from all frontal directions.

I remember my first moments of dragging myself out of the sea holding on to my Bren gun, magazine boxes and other kit. I looked around to see instant death and destruction all around me. But I was conscious that, even so, the beach was perhaps no worse than staying on the boat where I felt I should have died of seasickness anyway.

I sought cover behind an AVRE which had just been hit. I moved away quickly enough when I realized it was blazing away and that with its Petard explosive charges etc., it could blow up at any second. I succeeded in making for the bank of dunes at the high tide mark. I hoped that somehow I could get my Bren gun into a position to fire over and beyond the dunes in the enemy direction, wherever he might be.

I remember as well as anything else that happened just then — damned silly considering the circumstances — my annoyance and irritation at the sea lice or beach bugs, or whatever they were, that were crawling all over me as I itched, above all, to get my Bren gun alive and kicking to some good purpose. An attacking position was not easy because of the mortars, shells and bullets that were hammering down on to a relatively small and concentrated area. There were at least two occasions when I was sure I was an eye-witness to shells or mortars making direct hits on soldiers moving close to me — the phenomenon of seeing them literally disappearing in a flash. I was to learn later that besides the high number of assault engineers killed and wounded there were also fifty-four other ranks missing.

Until that time I had never seen a live or dead German soldier in my life. Here suddenly were two of them almost jumping over me as I crouched low behind the sand bank at the high water mark. One of the Germans appeared to throw a hand-grenade as he came over the top to land on the beach, although it was difficult to know one explosion from the many others happening at the same time. Another British soldier must also have thought a grenade was thrown because he managed to kick the German behind to send him sprawling, and then by blasting away with his Sten gun. I figured that whether a grenade was thrown or not was hardly a matter for a board of inquiry in the circumstances!

I moved to a position to be able to view the ground over and beyond the sandbank. The area all around seemed to be covered by bursts of creeping barrages of shellfire, raging and rolling over the ground as if threatening to overwhelm us all.

In the circumstances I decided to do something about helping some of the badly wounded soldiers — many of my own comrades among them — who were lying around in exposed positions on the beach. The best I could do was to drag a few of them to a low position in the sand dunes, where things were almost just as bad. I caught up with someone who had a stretcher, and the two of us worked as we never worked before. Truly in every way — emotionally, mentally, physically — the most awful job in the world. It was, I suppose, made worse for me because there were no medics around, obviously no hospital and no sanctuary other than a dip in the ground where we dumped those we carried. It is also true to say that quite a few of those who were placed there were hit a second time; some of whom were killed. I saw many mutilated bodies and grey-green-yellow faces on that morning; some who became silent and still forever. I was a stretcher-bearer until I was physically exhausted, depressed and sick, when I could do no more. I handed over the stretcher to someone else, being firmly resolved in my own mind that a stretcher-bearer's job would never, never again be one for me. Before moving away from the beach, my final effort was directed towards trying — though unsuccessfully — to plug a fist-sized hole in the back of another poor fellow who had himself been hit when tending to another wounded person.

Our task was now to leave the beach and if possible to move inland for a quick link up with British airborne troops who had been dropped earlier, a few miles inland on the left flank area.

The 6th Airborne Division had set off shortly before midnight from England. They were also under command 1 Corps with part of their main task being to capture the bridges over the River Orne and the Caen Canal at Benouville and Ranville — the two bridges being close together. They were to secure the area around the bridges, and with a bridgehead established to resist enemy attacks from the east.

It was towards these two bridges we were now directed, where other RE tasks were in the strategic pipeline awaiting our arrival.

The fire from shells, mortars and small arms continued to be heavy along the tracks and lanes leading inland from the beach. The ground was also well-laid with mines. Many dead bodies could now be seen, a number of them being our own soldiers who had failed to make the ground from the beach.

We were a small group advancing or taking cover as the situation demanded. There was a good deal of sniper fire around, and often our progress was slow. I had little idea of the time of day in the circumstances, but I guessed that it must have taken us a few hours to reach the area of Benouville and Ranville.

Unfortunately two of my group comrades were killed just before getting to the first of the bridges. They had moved — perhaps too boldly — ahead and were lying dead almost within sight of the bridge, with charred and blackened faces when I got to them. They had, I guessed, been killed by mortar fire.

Very much later I was to read an account of certain events that happened on that day, by someone who wrote, 'There will always be some doubt about who was the first of the sea-borne forces to meet up with the airborne forces. It is, however, believed to have been a small party of Royal Engineers . . .' In my mind there is absolutely no doubt whatsoever that it was my own group who must have been the first into the area, my two dead comrades for the particular credit.

The Benouville canal bridge was the first bridge we encountered. It was an iron bridge with a peculiar looking cantilever tank on its upper structure. There were no airborne soldiers around when I first saw the bridge — although I was of course to see and meet up with many of them later. The bridge and surrounding area were under intense fire and, in order to get to the far side with my Bren gun, I ran a pretty nasty gauntlet with steel and lead thudding, whistling and whining along the way.

The airborne lads had done their job pretty well concerning the bridges, setting out before midnight from England, a glider force — which included a Field Company RE detachment — landed exactly on schedule at two am within a hundred yards or so of the Eastern end of the canal bridge. They rushed the defences, with the REs looking for demolition charges. It was discovered that although the bridges had been prepared for demolition by the Germans the charges were not in place, but were stored in a nearby house.

I saw the crashed empty glider — to become a close and familiar feature over the next few days — which had landed with such marvellous precision to surprise the German troops — many of whom were literally caught napping in nearby fortifications.

Near the bridges some dead bodies of both warring sides were rather grim evidence that the bridges were not altogether easily surrendered and captured.

Other soldiers of our troop gradually moved up into the area, and it became clear that we were to be involved in the construction of two Bailey bridges which were required to reinforce, with heavier class load structures, the captured existing bridges which were of low class load designation. It was strategically obvious that we urgently needed sound lines of communication for the Allied force advance; but more immediate was the necessity for a way through to the airborne held bridgehead for our own heavy armour etc., to meet the heavy stuff of the enemy. Good as our chaps were it was unlikely that they could hold out for long against Jerry's Tiger Tanks, for example. It was therefore a critical matter — indeed a matter of life and death for a large number of our troops — that our Bailey pontoon bridges across the canal and Orne river were thrown across as quickly as possible. But we would, however, have to await the rather uncertain delivery of the bridge equipment from the beaches.

I think it was late afternoon when I heard and saw the bagpipes and pipers of a contingent of Marine Commandos led by Lord Lovat. They halted a while before crossing the bridge in the direction of Ranville. A short time later I was to hear the noise of battle as they engaged the enemy. They certainly made a din and no doubt must have accounted for many of the enemy, but I was to hear later that they really did take a hammering — almost to the point of being wiped out.

My own instructions were to take up a defensive position with my Bren gun at the enemy side of the far bridge in order to give covering fire and protection to the rest of the troops who were on the 'home' side of the canal bridge. I found a German foxhole on the far river bank alongside the bridge abutment and road approach. Steel duckboards lay scattered around, and some of these I used as a parapet for protection against bullets and shrapnel.

I settled into my lonely foxhole position. I felt isolated and pretty vulnerable. since opposite me were menacing fields and trees. I recall my first panic situation a short time later when an airborne vehicle came belting back just a short time after it had gone forward. The guys on the vehicle were shouting about Tiger tanks approaching and that I would be wise to get the hell out of it quickly back to the other side of the bridges! I remember spending some tense moments with my Bren gun positioned between concrete posts of a gateway to a house which overlooked the canal bridge. I waited with certain expectation of seeing a 'Tiger' pop up somewhere on the other side of the bridge. In any case if it had done so, it could not cross over bridges much too weak for the sixty odd tons of TT armour. A bit of a false alarm, I think it was, and I was soon back across the bridges again to my earlier foxhole position.

It was getting to be late evening with light falling fast, and I cannot say that at that moment I was looking forward to passing my first night on foreign and hostile soil. I was not particularly cheered by the immediate company of corpses I found close to me. I could almost reach out and touch the most gruesome of three, who was a German who had his brains blown out through a great jagged hole in his steel helmet. There were two Germans and one of our airborne, obviously one who was a stricken warrior in the earlier battle for the bridges. Before light fell I found it difficult not to think of leaving the three mutilated bodies to the dark of the night without my presence, which I felt would be better by far on the other side of the bridge. Instead I had the opportunity of pondering long and hard about the position of one of the corpses. It seemed to me to be almost impossible in the way it was lying on the steep river bank without rolling down. I concluded it could only be a very dead body indeed — rigid muscles, rigor mortis etc. — that could cling in such a way.

For me, what better way to spend my first night in action? I was, in truth, cold frightened, confused, terribly tired and hungry; a not very brave young soldier who had been cast in a nightmarish world of awful reality. Before being swallowed up by the night I reflected on the long long day called 'D-day', and consoled myself with the thought that if 'D + 1 day' was perhaps just a tenth as bad, I should only have to endeavour to survive a mere ten possibilities or situations of getting killed!!

4

The River Orne Bridgehead

It was early morning and the beginning of a day known as 'D + 1' on the Normandy invasion's strategic calendar and timetable. The cock-crowing of the morn was stilled, silenced and awed by the clamour of the German and British guns blasting away in thunderous opposition.

Many of our offshore crafts and ships were also contributing greatly to the British exchange with a pounding of rockets and shells on to enemy inland positions — perhaps reducing the cockerel population in the process!

From my foxhole position close to the River Orne bridge near Ranville I observed the occasional airborne figures and stretcher-carrying jeeps moving speedily in both directions across the bridge. There were trees along the path on the river bank, and against one of them I could see, in the early morning light, a solitary airborne figure leaning or taking cover. He was not far away from my own position, and it was therefore an opportunity for me to get some information as to what was happening around me. He was a weary and contemplative looking fellow who had obviously been around on this dangerous side of the river for more hours than I had been. I spoke to him and discovered him to be the officer who was — or had been — the OC of the party from the nearby crashed glider. It was he and his party who had made such a marvellous job in capturing the 'Pegasus' and 'Reinville' (Benouville and Ranville) bridges intact more than twenty-four hours earlier. But the officer seemed to be rather anxious, even rather depressed, at having little or no news himself. I was later to see a number of his Airborne Division comrades lying dead in the area, which could perhaps explain his anxiety and sadness. He queried the situation concerning reinforcement troops from the beaches.

Our chat did not last long, however, because the bridge was all too obviously a bottleneck hotspot in the general layout of battle and was therefore anything but a safe and healthy place to be. Airborne troops in the area appeared to me to be very thin on the ground, and some of them, as I was to see, were often driven back to the bridge by enemy infiltrations. This was making the situation difficult to know who were the attackers and who were the defenders. Young German snipers were found to be in the area as late as 'D + 3' day.

Our bridgehead, although hardly well-defined, was thought to be a semi-circle of about two miles from the position I had covering the enemy approach to the River Orne bridge. The semi-circle, however, did not extend to the sea at the mouth of the River Orne, which meant that pockets of enemy resistance and enemy infiltrations were dangerously active from that direction also.

The bridge was obviously a bull's-eye in the enemy's critical target, and we could expect him at all times to strike with desperate attempts to throw us back into the sea.

I was here at this point with a Bren gun to defend against enemy counter-attacks, and it was necessary to give protection to working parties of REs back on the other side of the bridges.

It was 7th June, with the tasks of 3rd Div RE being the clearance and improvement of forward routes for the Division. Also when not taking up positions with the infantry in repelling numerous enemy counter attacks, there were mines to be laid or cleared, bridges to be built, etc.

Amongst the tasks scheduled for early attention were two pontoon bridges of class forty tons to replace or reinforce the existing captured bridges at Benouville and Ranville.

Although some bridging stores and equipment had been landed and moved up from the beaches, it was soon to be discovered that most of the bridging necessaries were held up, causing a delay of some twenty-seven hours or so before arriving. This excessive delay inevitably resulted in bridging teams waiting around impatiently before being able to begin the vital construction tasks.

In the meantime I could only hold on to my position and hope that all the blind spots — trees, ditches, fields, hedgerows, etc. — in front of me posed dangers more imaginary than real.

I really had no way of knowing just how close the enemy was, or sometimes came, except by seeing the occasional speedy retreat of an airborne vehicle flashing past with shouts that 'the enemy had broken through!' This happened a few times leaving me feeling vulnerable and insecure, to say the least. On such occasions I was, unlike the others, not able to escape quickly on a vehicle, and this left me with little choice but to defend myself as best I could, with a Bren gun from my little hole in the river bank. Anyway I was confident that a Bren gun was a great defensive weapon, one which I wouldn't change for any other.

Although the situation was tense, I was becoming all too aware that I was hungry. I had nothing to eat and drink since shortly after leaving the shores of England. My severe seasickness had left me with a very empty stomach and loss of appetite — but which was now, after some thirty hours or so, well past.

Perhaps it was the smell of the frying bullybeef sizzling away in my mess tins, or perhaps more likely the fact that I was moving around a little too exposed and not being sufficiently on the lookout, that led to what happened next.

A sudden burst of machine-gun fire viciously threw up the ground around me and sent my bully, tommy cooker and mess tins spinning away as if it was some kind of sharpshooting scene in a Wild West film. This was for real, however, and I was indeed fortunate to get away with it. I was pinned down by a few more bursts of fire, from what was obviously a German Spaundau MG. I was unable to pinpoint the source of the fire, though I suspected that it came from an extreme right position. Possibly from some lone infiltrator who had somehow come down along the river.

He could not have stayed long, because I was made aware of the fact that he was no longer around when a despatch rider from my troop, who was somewhere back across the canal, managed to get up to my position. I was told that sniper fire had prevented an officer reaching me on a couple of occasions earlier, and was part of the reason why I was isolated for so long. Perhaps I could do something about the fair amount of small arms fire that still seemed to be firing in the wrong direction? Instructions were that I was to stay until I was relieved.

The DR's apparently untroubled arrival and departure encouraged me to move around more freely. Since my earlier ordeal of being pinned down by gunfire, I was beginning to feel that my foxhole position was, or could be, something of a trap because of the limited view I had of both background and foreground of the danger zone. I had, a few times earlier, entertained the idea that it might be better if I clambered up one of the trees that lined the pathway along the river bank. In that way, hidden among the leaves in the treetop I might be safer, more dangerous to any approaching foe, and certainly better able to view the landscape around me. Also, if a sniper became active from out there again, his position might be better spotted from such a fine lookout post.

There were a few pieces of rope lying loosely on the river bank among or near the German duckboards which were scattered around the place, perhaps used earlier by German troops for their own bridge or river crossing training. With a good piece of rope I succeeded in getting a running knot fastened to a stout branch of a well-selected tree. The loose end of the rope I tied to the Bren gun for heaving up to a roosting position in the tree — while ensuring my own protection behind its broad trunk.

In a short while I was aloft and feeling quite exhilarated. Was I perhaps setting up a new kind of warfare tactic by taking a Bren gun up a tree? Visions perhaps of super sniping on a grand scale!

I spent the next ten minutes or so gazing down not so much at the world in general but rather intensely at certain objects in particular. Here I felt more of being hunter than hunted, and I was intent on seeking out prey, if any were around.

It was the scream and explosion of a shell that suddenly changed my perspective of the situation and brought me somewhat down in the world. Up a tree was certainly no place to be when the flak was flying, and I quickly grabbed my MG and slid down the rope. Almost before I hit the ground I was showered from above by splinters and foliage caused by a hail of bullets pumped and directed into the tree top I had just vacated. Obviously the shaking and disturbance of the tree, as I hurriedly descended, had drawn somebody's attention and fire to the spot. Yet again I was lucky to escape the awful danger I had so foolishly — as it seemed in hindsight — placed myself in. My little foxhole was not, after all, such a bad place to be, considering the changed situation.

For quite some time I was glad to be below ground because of a spell of intense shelling, which was obviously aimed at damaging the bridges, or preventing British troops from crossing the river.

The foxhole I crouched in was one of a number around the area, and would have been dug by Germans who must have been given a rough time by the many RAF aircraft savagely attacking enemy communications prior to our arrival.

In the matter of field warfare, I understood that the trench for the German was no longer the 'in' thing, preferring for himself instead single well-spaced foxholes as affording better protection and defence. The British on the other hand — according to military training manuals — having a long-standing preference for the 'two-man-V-trench.' The argument favoured by the British was that the morale of single soldiers in isolated positions could not be maintained as well as for the 'duo-in-the-trench' system. However, things in practice do not always work out in accordance with military theories and training manuals. Here I was, glad to be in a somewhat reverse situation, in a predicament when half a hole was better than none!

A lull in the shelling brought me my second visitor, who was sent over with instructions that I was to find my way back to troop HQ for rations and briefing. My visitor, having delivered his message, was off as fast as his fat little Scotch legs would carry him. Tommo was quite a character, of whom I shall have something to say later. There was obviously the danger of shelling starting up again, leaving him on the wrong side of the river.

Before joining up with my troop, however, I had made up my mind that a visit and search at a certain spot on the seaward side of the bridges might be worthwhile. From information received earlier I understood that when the airborne troops captured the bridges, they had, in the process, surprised and destroyed a fortified nest of Germans — some of whom were asleep when they were killed.

My recent experiences made me feel that personal possession of a revolver might be no bad thing for my survival in these dangerous times. If I could get to the fallen German group, I had no doubt I could obtain a good German pistol from some poor soldier who had no further use for such a weapon.

It was not to be, however, because I had not proceeded very far, when the enemy started shelling again; this time with a vengeance! It was the heaviest shelling I had yet encountered, and it seemed that I was suddenly at the very centre of it all. After being hurled all over the place by terrific blast, I found myself sheltering in a small brick building near, and between, the two bridges. It may have earlier been used as a sentry or guard building, or more likely a control point structure for a tidal waterways and bridge attendant. Inside was a good solid table, which certainly saved me from injury from falling brickwork. We were at a geographical point that was well within range of the enemy's heavy guns at Le Havre, and there was little doubt that these were the ones now brought to bear, to give me the most shattering thirty minutes or so of my life.

It is no exaggeration to say that the building all but collapsed around me in a pile of rubble, on top and around the table, with me in the middle. Several times I tried to escape the raging, razing inferno without success. A few times I braced myself for a dash into any newly created shell hole, believing the old soldiers' tale that no two shells land in the same shell hole — each time driven back by violent explosions.

The very big shells, shattering the air and ground all around me, was too much even for the tough guy I imagined myself to be, and although I and my body managed somehow to retain a correct number of limbs and pints of blood I was not so fortunate in holding on to my nerves; most were shattered if not gone altogether!

With the first good hint of a lull in the shelling, I was off like some rabies-stricken greyhound running for dear life along the canal bank to get anywhere as far away as I could from the murderous Hell of a place where I had spent such a terrible half hour. I ran till I could run no more and, totally exhausted, I slumped down into a patch of greenery somewhere in a field along the canal in the direction of Caen.

I was shattered and in every way at a very low ebb. My last forty-eight hours or so had been a Hellish and ghastly war experience. It was a time now when I was only dimly aware that some of my less obvious biological bits and pieces had been scattered; a time and condition when nerves, brain, character etc., are all in conflict, and when some inner genealogical sense is tested to the limit in trying to restore order again.

It may be true that it takes a shock to counter a shock — and it was just this kind of thing that seemed to be so well-ordained or arranged for me in what was to happen next.

I was flat on my back gazing at a clear blue sky. As I did so a British Spitfire came into view. It was flying rather low and was directly overhead when an amazing thing happened. As I gazed blankly at the aircraft it suddenly exploded over my head, leaving a front and rear section of the shattered craft spinning down on either side of me within a space of fifty yards or so.

The shock of seeing such a thing — which really was a million to one chance spectacle — brought me quickly to my feet and off for a rescue act if such was possible. As I moved towards the cockpit end of the wreckage, I could see the upper part of the pilot's body, unmarked and looking in such good shape that for a moment or two I thought he might have miraculously survived — until I saw that the lower half of him was concertinaed with the underside of the wreckage into the ground. I tried unsuccessfully to pull him free. He was obviously dead and there was really nothing I could do for the poor fellow. A sad and tragic end for someone who looked to me to have been one of the older veteran types of pilot.

The incident, however, did much to lift me out of my shell-shocked stupor and set me wondering as to how it could have happened. If it was caused by enemy action then it was likely I was in hostile territory with the enemy somewhere close by. The sky space seemed to me, though, to be over our own captured ground. I had a vague notion that pilots were usually advised to fly well above space zones occupied by flying projectiles from artillery and gunfire exchanges, etc. It seemed to me that he was flying low enough to have caught a packet in just this way — perhaps from one of the British guns. All speculation, however, and time for me to move away quickly, just in case some jubilant Germans came whooping or snooping around.

As I moved back along the canal to find my troop I pondered on the three strange, coincidental and somewhat similar happenings in which I was a 'split-second' eye witness — my head used and manipulated by providence like a camera. First seeing the explosion and sinking of the destroyer; then to see a nearby soldier on the beach disintegrated with a direct hit by mortar bomb or shell, and then the latest incident of seeing the aircraft shot down, each occurrence somehow happening when my soldier's morale was low — as if to switch introvert knocks to extroverse shocks! But a soldier in battle, I reasoned, could expect to see at first hand many of the horrors of war and doubtless there would be more coming my way if I was to survive long enough!

5

We Build The First Bailey Bridges In Normandy

As can be imagined, food for soldiers in the front line of battle was never, in the history of wars, an easy provisional, distributional and consumptional matter. But here in Normandy, however, things were not at all bad, and it was unlikely that anyone on the British front would die of starvation by neglect.

In the concern of field kitchens and 'grub-up', my own unit was, I suppose, similar to most other units in the British Army in that it was organized on a 'company — or platoon — or section — or individual' system and arrangement, depending on the circumstances in the field. Usually the cook or cooks would be more safely placed somewhere in the rear preparing food and drink and then moving it forward to troops up front.

Cooks, however, were these days finding their work very much easier thanks to the clever W/O planners and dietary experts who had obviously put a lot of skill and thought into a system of rationing which came in the form of ready-made tins, packs and cases. It was a system — quite a mystery to me — of letter-coded containers as 'A-packs', 'D-packs' etc., which appeared to be designed to cater exactly in terms of numbers and times (i.e. six man forty-eight hour pack, etc.).

Besides the excellent variety and quality of canned foods, a few boiled sweets and cigarettes were also provided. It seemed that the only thing lacking was bread, which was probably the only item of foodstuff the boffins were unable to get into a tin! Hard biscuits were the bread substitutes which few of us had any taste for.

But even without bread I managed and relished my first meal since leaving England more than forty-eight hours earlier.

It is said that a good drink of hot sweet tea does a power of good for persons suffering shock or injury. Hot sweet tea together with some food in my belly certainly did much for me in that I quickly recovered from my earlier state of fatigue and shock which was probably caused by weakness through hunger as much as anything else. Being among familiar faces in my troop also helped boost my morale, as did having information as to what was happening generally.

It was understood that the Germans were pressing on all sides of the bridgehead, giving our paras a tough time — particularly as the element of surprise was fast diminishing, with the Germans moving in fast with armour and throwing defensive perimeters around us.

The race was now on to get our own armour across the canal and Orne river into the bridgehead to meet the increasing threat of that of the enemy who could otherwise run riot with their almost invincible Tiger tanks.

My own platoon were key troops in the race in that we were to build the first of the pontoon bridges, later named LONDON I and LONDON II, across the canal and River Orne.

I was instructed to recross the waterways to take up my former position with my Bren gun, and to be on guard against expected German counter-attacks.

From my foxhole position on the far side of the bridges I had little idea of what was between me and the enemy. I knew that British paratroops had been dropped in the area and that part of the military plan, as well as seizing the Orne and canal bridges, was to secure the area in the neighbourhood of the bridges.

Thickly wooded high ground divided the valley of the Orne from that of the parallel running River Dives which was about five miles away on the enemy side. The paras were scattered somewhere within a two mile radius of the bridge, with the ground appearing to be dangerously thinly held.

It was because of my somewhat isolated position in my foxhole, and the fact that I had but little knowledge of how close the enemy were pressing, that I came close later in the afternoon to making a deadly mistake.

The most efficient, well-trained soldier is likely to be also the most trigger-happy one when in and around at the height of battle. Obviously in the struggle for survival — which is what war is all about for those 'PBs' in the thick of it' — the usual thing is to 'shoot first' where the enemy is concerned. Circumstances of battle seldom permit clarity of thought, correct procedure and civilized conduct. The battlefield is no place for a real gentleman, to be sure!

My near deadly mistake happened when I caught sight of a file of German soldiers emerging one by one from a wooded area way out to the left front of the bridge. Seeing the first of what became a good dozen of them made me quickly take aim with my Bren gun. They were running and emerging in file and were bent low as if holding to the ground for cover. Not knowing how many would emerge I held my fire, hoping that none should escape to threaten my own position. My trigger finger applied the first pressure in readiness for the rapid fire I was about to deliver, when suddenly at the rear of the file came two British paras also moving rapidly behind, with guns trained on what obviously were their prisoners of war!

They were all so damned lucky, because in this particular instance for some reason the prisoners did not — as one might expect — have their hands above their heads. I wondered later whether this was because they were moving quickly through a wooded area, or whether it was stupidity or ignorance because of the heat of the moment. It was also, I was to reflect, a moment when I, like others in wartime, could either be a hero or an idiot, depending on witnesses, if any, around at the time!

The next incident to happen was of a kind I had experienced before, though, this time, rather more desperate and compelling. A jeep carrying a couple of our airborne soldiers came speeding along the river pathway, slowing down as they approached, yelling for me to get aboard the vehicle. If what they were shouting was true, then perhaps there was reason enough for panic — something about a Tiger tank being only a couple of hundred yards away. The guys in the jeep gave me no time to ponder the matter, and I was hard-pressed to grab my weapon and catch up with the accelerating vehicle, strange feelings galloping away from the imminent approach of a Tiger tank, with the small of my back feeling as if it was spot marked for target practice!

As the vehicle retreated speedily across the first of the two bridges, I asked the driver to ease down to pick up a figure I recognized coming towards us. It was the tubby little Scot

'Tommo', who was on his way to join me, unaware of the latest predicament.

As the airborne fellows seemed intent on moving back further to the rear than I expected, and also that they were not intending an early return, I thought it best to get off the vehicle and find my way back to the river. For me there could be no better defensive position than being behind, and close to, a river.

Tommo and I were soon off the jeep and wondering about some quick way of getting back to our platoon, which we believed was back there somewhere.

In contrast to my earlier forward position where few if any troops could be seen, here a mile or two to the rear, lines of troops could be seen digging trenches, or were in dugouts already. British infantry seemed to be around in some strength, and I was puzzled as to why so many were to the rear instead of up at the 'sharp end' where I had just left and was now returning. Was it some kind of reserve strategy, I wondered? If we were to lose the two existing bridges then it would be damned poor strategy, I reckoned!

The troops here appeared to be green and fresh from recent landings and arrivals from the beach. They seemed bewildered and threatened as if enemy air and ground attacks were imminent. An infantry captain stood close to a long trench in which a number of his squad were taking cover. As Tommo and I stood nearby wondering about the possibility of a chance vehicle for our return, the captain — in the absence of real enemy — turned on Tommo and me. 'Shove off you two! These trenches are for my blokes, not for RE, P--- off!'

Tommo was a tough little Scotch terrier type who could be relied on to give as good as he got. 'You bloody gutless wonder! Who the Hell wants your lousy trench anyway? You should be up there mate, where we've just come from — not back here with the f--- Home Guard!'

Such insubordination the poor captain never had before. His face was visibly purple and his eyes popped. He whipped out his service revolver and stepped forward to jab it viciously against Tommo's head. 'Talk to me like that again, laddie, and I'll blow your blasted brains out — if you've got any!'

Tommo's mouth opened and shut like a fish out of water as the gun was directed with deadly intent. It looked as if

Tommo was a definite loser, as well as a goner, if he didn't concede — and I was kept holding my breath for some awfully long seconds before he appeared to do so.

I pointed out to the captain that he could rest assured that we had no intention of stealing his place in the trench, that we were a vital part of a critical bridging task ahead, and would he therefore kindly allow us to proceed.

We left the captain still waving his gun around, and we wondered whether being up front among enemy Tiger tanks was perhaps a safer place to be. With such allies who needs enemies?

Indeed, another incident not a hundred yards away, served to remind us that our brief detachment to the rear echelons was fraught with danger. This time it was an infantry RSM — a massive hunk of a fellow — who came up and ordered us to go with him to do a 'little job', as he put it. He explained that he had been looking around for some REs to remove a nearby danger to members of his own unit. We were led to a deserted or abandoned German armoured truck which was tucked away in a corner of a small field. The RSM thought that it was booby-trapped, and was indeed found to be so when I examined it. The vehicle appeared to be designed or adapted as a transporter for Teller-mines. Inside the vehicle were racks upon which were a great number of mines neatly stacked and secured. It was no doubt a sort of German 'quickie' system of distributing and laying mines rapidly to close the gaps caused by the increasing shortage of manpower in German lines of defence. It was, or should be, all too obvious that such an abandoned vehicle loaded with mines — which were themselves designed to hold booby-trap switches — would be a trap.

After careful examination I discovered two booby-traps, one a 'pull switch' which would be activated by opening the back door of the vehicle. The other was a 'press switch' booby-trap and had been placed under a stiff cover on the driver's seat. A live mine was attached to both igniter switches. Other mines in the rack could also be presumed to be made sensitive so that one big hell of a hole in the ground would be made if any of the booby-traps were triggered. This was one disarming job I would trust only myself to do, and, as I didn't like the idea of possibly being another 'missing person', I told Tommo to watch proceedings (or at least the vehicle) from a relatively safe distance. The RSM had already vanished! I was not — or indeed could not — be absolutely sure that the two booby traps I found, and tackled successfully, were the only ones around. It was always a possibility that something more cunningly devised could be concealed underneath or within the mechanism of the vehicle. I therefore fastened a scribbled warning note to the window. 'Some booby-traps removed. Handle with extreme care!'

Tommo and I were both of the opinion that the quicker we got back to the company of the devils we knew the better! Fortunately we had but little walking to do before clambering aboard an ambulance vehicle which comfortably took us to a position not far short of the canal bridge at Benouville.

We found most of our platoon dug in along the riverside bank of the canal. Some preparation had been made for the start of the pontoon bridge, but little progress could be made because only a few items of bridge equipment had arrived from the beaches.

Spasmodic bursts of shelling around and about the vicinity of the bridges did not allow for casual activity. It was more sensible by far to keep heads down and guns at the ready until the pontoon bridge operation could properly begin.

With night-time approaching some of the platoon were spaced out between the two waterways, with myself and another soldier positioned on a high bank overlooking the River Orne in the direction of the enemy. It was possible, even likely, that the Germans would, for many good reasons, attempt river crossing raids under cover of darkness. We were therefore to keep close watch on the river; to cut them down if they posed a threat.

My Bren weapon ensured that my position was furthest along the river in the direction of Caen, to cover the squad's right flank as well as the river.

It was remarkable just how quickly men became moles when up in a forward position on the war front. Getting below ground was a life-saving priority for anyone not protected by thick armour. Remarkable also how effective a pair of hands and a bayonet can be, in the absence of better implements, for digging a hole in the ground.

The two of us — myself as Bren-gunner and my No. 2

(Bren-gunner's mate) — being together allowed us to have an agreed system of guard duty of two hours on and two hours off to give each of us in turn some sleep in our one-man dugout.

I needed no reminder that it must have been several nights earlier, the night of 4th/5th when I last had a night's sleep. We were now into night 7th/8th, with the intervening couple of days being by far the most dangerously frightening, fatiguing and longest I could have possibly ever endured. The time was around ten pm and I was on first watch.

I was tired and cold when it came to midnight, with the rising damp of the river enough to dampen those warmest of spirits far removed from my own. The night darkness was worsened by fog or mist along the river, making visibility no more than a yard or two at most.

I spent impatient minutes trying to rouse my partner for his spell of duty, before claiming my own two hours of merciful oblivion.

Despite my shivering and cramped position in a rather small wet hole in the ground, I was as ready as anyone could be to 'pull the blinds down' on a violent and cruel world.

I had no idea of how long I slept, but it really did seem to be no time at all before I was semi-consciously aware that I was being rudely awakened by an almost hysterical partner. 'The Germans are here! Quickly — the Germans have come across the river!'

I was dazed and almost sleepwalking as I let myself down the bank into the high marshy grass of the lower ground between the bank and the river's edge. I had no way of knowing what the true situation was and I could only grope and stumble in the foggy darkness, tall weeds and rushes, sleepily to search out and combat the enemy. My eyelids seemed unable to shake away the heaviness that pulled them downwards so that it was my ears only that would have to do the searching.

I listened intently and caught sound of something moving close by. I took to the kneeling position with my Bren gun cocked and ready for rapid fire as the sound moved closer. The sound approached from the right — the direction of anticipated danger — and because I was fast awakening to my own dangerous predicament, I was conscious and aware of the dire consequences of letting bullets fly before being sure of my kill. I had it in mind to fire one quick short burst and then to move away fast from my give away position. I might possibly hold an advantage in this way since I had no idea of how many of the enemy had crossed. Patrols were usually in groups of about six or so.

The moving object was almost upon me, and I was as close as I could ever be to cutting it down and then bolting away from the 'scene of my crime.' Miraculously the first thing I saw emerging from the high grassy growth and foggy darkness was a steel helmet — a British one! My voice was hardly my own as I croaked out my recognition of our unit platoon L/Sgt.

I shuddered to think that I had, within a short number of hours, come so very close to making two terrible mistakes. I was to wonder later on just how many soldiers are killed by own troops in the battle confusions that abound in wartime.

It seemed that the sergeant had also been alerted to a message that the Germans were passing on the other side of the river. He had come looking for our position and had gone astray in the darkness. He left soon enough when I explained that he was at considerable risk in wandering around in such a manner.

I found my number two who, I discovered, had been badly shaken by a couple of very close shell bursts shortly before disturbing my short sleep with such panic. He had in his somewhat shocked and nervous state caught sight of the blurred figure of the platoon sergeant groping around in the dark, and mistook him for one of the enemy.

Early morning came and went, with a very bleary-eyed Bren gunner having very little enthusiasm and in no great shape to be a dominant figure or factor in winning the war for the Allies. But whether weary and unwilling or not, I still had my part to play in the Normandy battle, which would surely call for a good many more sacrifices yet!

It was some time in the morning that the platoon was mustered for a concentrated effort in putting the first Bailey pontoon bridge across the canal, near to the captured bridge at Benouville. A number of pontoons together with a fair amount of bridging equipment was at last getting through from the beaches.

The start of construction saw also the beginning of a few problems. A couple of pontoons were found to be holed when they were put into the water and a few were damaged and sunk by shrapnel from occasional nearby shellbursts. Recovery and repair work on pontoons and other equipment caused inevitable and unfortunate delay.

Individual pits and trenches were dug along the riverside bank of the canal, providing at least some cover against enemy attack. However, as every available soldier in our unit group was to be employed on the bridge task, no one could be allowed the luxury of a 'trench warfare stance.' Battlefield engineers know well enough — much to their cost — that such bridges can only be built in the open by dangerous and brave sapper exposure.

Despite propaganda and media accounts that would have us believe in the inferiority of German soldiers, there was little, if any, disposition on the part of Allied soldiers to despise or underrate the enemy. It could only be foolish and dangerous nonsense to think for a moment that he was anything less than a courageous, clever and formidable foe.

It was therefore expected that some kind of opposition to our bridge building would be forthcoming from the enemy. Even so, it still took us by surprise when it came in the shape of low flying German aircraft. They were upon us in an instant, blasting away with cannon shells and bullets.

We were extremely lucky in suffering few casualties, none serious. Perhaps this was due to being close to quick cover in the dugouts along the bank, and also by taking cover behind the bank itself which ran crossways to the aircraft approach. All things considered, it really was a miracle that we got off so lightly in Jerry's lightning aerial attack.

We certainly had no intention of being caught 'on the hop' again. So an arrangement was made for an NCO to stand guard with a whistle, keeping an anxious eye on the sky. He would alert us all by blows on his whistle at any further approach by the enemy aircraft. But our early experience made us aware that even with a whistled warning it would have to be a split second dive for cover, in order to dodge the incredible approach speed of such extremely low flying aircraft.

I mentally fixed the position of my own little dugout so as to accord to quick facility or access from whatever direction I might be forced into very speedy retreat.

The important job in hand — the construction of a pontoon bridge — involved a great deal of hard physical labour, allowing little or no time to dwell on possible dangers from enemy aircraft. We were therefore very much in the hands of the guy with the whistle. Thankfully he was a reliable fellow, with good eyesight, hearing and puff whose first warning blow on the whistle would have out-tooted a factory hooter. It sent us scattering like rabbits diving for our own little burrows. I certainly dashed for mine, only to find that someone else had beaten me to it. I was trapped, out in the open, until I realized that closeby was a walled cutaway part of a culvert or sewer in the bank. But whether sewer or drain was a matter just then not to be questioned, and not a moment too soon I dived deep into the most obnoxious foul-smelling sludge.

I emerged with a distinct feeling of sympathy for sewer rats, and with a feeling also of being very fortunate in dodging the murderous swoop of a line of four German aircraft. I was saved by the dirty ditch in the nick of time and I had good reason to bless it. Who knows but that it might be my shrine for a future pilgrimage?

At that moment, however, I was not particularly keen on any more similar dives, and I resolved that the next time around would see me behind my Bren gun firing at the blighters with hundred-round magazines.

We live and learn! I was fortunately alive and already learning that if the Germans were to give repeat performances, we could set up and sight our MGs from two spaced positions on the canal bank so that our crossfire could be brought to bear on the low flying aircraft travelling the same flight path. My own hundred-round magazines were already loaded with a one-in-five ratio of tracer (flare) bullets so that I could visually direct the stream of bullets into the attacking aircraft.

It was some time later when the whistle blew a warning for the delivery of the third German air attack against our bridging operations. This time, however, the enemy found himself flying into two visible convergent streams of fire — that from my own MG and that from another Bren-gunner who had collaborated. My own position when they came almost head on was lying down behind the cover of a good sized lump of rock embedded near the top of the canal bank.

They came in quick succession, one directly behind the other, flying low and in almost perfect alignment to my own line of fire. I almost felt sorry for them as I directed and traced a line of glowing bullets bang into the aircraft as they swooped spot on. Poor bastards! I preferred my own situation to theirs which, when I thought about it later, must have been a frightening experience even for the bravest of Huns. My own experience, although perhaps less frightening, was strange and peculiar to say the least. Pumping death and destruction into one-two-three-four zooming aircraft and their human parts was an experience not easily forgotten — particularly as they came so close that one could use stones as missiles.

I am unable to claim with certainty that my fire brought down any of the aircraft, but I do know that one big Hell of a bang followed immediately behind the last aircraft as it zoomed out of sight below the tops of hedgerows.

It was an experience that taught me that the use of hundred-round magazines was one not always to be recommended because of the tendency of gun barrels to overheat, melt and bend. I was left with one that was totally and completely useless.

I like to think that the confrontation must have had an off-putting effect on the enemy, as there was afterwards but little trouble from that direction against the construction of our pontoon Bailey bridge.

The completion of 'London I Bridge', as it was to be called, would no doubt be recorded in military history as being some time early morning 9th June, 1944.

6

A Time Of Uncertainty

Considering the bridgehead situation and surrounding features of Normandy countryside, the town of Caen was very much a vital and fortified position in the German Army's tightening defensive perimeter and despite the many days of furious onslaught by British forces, Caen was proving to be a tough nut to crack. It would take a few more weeks yet before the important strategic breach could be made.

In the meantime there were those of us within the bridgehead enclosure who were kept like ants inside a deadly volatile matchbox. It was a time of grave uncertainty as to how the tide of war and battle would turn, and we could only hope and pray for the urgent breakout into broader, less dangerous, fields. From the combatant British soldier's point of view there was very little room for manoeuvre, and there were days when the sea behind us was much too close for confidence and comfort. It was, to be sure, a pretty long swim for us to get back home again if the battle favoured the Germans — if only for a short time and distance!

The uncertainty was manifest in several ways, not least in the positive steps being made against the distinct possibility of a reversal of our territorial gain. It really was a time when many of us began to wonder whether the bridges we constructed — with courageous and determined intention to facilitate a speedy Allied advance — might now perhaps be of more help to enemy traffic in pushing us back to the sea.

Although something of a paradox, the preparation of our bridges for demolition by explosives so soon after we constructed them was essentially a critical defensive measure during a particularly critical time in the Normandy battle. There were, of course, the vital bridge crossings over the canal and river at Benouville, with others — including a newly completed Bailey Bridge near the waterways complex (lock gates, footbridge, etc.) at Quistreham towards the mouth of the River Orne. All were wired up for demolition *in the face of the enemy*, and it was during spells of 'standby for detonation duty' at both places where I was to experience a few more peculiar happenings which again, perhaps, are worthy of mention.

One of the incidents occurred near the Benouville bridges (Pegasus) at a time of desperate pressure and danger from the enemy who, during the early stage of the Normandy battle used night-time to best advantage for their military movements. I was on night watch duty in the company of a junior NCO, with both of us jointly having the somewhat heavy responsibility for the possible 'last ditch' destruction of the bridges as decided (a) by the personal command or signed order of a superior officer (CO/OC) or exceptionally (b) in the most clear circumstance, or danger, of being swamped by superior enemy forces.

I am unsure just now as to what then was the exact layout of the demolition charges; for example, as to whether it was only the forward bridge 'on tap' or whether its companion bridge was also connected to the ring main circuits for simultaneous detonation and demolition. I remember clearly, however, that on this occasion my companion and I were crouched together in a shallow but well-concealed scooped-out ditch which was our place and point for initiating the demolition charges as might be deemed necessary.

I had not, in this case, been involved in the preparatory work for the demolition job but I was, of course, well-trained and aware of the general drill and standard involved in such a task. The training of sappers in the deadly business of explosives and demolitions is, as one would expect, comprehensive and thorough, being altogether a subject not to be misunderstood in any way.

Here then our ditch, being the point of initiation for the possible demolition of the bridge(s), contained the nerve endings and beginnings for the 'big twitch' in any awkward development. Fuse, cable, exploder/test box, etc., were all connected and within easy reach of both my companion and I as we waited tense and alert for the worst to happen. (The ordinary battlefield soldier has a very small and limited view of the general war picture or battle scene and can therefore only think and act accordingly.) It was late night as we peered into the misty dark direction of the forward bridge and towards the enemy somewhere not far beyond. Jerry, we knew, was no more than a mile or two away, which allowed little time or warning in the event of a sudden push or infiltration through the bridgehead shell, which was certainly not impenetrable by a particularly desperate foe. We kept our eyes skinned and our limbs ready for the dreaded emergency of setting the fuse alight and activating the detonating handle of the exploder.

It should be explained that the demolition layout and task before us followed our usual sapper practice of having two alternate ways of detonating the charges in case of the failure of any one of the methods through battlefield incident (shelling etc.), fault or accident. The two methods involved two different circuits (or ring mains), one of them being standard electric wire cable connected to the series of electric detonators (dets electric No. 33) which — after careful testing and calculation of the connected circuit's Ohms resistance — would normally be activated by the electric current generated manually via the handle of the exploder box. With this method a small battery-powered test box would be used to pass and receive a low inactivating current so that a positive meter reading of a flickering needle ensured that the many connections were properly made and that the circuit was complete and ready for the generated activating current.

The second method was the use of a circuit (or ring main) of 'American Cortex' which might best be described as explosive cord (or cable) which had the explosive (or detonating) speed of 2,000 feet per second. This was connected to the main demolition charges by a series of knots and bindings etc., being itself initiated by safety fuse (burning rate of two feet per minute) inserted into an ordinary detonator (detonator No. 27) which together with a primer would explode the cortex.

The enemy had shelled the area intermittently during the night and we had therefore made the occasional circuit test for assurance of positive readings in case bursting shells or flying shrapnel damaged sections of the long lengths of cable running above ground. I remember that it was close to midnight when a circuit test was made, and a positive reading obtained, about ten minutes before a visitor stealthily made his way to our position from the rear. Our OC had come personally to check on the situation, in particular our state of readiness because of increasing tension and threat from the enemy. He soon went off in the direction from where he came after obviously acquainting himself with our live and able presence and on being assured that all was operationally functional for the possible critical moment of awful and dreaded emergency. It was a time which had me thinking as to what commander — if indeed any would dare — could make such a decision and give such an order of grave finality — much too grave and final perhaps? Too many known and unknown factors would have to be involved to allow for careful and deliberate planning for the actual destruction of such vital bridges — factors such as precise timing, correct appraisal of enemy strengths, threats, etc., and exact minute-by-minute knowledge of positions and intentions of own troops; their defensive/rearguard actions, etc. Also, our own bridgehead situation was such that we really had no place to retreat or retire to. Our success and survival could depend only on our moving in a forward direction. It was, I thought, altogether the weighty problem, when under threat, of whether or not to blow up vital bridges, and I wondered how many stories could be told of historical vital bridges captured in war because of delay in decision and demolition. Here then, for the life of me, I just could not imagine the decision and order being made by anyone other than by a lone, desperate and doomed hero whose eye was on the enemy and whose hand was on the detonating plunger. Could be me perhaps...

Such speculation, I suppose, and the fact that there was little else to do, must have prompted me to carry out another circuit test for a positive reading of the meter indicator — just in case! But alas! This time there was no movement of the needle, and it seemed most peculiar indeed that in the space of the twenty minutes or so between tests — ten minutes before OC's arrival and ten minutes after his departure — the demolition cable had somehow been interfered with, resulting in the circuit failure. There had, in the meantime, been spasmodic shelling, but it hardly seemed close enough for such damage. It could well have been a -dud line' at the time of

OC's visit which, had it been discovered by him, would certainly need some explaining. He himself had come from an opposite direction, returned the same way and therefore was not thought to be in any way responsible.

Action, then, was needed urgently to put right the failure and, after checking that the fault was not at our end of the line, I went off to chase the cable, leaving behind my colleague at the critical control point. I took with me the few requirements necessary to do the anticipated simple task of reconnecting a broken or disjoined piece of wire cable. I was not — as explained earlier — acquainted with the layout of the explosive charges or this particular prepared demolition task, but I was fairly certain that it followed the usual RE method with which I was well familiar. Sapper-training and experience had taught me the different characteristics and uses of different types of explosives (i.e. Ammanol/Baratol for cratering and lifting effects; gelignite/808 for bore-hole charges and blasting effects; gun-cotton for shearing and shattering effects, etc. (plastic HE being a newly introduced versatile type of explosive)). I guessed that the explosive charges here would be the usual well-placed bundles of gun-cotton slabs with inserted primers and electric detonators, besides the connected explosive cortex cable. But I doubted whether the fault was caused by any of the separate branch lines from the 'ring main' cable which must in some way have been damaged and was itself the likely problem.

An army torch was useful in the circumstances, provided it was not flashed around in the direction of the enemy. German snipers were still around, as was the ever-present danger of enemy patrols who were particularly active under cover of darkness.

I moved along on hands and knees carefully, feeling and searching for the break or damage in the cable, and I must have travelled a good eighty yards or so before I found what I was searching for. I was much astonished to discover that the cable was cut — as if with a knife — and with both severed ends lying several inches apart. But, as every soldier knows, flying shrapnel is no respecter of man, his person or his artefacts, is designed and directed to shatter, crush, spill, pierce, chop, slice and cut a good many things — perhaps especially the vulnerable composite bodies made up mainly of blood, flesh and bones. It could, of course, have cut the cable like a knife . . . but upon looking around further I was more astonished to find that more than one cable had been cut. It seemed to be more than coincidence that both the cortex cable and electric cable had been severed in much the same way with a clean cut, and at the point where they ran close together, being a few feet apart.

But the situation allowed little time to ponder the matter or to draw conclusions since the obvious priority was a rapid repair job on the broken cables.

There was no trouble in sorting the matter quickly, but the incident had the effect thereafter of making my companion and myself rather jittery and anxious for what hours remained with us on duty.

I certainly had time to ponder the matter later, but without any proper evidence to indicate exactly what happened to the cables that night I was unable to have definite views on the matter. What I was left with, however, were some peculiar thoughts, not least was the idea that it was done — with much justification — by someone more likely to be British than German. When I thought about it I could so easily conclude that the demolition of the bridge(s) would be a much more disastrous thing to happen than not at all — *given any circumstance whatsoever*!!! It may have been no faint probability that divided opinions existed about the strategic advisability and preparation for such a critical demolition — a kind of unwise decision in a panic situation?

Later, much later, when I dwelt on the matter, it would for me have made better sense if the cables had been cut a hundred times or more at that critical time. 'Heaven help us all' would have been my prayer had I been forced to cut such vital arteries in such a situation.

I often wondered afterwards as to when exactly those demolition charges were removed. . .

I am unsure about the time gap between the above incident and a second of a similar kind which I guess must have happened just a day or two later. This time it was at the site of another newly-constructed Bailey bridge across the canal at Quistreham. Nearby — as much as I remember or know of the situation — were lock or sluice gates and a long narrow footbridge of some kind which were all prepared for demolition in the emergency of a particularly critical time.

Again the same two of us were very much in the same position as previously, with our orders to stand by to detonate the demolition charges on the verbal or written instructions of OC/CO or in the face of superior enemy forces. This time, however, it was daylight, sunny and bright and all around very much on the boil with the sight and sound of warfare.

High banks on both sides of the canal offered good cover against the considerable number of shells falling in and around the area, and from our control point in a shallow trench near the top of the far bank we could observe the field before us in the direction of the enemy while protecting ourselves reasonably well. Our position was such as to be on the wrong side of the water in the event of the canal bridge being destroyed and we should therefore have the not so difficult task of having to swim the waterway to get back on to the home side. Strange that at the time I never gave a thought to our peculiar situation — one decided by I don't know who.

From my position on the bank I could see across the ground before me the distant and not so distant shellbursts spewing up the usual clouds of dust and smoke. The enemy heavy gun emplacements at nearby Merville had, from all accounts, been knocked out, but it was apparent here that Jerry still had some fair sized artillery concentrating on the area. I had sometime heard it mentioned that we were within range of his Le Havre guns, which could perhaps explain some of the difference in the explosive power of descending missiles.

But one thing for sure, judging by the sound and activity of our own guns, was that he was getting a much greater return in delivery of such explosive packages. In particular, just a comparatively short distance away at sea, our warships were also demonstrating a vital support rôle by pounding enemy inland positions with tremendous naval fire power.

I watched and was fascinated for some time by the cool pluck and steadfast devotion to duty of what obviously was the figure of a British naval officer observer. He was high up on what could only have been a coastal look-out tower hardly more than a few hundred yards away. From his high 'crow's-nest' position he was extremely well-placed to signal and observe for his offshore naval gunnery command, but he was also at considerable risk in being perched high on a conspicuously tall white landmark. Again, strangely, it was as I was thinking of the brave man's exposure and vulnerability that I witnessed what was truly a remarkable example of enemy artillery marksmanship by seeing the top of the tower being taken away by a shellburst, leaving behind the jagged cut just below where the navy man had been operating. The man and his tower-top catwalk disappeared in a cloud of smoke and dust — a bull's-eye strike for the gunner in his Tiger tank maybe.

But the demolition incident which concerned me more directly occurred a short time later when the bombardment of enemy shelling was at its worst and close enough to force me to keep my head down. I had, however, seen flashes of exploding shells on or close to the nearby footbridge which was connected to our demolition ring main and therefore carrying a number of fixed explosive charges. I was concerned about the possible danger of a direct hit, or even of sympathetic detonation which could set off the ring mains series of demolition charges.

I waited for the duly obliging lull in enemy shelling before risking a quick inspection of the bridge section, where I considered possible damage to be done. In such a situation, or course, one would be expected sensibly to note and report any serious damage done to the bridges and, in the case of displaced charges or broken cables, to make good the damage as soon as possible.

Taking advantage of lulls in enemy shelling and having to run the gauntlet between unpredictable bursts of flying shrapnel was always, one might say, a kind of occupational hazard for battlefield soldiers whose unfortunate predicament is to live, work and fight midst the guns of war.

This time, however, the break between Jerry's shelling bombardments was little more than a few minutes' pause, and I was caught out in the open between the Bailey bridge and the more forward footbridge. It appeared to me, as I pressed flat to the ground, that a few more shells landed on or very close to the footbridge, which again was a matter of concern because of the explosive charges on the bridge. The thought occurred to me that it was one thing for the lightly structured and decked footbridge to be demolished by the chance ignition of an exploding shell, but altogether another, far more serious, thing for the canal Bailey bridge to be destroyed because of the cortex ring main connection. Perhaps some initiative on my part might well be directed towards cutting off one from the other . . .? But in the heat of the moment I was unable to make a decision and no positive action was taken.

I was happier later when a period of continued cessation of the shelling allowed me to take stock of the situation more closely. I had imagined that much more damage had been done to the footbridge than was actually the case. Close examination showed that only a couple of shells, 88 mms probably, were registered as hits on the structure. But the truly remarkable thing about one of them was the fact that it was a hit directly or almost directly at the spot where a demolition charge had been placed. The evidence was the area of damage around which were powdery traces and flaky pieces of the explosive charge which had earlier been one of the taped bundles of gun-cotton slabs fixed to the bridge. It was really astonishing that what I had feared could possibly happen had actually happened, but for some inexplicable reason without the dire consequence of detonating the explosive charge and its connected circuitry of cortex.

As I set about repairing some of the damage done to the layout of the cables etc., I could only ponder bemusedly as to the result of such a freak happening if all had been destroyed in one big bang. But it would be much later when I would be historically wiser about the campaign, when I would give the matter more thought.

Another peculiar happening — although of a different 'demolition' kind — was an event at some uncertain chronological point during those early days in the battle for Normandy. I guess the occurrence was sometime between the two forementioned bridge incidents.

I recall that it was a hot sunny day, as I sat on the far river bank of the River Orne, close to the recently completed London II Bailey bridge at Benouville. I was there, as on earlier occasions, with a Bren MG in defence of the two adjacent bridges, the captured old iron bridge and the new Bailey bridge, should any danger threaten from the enemy side approach. But I knew that on that side also were many of our own tough and stubborn airborne troops who were bravely holding the line despite considerable initial losses to their numbers.

From my position on the bank I could see some of them come and go from time to time. Those who crossed to the rear of the bridges were usually the casualties and their attendants, while others going forward appeared to me to be those who had been treated, decasualized and returned to the 'sharp end' again. I had the opportunity of talking to a few of them and I was struck by their cheerfulness. I could only admire them for their spirit and high morale, for I knew that the fields around and about were strewn with bodies of their dead comrades. Jerry's attacks and counter-attacks around the bridgehead were having little or no success against our lads, dropped from the skies, who had every intention of holding on to the ground so desperately and dearly won by them earlier.

I am sure that the two particular 6th Airborne guys who lingered and sat chatting with me for some time well deserved their break and also the little diversion which followed soon after in the way of a spot of fishing in the river. The heat of the day, the cool tidal incoming waters of the river and the nearby mooring of a wooden dinghy were, I suppose, temptation for the three of us to indulge in a few minutes' fishing which would hardly have met with the approval of the likes of Isaac Walton. Battlefield soldiers could not expect to have the time or the luxury of rod, line and bait in such a situation and, instead, it was the hand grenades carried by my companions which would be the speedy method, perhaps, of getting us some fresh fish for tea.

Out on the river, with myself at the oars, I watched my companions of brief acquaintance prepare to cast the explosive tackle which would hopefully bring some concussed fish to the surface. I naturally expected the grenades to be lobbed at safe distance from the boat but, instead, I was 'a little uneasy' to see one of my fearless friends toss his grenade no more than a yard or two from the boat, while the second fearless guy simply put his arm out to drop his grenade over the side of the boat. It became plain that we were not exactly in deep waters of the river when shock waves of the exploding grenades struck the thin timbers below our feet. The effect was a couple of painful and paralysing vibrations which were like the cracks of vicious and powerful whip lashes. We were indeed fortunate that the bottom of our craft did not cave in to fill our own bottoms with wooden or perhaps even a few steel splinters. The timbers had, however, been split, holed or somehow damaged to let water pour in around our feet. I certainly had no wish to lose the Bren MG I had with me in the boat and I therefore pulled like mad at the oars to get the craft to the river bank before going under. The fish, of course, had to go by the board as we only just made it on to the bank. But it was not only the fish that were the 'ones that got away', and we had a few good chuckles about it all before the two nutty fearless fellows left me to go to their more dutiful and serious calling.

But that incident was the preliminary to a more peculiar and much less funny one which followed very soon afterwards. It happened as I sat drying myself out on the same river bank, not more than a couple of dozen yards or so away from the London II Bailey bridge on the side towards the mouth of the river. Civilian boat traffic on the river was unthinkable and impossible in the circumstances, and up to that time it was only our own military activity and equipment associated with our bridging operations that had been involved in our stretch of water. Our London II Bailey bridge was complete as it cut across the River Orne on low pontoons, and it was therefore a barrier to river-journeying craft, if any were so foolishly put to it.

The River Orne estuary was a few miles to the right of me as I sat looking in that direction. Something had caught my eye but I couldn't quite make out what exactly was the strange looking flotage in the distance that appeared to be coming in with the tidal waters of the river. It was looming larger and more menacing by the minute, and with the London II Bailey bridge close to the left of me, I was suddenly concerned with the possible danger of some cunning German device or craft, perhaps prepared with explosives and directed at the bridge.

I watched in amazement as it followed the winding course of the river, gradually taking the outline and shape of a motorized sea-going vessel of some kind, but without the sound of engine or the sight of any person on board. Relative to the width of the river, the mysterious craft appeared monstrously high and wide on the water as it came ever closer, with its huge bulk seemingly hell-bent on a collision course with our Bailey bridge.

It was ominous in the extreme, and I was spurred into action by the sudden realization that I was duty-bound to defend the bridge, that I was there with an MG for that purpose! I dived low behind my Bren gun, took aim and rattled off a number of bullets towards the oncoming craft as warning shots if nothing else, since I had no idea of who or what was on board. It soon became clear, however, that it would take more than the rattle of bullets to halt the forward thrust, size and weight of the floating steel structure imminently endangering the bridge.

My last brief hope was that a protecting boom cable had been laid, as is often the practice by bridge-building sappers who are aware of the possibility of dangerous floating objects such as enemy mines, etc., which would perhaps arrest the vessel or reduce its impact when striking the bridge.

But whether such a boom cable existed, or if it did, what difference did it make? I was unable to tell as the mystery vessel struck the bridge at its middle with an almighty crack. It seemed for a moment that much of the pontoon bridge would be swept away on the tidal flow of the river and in the sweeping path of the vessel. But miraculously the bridge somehow held together, although forced out of alignment and bent into a configuration like a dog's hind leg.

The bridge was badly damaged but fortunately not completely destroyed, as might well have happened by what we soon discovered to be one of those freak incidents that can so often upset the applecart and best laid plans.

The villain of the piece turned out to be an unmanned LCT (Landing Craft Tank), being one of the vessels used in the Allies' fleet of assault craft for the beach landings in Normandy. Abandoned, lost or perhaps without crew because of enemy action, it had somehow drifted on the incoming turn of the tide from the sea into the river mouth and followed the winding course of the river to smash into our bridge, as if remotely controlled by the enemy.

Such an LCT was a powerful craft, designed and sturdily built especially for the conveyance of heavy armoured tanks across the sea. It was an item of naval equipment not easily lost, overlooked or lightly disposed of, and I therefore wondered as to how it came about that such a significant piece of Allied Forces' equipment had succeeded to do what a massive enemy force around the bridgehead had failed to do — damage and almost destroy the strategically important London II Bailey bridge.

To make good the damage was to take many hours of engineer skill, man and plant power, since the removal and replacement of damaged sections to such a completed bridge was no easy matter.

7

Strangely Wounded In Search Of An ADS

To me this was just another village in Normandy which was a village in name only. It seemed that having taken so much pounding and blasting from the guns of both sides, most of what now remained was the usual by-product of war and battle — pollution.

Filth, flies, stink and dust were everywhere, with a persistence that was in no way diminished by the hazy afternoon sunshine of the midsummer day.

My task here was to tackle another kind of pollution — mines and booby traps. There were plenty of these around and all well-placed, well-concealed and well-intended to kill, maim or hinder.

For my part, I knew well enough that the German enemy was expert in the design, setting and laying of such devices. As a sapper, disarmer and neutralizer of these devices, I was ever more inclined towards greater respect and caution as my knowledge and experience grew in such matters. I was always mindful that their Mark I device could just as well be a new kind of Mark II, about to be replaced by a more cunningly devised Mark III. Also their minefields, which once had a regular pattern of type and spacing, were now becoming craftily more irregular, with mines having different features and being differently spaced out, all done to baffle and confuse!

There were just two of us, in a partnership that usually worked well on this kind of operation. Our position was rather close to the enemy position and was therefore motivation enough to see the job done and then to get to Hell out of it as quickly as possible.

Handling mines in a minefield, however, is a matter which is hardly conducive to great speed, particularly so with the

93

deadly mixed-up lot we were in the process of finding and unearthing. By patient prodding and careful examination of long stretches of road verge we were surely — if not speedily — harvesting the deadly German crop of metal 'Teller' mines, wooden 'Box' mines and 'Schu' mines; 'S' mines and glass 'Tophf' mines.

It may perhaps be of interest to offer a brief description of these particular nasties so that some appreciation can be made of the danger and difficulty of such a task. A 'Teller' mine, for example, was about the diameter size of a large dinner plate, an inch or two thick, containing enough high explosive to blow man and vehicle to pieces. Besides having a detonating fuse for downward pressure, it also had two screw holes into which — all too often — were inserted small pegged booby switches, one which could be felt with sensitive fingers along the outer edge, which would then indicate that the other could be found underneath at the 'four o'clock' position. It had for some time been the usual disarming and safety practice to simply unscrew and separate the fuse from the mine charge, but it had lately been discovered, after many people had been killed in the unscrewing process, that safety depended on turning the fuse a precise number of times, which were certainly not to be exceeded. Removing the fuse here would be the death trap. It may be evident, therefore, that to find this type of mine was one thing, making it safe was another!

The 'S' mine was in every way an anti-personnel mine. It was one that must, I believe, have caused many British casualties in World War Two. It can best be described as a device having two small metal pots — like jam jars — with a smaller one being inside a slightly larger one. The inner jar contained approximately 360 ball-bearings. A peculiar antenna on the mine was a detonating system having three switches, i.e. press, trip and release, which meant that it could be activated by walking on it, tripping off a loose wire leading from it, and by cutting or releasing a taught wire attached to it. When triggered by any one of these switches, the smaller jar containing the steel ball-bearings would be propelled or hurled like a jack-in-the-box into the air to a height of six to eight feet before exploding and scattering the ball-bearings like bullets.

The 'Box' mine and 'Schu' mine were wooden-cased mines

which were deliberate non-metal mines to defy discovery by metal detectors, which formerly had been used extensively and successfully against the more conventional metal mines. Prodding the ground patiently and laboriously was the only way of tackling the problem. There was, however, always the danger of becoming a little careless, particularly after some barren patch, by prodding a little too hard. The 'Schu' mine was the smallest of the German mines, having only about four ounces of explosive — sufficient to take some poor blighter's leg off and cause him blindness as well. A view seemed to exist that a badly injured and maimed soldier was worse for his country than a dead soldier!

The 'Tophf' mine was a kind of experimental glass composite type. The idea, I suppose, as well as being non-metallic, was to scatter bits of the rock-hard substance on explosion.

I had lifted mines many times before. Indeed, it was just possible that I was a champ since I did, after all, a possible record number of about 700 in one shift on an earlier occasion. But alas! I knew of no one who was around long enough to keep records. I had, however, already received a piece of paper in the form of a certificate, with neat copperplate writing and which read as follows:

'As Commander-in-Chief 21st Army Group I award you this Certificate in token of my appreciation of the outstandingly good service which you have rendered. I have given instructions that this shall be noted in your Record of Service. Signed (personally) Bernard Law Montgomery (General).'

So besides being a nice 'thank you' for services rendered, my wartime certificate was also a qualification and passport for the even better pickings ahead.

Here, I pressed forward 'doing the job I loved to do most.' My throat was dry from the dust — maybe it was also just a tiny bit due to a number of tricky disarming operations — when I remembered that somewhere in my pack was a treasured can of plums. (I think somehow that it was perhaps not the 'official ration' sort of issue.) This, however, was the right moment to appreciate the juicy delight after having lugged it around for so long. I opened the tin and was not slow in spooning the fruit into a hot, dry and dusty gullet. In fact, I gulped at it too fast to notice another thirsty creature that descended for uninvited partakence of the syrupy succulence. A wasp went in with a plum, and it was then that my moment of ecstasy became a time of agony. The wasp (obviously a well-trained German one) went into the attack and 'over the top' with its own deadly little bayonet (sting) to the fore. It caught me somewhere at the back of my mouth or throat, causing the most excruciating pain. I coughed, spluttered and spat for several minutes, with tears running down my face. I cursed and really felt quite mad to think that I had survived a great deal in the way of explosive, shrapnel and bullets, etc., only to succumb now to a blasted little insect.

My throat began to swell dangerously, and it was clear that I would have to get medical treatment quickly because of the possibility of suffocation with closed windpipe.

I had a fairly good idea of where the nearest ADS (Advanced Dressing Station) was. I reckoned that it would be quicker to get there by running and walking, as the crow flies, across several fields and ditches to the higher ground where I remembered seeing tents with red crosses.

My partner was sympathetic and urged me to move with haste, to return only after medical treatment and reassurance.

I went off well aware of the possibility that my short cut to the ADS could take me into other minefields. It was, however, a chance I had to take. I was fairly sure that the direction I took was the right one and that I should make the ADS in about ten to fifteen minutes or so by moving fast.

Because of the danger of trip wires, etc., I avoided areas of likely placement and preferred sometimes to travel along dried-up or low ditches. There were, however, some open field areas I could not avoid altogether.

Dead and dying cattle were a common enough sight in many battle areas. I had become quite inured to the butchered appearance of many a cow's carcass in the Normandy fields. Two creatures I came across here, however, I could not pass by without ending their misery with close-range Sten bullets. One of the cows I found had somehow remained stumbling about on all fours with only half of its head left, this a black mass of swarming flies. The other creature was also a dreadfully sad sight because it was slowly moving around trailing a good part of its own hide behind itself. A bomb or shellburst had at some time half skinned it alive.

I was shortly to encounter an even worse sight, too much even for my battle-hardened eyes and stomach.

At the end of a field, almost within sight of the ADS, was a long and wide ditch which I would have to cross. Otherwise I should have to retrace my steps to find another direction by way of a detour to get to the ADS.

I approached the ditch and was assailed by the most horrible stench. The reason was obvious enough when I gazed with sickness and revulsion into the ditch which had obviously been used as a burial trench. In both directions as far as I could see were hundreds of rotting dead bodies of what evidently were German fallen soldiers. Because of the summer heat and the uncovered state of the corpses, the ditch was a moving maggoty mass. I wanted to get away from the ghastly sight as quickly as possible but my problem now was somehow to get across the heaving trench. I saw that it would take a very good jump indeed to strike the bank firmly on the other side.

My throat was extremely painful, and by now swollen enough to give me a great deal of concern. I looked again at the ditch and wondered whether my present state of doubtful physical fitness would be enough to see me safely across with one good jump. I threw my gun and small pack across without difficulty so as to make my flight more assuredly an airborne one. Fear of falling below into the grizzly swamp-mire must certainly have lent wings to my feet, for I landed with a good inch or two to spare.

I moved quickly away, gradually leaving the stench behind, but with the gruesome picture still lingering on.

The ADS was little more than an encampment of tents, to which came the stretcher bearers, field ambulances, etc., bringing in the casualties directly from the battlefield areas. As with many, if not all Advanced Dressing Stations, this one was little more than an emergency treatment area marked by a few red crosses, too often disregarded in forward area gunnery exchanges. Stretcher loads would be placed on the ground for quick examination by some anxious and overworked military medic, then allocated to one of a number of small tents called 'wards.' Here, of course, the emergency dressings are applied before casualties are transported to secondary or base hospitals.

Seeing casualties arriving with their awful injuries made me feel more than a little embarrassed, with a feeling that here I was among so much blood and guts, with a ridiculous wasp sting complaint. I began to feel guilty about imposing myself on overworked medics and perhaps gaining attention for myself at the expense of some other poor devil. I felt like hoofing it back there and then until I remembered my unpleasant journey to get here. It was just possible, I thought, that a tablet or two might do the trick and that I might see much of the journey back from a perch on a jeep.

In any case my throat was throbbing painfully enough for me to approach someone who had the least red-blotched white coat. He was the fellow standing in front of two bandaged soldiers — one of whom looked more like an Egyptian mummy with head completely swathed in bandages, except for the small eye-slits. The other soldier had both arms bandaged up to the shoulders. I noticed that the medical officer — for such he undoubtedly was — was not so much dressing the soldiers up as 'dressing them down.' I thought it strange — no doubt in other circumstances I would have considered it downright funny — to see the MO, standing in front of the mummified figure, moving an admonishing finger and shouting 'You damned oafs — you should be charged with having self-inflicted wounds — that's how I look at it. Anyway off you go to No. 2 ward. I'll see you two clowns later.'

It was a case of murmuring to myself 'Oh dear!' as the officer came up to me, still apparently a bit hot under the collar. 'Those damned soldiers who get themselves scorched, burned and blown up when making blasted cups of tea for themselves. Negligence — making themselves incapable of carrying out military service, that's how I see it!' He speaks to me, 'By God, you know there seem to be more casualties in the British Army through making cuppas in the field than through enemy action in the field! Anyway, what can I do for you?' I put on a bold face and endeavoured to play it casually, 'Just popped in for a tablet or something, Doc,' my voice had somehow become just a faint whisper. I gulp, 'Bit of throat trouble — wasp sting,' pointing to the painful lump of anatomy that held my head up.

He looks into my mouth and feels the swelling around my throat. Then he looks at me with a degree of sympathy I least expected just then. 'You've got something nasty there, haven't you? Very dangerous! Sorry lad, but I shall have to keep you here overnight under observation. People have been known to choke to death with that kind of thing. If the swelling gets worse I shall have to do something to keep the tube clear.' He then instructed me to report to the orderly in ward No. 4, where he said he would visit me.

I really didn't like the idea very much of staying at this place for several hours, and I could understand the doctor's apology for his keeping me overnight. Anywhere else must surely be a better situation that being placed here in the centre-flow of war casualties. Smashed, bleeding and dying bodies were all too plain to see as they were shuffled around the place.

Ward No. 4 was the inside of a canvas tent with about six stretchers lined up on both sides, on the grassy floor. One stretcher was empty. The medical orderly took some details, then told me to rest and make myself comfortable on the available stretcher.

I was, by now, more than a little weary, and a lie down, even with a few moans and groans going on around me, was a state of inactivity that was in no way unwelcome. I went to lie down on the stretcher only to find that the previous occupant had left half his blood behind in a thick congealing pool on the canvas. I was angry and I certainly would see to it that not even war and battle would ever reduce me to a state of ready willingness to wallow and sleep in another human's blood — I told the orderly so in no mean terms, and demanded if not another stretcher then at least a couple of blankets. He went off muttering something about, 'Some people being afraid of a drop of blood.' He did, however, return quickly with a waterproof sheet and thick blanket.

I settled myself, though not at all comfortably, on the stretcher with a feeling that somehow I shouldn't be here, that my particular war wound was hardly the kind confidently to give me that 'belonging' feeling. I felt sure that my membership of this little club would be resented or ridiculed when it became known by the genuine and real battle casualties — heroes all — that I was among then with a little sting problem — put out of action by a bloody wasp!

Before falling quickly asleep, I determined my secret was safe if I got up at the crack of dawn and moved back to my friendlier and more familiar places — my beloved minefields!

8

Somewhere In Normandy's Bocage Country

Midsummer 1944, when there could be few complaints about the weather. Mother Nature's sunny treat in the fields of Normandy was being most improperly appreciated by man's savage acts of war. But complaints about these matters, however, were pointless and not at all in accordance with the demands, conduct and heroics of warfare if the war was to be won and its duration shortened.

Moans and groans, though, were usual enough since they were the soldier's natural safety-valve, his emotional release from the tension and stress of viciously cruel combat.

There were, indeed, plenty of moans and groans in our platoon when we were told that yet again another dirty job was to be ours, which was an extensive mine clearance task in the area of a small village, or hamlet, located at the foot of a hillside. The problem was that the hilltop and the ground beyond were occupied by enemy troops, who had the obvious advantage of dominating the lower ground with considerable fire power, an unhealthy situation because the operation would put us well within range of Jerry's bullets, shells and mortars for a considerable period of time.

I had long given up wondering about the apparent craziness of sending troops into such impossible situations, having reasoned that such a war demanded sacrifices from everybody — but especially and more particularly from the suffering souls of the lower ranks. We would never know whether we were put into such situations simply to draw the enemy's fire and test his strength, etc., which might be damn good strategy as reckoned by the gods and geniuses of higher rank, command and echelon. Or again, one could never tell just how important it was in such situations for a few of us to die so that a few more of them may live. 'Such honour and glory, chaps. . . and don't forget, soldier, yours is not to reason why. . .!'

I had already been with a recce party to the place — which to me was a geographical point somewhere in the Normandy Bocage country, since their place-names always confused me — when I then had the ominous feeling that it was a place where it was all too easy to die by enemy action, even if you didn't have to work out in the open lifting mines!

Silence and stillness hung over the place when, during this recce, I searched the couple of streets and rows of houses which mainly made up the village. The houses were deserted — some badly damaged — and a quick look into many of them showed that they were the houses of extremely poor Norman peasants who, I am sure, would not have lost much sleep over the value of possessions left behind, the exception being one hut, or outbuilding, containing a collection of tools.

The line of the two parallel streets ran at right angles to the vertical line of the hillslope, which, for an infiltrating reluctant military 'Aunt Sally', could be considered a considerable advantage when taking cover from the deluge of hot steel expected from the enemy's high ground positions.

Two sections from our own platoon were detailed for the operation, with a working party of eight men from each section to do the actual work of sweeping the area clear of mines and booby traps. I was included in one of the sections.

A road passed close to the edge of the village and came from a crossroads junction about half a mile or so from our own lines to pass up the hill to disappear somewhere into enemy territory.

A couple of daylight runs had already been made by our recce vehicles along the road from the crossroads to the village without causing much of a stir in activity by the enemy, who may have had their own good reasons for keeping a low rather than high profile. It was therefore considered not too dangerous to move our section vehicles along the road to within a short distance of the village.

The day was early as we set off for the commencement of our task. Besides carrying section personnel, our vehicle also carried a couple of Company HQ guys who had for certain reasons asked to come along for the ride. One of them was the CHQ handyman who somehow had been told of the tools lying around in the village shed and he wanted, perhaps, to see how he could make good his own deficiencies in tools. He was, as I knew, an excellent Jack of all trades who did everything from signwriting to boot repairing. The other fellow was a L/Cpl who was the unit's medical orderly. He was a particularly striking and likeable chap, being a handsome, cultured and gentlemanly type. I had been told he was studying and training to become a Doctor of Medicine before his call-up for military service. Or he may indeed have been a volunteer to gain valuable practical experience, since he appeared to be a dedicated medical type. In every way a respected and popular NCO by everyone throughout the unit, which was hardly surprising since everybody at some time had been treated by him. I had no idea of what it was that brought him along with us, unless maybe he wanted to see more of the action and countryside. It would make a change, perhaps, from the cramped environs of his usual First Aid post.

But for whatever reasons the CHQ pair had for making their journey with us it was soon to be decided that they were fatally wrong ones. But perhaps their fate was decided long past in the infinity of time and space by the mysterious unfathomable forces which created, controlled, assessed and finalized everything, be it a single blade of grass, volcano, waterfall or an Emperor penguin's egg. I no longer believed man was master of his destiny, captain of his soul, etc., as I had done earlier. Too many strange incidents had happened to me to hold on to that line of ego philosophy. Here again with the CHQ pair, I was to find more examples of the funny games played by the Grand Master of all our destinies. For example, their positions at CHQ gave them more safety and security than anyone else in the entire unit — although the situation was hardly a bed of roses for anyone. Yet somehow here they were tagging along with us of their own free will — probably the result of a fleeting impulsive thought — heading for their doom!

We arrived at the task area and were soon put to work searching and clearing the fairly lengthy tracts of ground which surrounded the oblong shaped block arrangement of the hamlet. We worked as individuals or in pairs, with each being allocated an area or plot for mine-sweeping and clearance. My own area of ground was to the right of the road and nearest to the lower slope of the hill. On my side of the road — which road passed to the right of the village to wind its way up the left hand side of the hill — an ancient four foot high stone boundary wall cut across in front of me, conveniently to offer stout covering protection. Early experience of enemy fire instilled in me the urgency and importance of ground cover availability. I therefore lost no time in marking out a foot high small semi-circle of loose stones at the base of the wall for protection in case of fireworks.

First indications were that there were no mines in the ground to the right of the road, although one could never be certain of anything where mines and booby traps were concerned. Suspect ground was always treated with caution and respect, and sappers in particular were unlikely to be the 'fools who rush in where others fear to tread.' But it was also true that for many of us mine clearance was all too often a slow, tedious and laborious job.

But situations and patterns of battle can change very quickly, with the ordinary soldier, more often than not, poorly in the picture with developments in the field. But then even the best informed and enlightened military commander must be often as much in the dark about enemy intentions and positions.

Difficult therefore for me to know what the Germans were up to, or whether they were as close to us as we had earlier believed them to be. So far things were not as bad as expected, and it was not an unwelcome sight for me to see a couple of drab elderly-looking peasant women walking in our direction along the road from somewhere up the hill. They had perhaps considered it safe enough to move back into their village homes? I noticed however that they continued along the road and went past the hamlet to move out of sight towards our own lines.

They were most fortunate because just a short time later the enemy's deadly missiles began to descend. Their series of bombardments were not very heavy and did not last very long, but even in such situations it is not always easy, when your head is down, to see where such missiles land. It seemed to me, however, that most were landing on the enemy side of the old stone wall. It was from my protective spot at the base of the wall where, from time to time during the volleying bursts, I heard the most amazing medley of sounds as the shrapnel and debris fragments, of varying size and material, ricocheted, whined, whistled and thumped around me. I had heard the scream and explosive sound of shells often enough before, but I had never so clearly experienced, or so keenly sensed, the high and low key sounds of flying objects — sometimes like the fading buzz of a giant bee, or the sound of someone flicking the pages of a book in my ear, or that of diminishing swooshes of a boomerang curling past my head. In my case 'hearing was believing' such sounds could be made by the duet of projectile and airflow.

For a considerable time later, however, little was heard and it was tempting to believe that Jerry had moved to less proximate lines, or that maybe he was extremely short of ammo. But experience had taught me that the often quite long intervals in Jerry's bombardments were craftily deliberate so as to create, within our ranks, a false sense of security and to lure us into a situation of greater vulnerability.

In this case, however, Jerry was generous enough to let matters rest for quite a few hours, which was a sufficiently long enough period to allow many of our party to become more relaxed and somewhat a little off guard. When the afternoon's 'grub up' was called it was easy to believe that squatting around the food containers and tea urns within the confines of the hamlet block, with its protective surround of buildings, was as safe a place as any — certainly much safer than the exposed areas we had just left.

It was a fine warm afternoon with all of us making the most of the matey get-together: the refreshing food and drink, and the respite from dusty, tiresome and dangerous labours. So darned easy to forget about the enemy!

It should be said that because of their varied tasks and often individual operations in the field, sappers are generally more casual and much less regimentally directed and minded than their infantry brothers in forward battle zones. Because of their limited, but intensive, drill and training, infantry soldiers have a single-mindedness for attack or defence. Fighting as they do in numbered formations, yet moving as a single unit, they are probably much more combatively alert than your average bunch of sappers — who may at times be much too casual where their own safety is concerned.

Joined in with the group was a young Troop Officer who had probably arrived with the field rations. He was a good-natured and popular chap who was usually around even in the worst of situations. He had a double-barrelled Welsh sounding name, which may be why I took to him so well, although he might not have been a Welshman at all as he had not the slightest trace of a Welsh accent when he spoke. He was anything but a serious minded regimental type of officer who perhaps fitted the image of a student teacher more than anything else. He was, however, a brave enough soldier to have had some pretty tight skirmishes with the enemy if all that was said about him was true. One such incident reported was that on the D-day landings he had somehow got cast adrift to later find himself washed up and wandering among Germans on a sector of Normandy coast not in the invasion front. He had quite a genuine tale to tell about how he got out of his predicament.

One incident, however, was hardly to his credit and he was finding it hard to live it down within the troop. It concerned a recent foolhardy prank of his which nearly had serious consequences — a matter not easily forgotten by those of us involved. The incident is worth mentioning as an example of his disregard for safety.

It happened just a week or so earlier when the officer accompanied the troop for an overdue trip to the RAOC Mobile Bath unit for a shower and a delousing session. The officer was in the cab of the open ten ton vehicle tightly packed with troops of our platoon. After travelling some way across open country, the vehicle was brought to a halt because of a bombardment of shelling which could clearly be seen churning up the dust and ground in the direction we were to travel. Our road ahead crossed a small iron bridge which was a couple of hundred yards or so away — a kind of bottleneck situation the enemy obviously wished to exploit in his efforts to resist the infiltrating process. The shells were falling pretty close to the bridge. We watched and timed the sequence of falling shells and lull intervals, and by my own reckoning we had a minute or so to get to the bridge, to get across it and to get clear of the danger zone if we were to make it a less dangerous journey. As so often happens in war, it was another case of running a gauntlet of enemy fire. Little thought was given to the possibility that the enemy was pressed to cut the road from his position somewhere to the right of us.

It was a moment not without excitement when the officer signalled the start of the dash of the vehicle, amid plenty of yells to the driver to put his foot down like Hell. To the bridge then, Hell for leather we went, with everybody having tense and anxious moments of desire to see the iron structure fast disappearing behind us. But to everyone's amazement, anger and near panic, the vehicle stopped dead in the middle of the bridge.

Out of the cab came the officer, wearing a big grin and rubbing his hands together in an attitude of exaggerated bravado, to ask how we were, how we felt and were we enjoying the trip. Such fury by a bunch of soldiers towards a superior officer have I seldom seen, and had the officer not moved rapidly back into the cab he was in danger from those who waved their rifles dangerously close to his head. The vehicle raced away not a split second too soon. Perhaps it is more true to say that for many of us in the vehicle it was almost a split second too late, as a burst of shelling caused a rattle of exploding fragments along the side of the vehicle as it sped away. A later examination of the vehicle showed a few small pieces of shrapnel embedded in the stout metal sides of the truck. Fortunately on that occasion nobody suffered anything worse than a few shattered nerves and some badly gnashed teeth.

But to get back to the hamlet situation, however, some of those same troops were to be much less fortunate as was the fate of the same officer who had joined in with the group's meal break.

A good helping of food and drink does perhaps have a biological effect of easing anxieties and nervous tensions, since under man's natural and primitive laws of existence it is a prelude to relaxation and sleep. It seemed to me that nature's intentions were always that the less fed should be the hunters and the well-fed the hunted. It may not therefore be such a ridiculous thought to think that a good bellyful of 'army nosh' might make a soldier more, rather than less, vulnerable to danger from the enemy.

For here again something was to happen about which one

could argue as being something man brings upon himself, or as something out of the control of man because he is unable to decide his own fate — what will be will be, etc. For me, as for those who have gone before me, the perplexity of the dual philosophy of logical explanation for the pattern of man's evolution and progression, or that of phenomenal happenings caused by mysterious forces of the unknown.

The situation was that as we sat or stood around in the bright afternoon sunshine I was — like some of the others around — just about to tackle the excellent tinned rice liberally sploshed into our mess tins. From my pavement position in the street between two rows of houses I was able to see a short stretch of the road which passed at the top of the avenue. For just a brief moment or two before they disappeared from view I caught a glimpse of the same two figures of the women I had seen earlier in the morning passing down from the hill. Although the rice tasted good enough to deserve my undivided attention, for some reason I dwelt on the reappearance of the two old dears. I was puzzled that they had again come down the hill, moving in the same direction as before, I could not recall seeing them moving back in the opposite direction earlier, as I should have done. It was a matter which caused me to think that they must be a daft old pair to move around in such a way. I remembered thinking earlier just how lucky they were to have missed, only by minutes, the spate of enemy shelling after they had passed me by in the morning. I was struck by the unpleasant thought that moving around as they did between enemy lines and our lines was altogether a dangerous kind of journey and exposure. Who the Hell wants to be caught in crossfire? — unless of course they had some kind of assurance that they wouldn't be, assurance which, if they had, could only have come from the enemy. The thought of their possible — or indeed probable — contact with the enemy made me feel suddenly very uneasy and it was not on impulse that I decided to finish my meal elsewhere. I went into one of the houses close by and sat down in a spot which I considered to be a much safer place — a pantry floor. Above my head was a great thick flagstone and around me thick walls for good protection.

Although I hoped to finish off the rest of my meal in peace, my nagging doubts increased by the second. I sat and ate while at the same time expectant that something was about to happen. Amazingly, as if in direct response to my straining senses, it really happened, and with a violence that shook me and the pantry around like a rattled penny and money box. A series of mighty explosions smashed and crashed around my ears, to leave me shocked, stunned and choking with dust for several minutes after they ceased.

I was able to crawl out from the place which had protected me well, but it was not without pushing aside a fair amount of wreckage and debris. Outside, although partly blinded by the strong sunlight and dust, I could see well enough to recognize that what confronted me was a very sad sight indeed. Most of the group who just a short time earlier were cheerfully bunched together, in hindsight rather foolishly, were now lying scattered around in pathetic bundles — some were lifeless and others badly wounded — all victims of a German barrage of missiles directed with almost pinpoint accuracy.

The officer appeared to have survived because, although remaining flat on the ground, he was already issuing orders and instructions to the fortunate few who were mobile. Someone had already dashed off to bring in the section's vehicles, including the sigs/radio vehicles, which fortunately were kept behind in waiting somewhere not too far away. This was a time when the stretchers carried on them were also urgently needed.

It was left to myself and a slightly injured corporal to tend to the wounded until the vehicles arrived. It was soon discovered that there were five dead bodies, six wounded — two critically — and with two persons missing.

The officer remained lying on the floor and insisted that as he was all right himself we should direct our attention to the others. But in the activity of sorting out the casualties it became clear that the officer was also wounded and unable to move. Again he insisted on being the last man to be put on a stretcher, only for us to discover as we did so that he was a dying man. He died a few minutes later with a fist-sized hole in his side. I felt bad and sad about the death of an officer who really could put on an act of bravery — his final act supreme in every way.

There had been two missing men, but one of these we soon

found as having gone to ground — forever, perhaps, if we had not been around to quickly dig him out alive and well. The other missing person was the L/Cpl medical orderly who was one of the two from CHQ who had come for the ride. It was I who eventually found him after searching in and around one of the houses, in a position almost as if peering to the outside. He was dead and could well have been hurled through the window from the outside by the explosive blast which had obviously been the cause of his death.

His fellow traveller on the truck — the CHQ handyman — was also dead, he being one of the five who, it seemed, were caught by the first delivery of what was said to be a simultaneous clutch of projectiles. The Germans apparently had a weapon — the Nebelwefer — which was a kind of mobile multi-barrelled (five to ten) mortar that could rapidly throw a great poundage of explosives over a good distance. It was probable that this was the weapon of slaughter used here.

The death toll had risen to six, and I was to reflect later it would almost certainly have been seven had I not been mentally primed and forewarned by somehow being urged to move away from the danger spot at precisely the right moment. I found yet again a buzz from my guardian angel had rescued me from a nasty end. Or was it really nothing to do with any mysterious and inexplicable agency, but more simply that I had that amazingly good piece of luck in having my body, head and eyes turned and tuned perfectly to spot, for this brief moment, the two females whom I had rightly sensed to be the harbingers of danger and tragedy?

That there was something about them that had somehow raised in me a kind of semi-conscious question mark, became rather more explicable a few days later when, by chance, I overheard a piece of conversation which concerned the interrogation and custody of a couple of French girls. The information I gathered was that a DR, being somewhere to the rear of the calamitous hamlet on the same calamitous day, stopped and checked two wandering females. He discovered that they were two young French girls who had altered their appearance by dress and make-up — long garb, grey hair, etc. — too look like older women, not such an unusual or bad thing to do in the case of young girls putting themselves at risk by having to move among unknown active service soldiers.

Their eventual interrogation, and information given by another civilian who knew both girls, revealed that they had cohabited for some time with German soldiers and that they recently had German lovers with whom they collaborated.

I was unable to confirm such information, but it seemed to fit the picture rather well that together they had in some way communicated or signalled to bring the fire upon the heads of our party when most vulnerable.

The girls were certainly in for a hard time if it was all true, the liberated French folk had their own way of dealing with collaborators.

And so for me, losing more of my friends in this way, was another sad experience but which again was just another deal in the bloody business of war.

There was, too, another strange sequel to this particular chapter of events and concerned the death of the CHQ medical orderly.

In the months that followed it so happened that, with the usual notification of a soldier's death to NOK, the mother of this particular soldier refused to accept as fact her son's death. It was understood that she was clairvoyant and a spiritualist who believed for a long time that her son was alive, that he was wrongly reported dead because of confusion and mistaken identity in the battlefield. She made repeated claims that she was in contact with him, and she continued — until the unit was disbanded, I believe — to send strange messages to the unit HQ. She also sent regular parcels of cigarettes, food and drink etc., which she instructed should be shared out among the soldiers of her son's troop. Poor lady! I often wondered about her and whether God and nature in their wisdom gave her a defensive barrier of deception in order to protect her from the overwhelming flood of grief. Knowing her son as I did, I hoped so!

9

My Mademoiselle From Armentières

You could really be a most intelligent and observant soldier, yet still find yourself often totally lost and disorientated in the battle zones and campaign areas of war. This was particularly so with a squad of REs like ours, when a sharp order or two would often see us travelling at the dead of night in the back of the section vehicle without the slightest notion of where we were, where we were going or what we were going to do when we got there. In any event it was most often the case that travelling in a truck was an opportunity for weary soldiers to doze and 'get some in' before the next bit of Hell was let loose.

In this way we were shuffled around for the many different tasks we had to do, which were often miles apart so that there were times when we had but little idea of whether we were travelling north, south, east or west. Place names, if anything, added to the confusion since often you could be dozens of miles away from the place you thought you were at.

So it was that travelling and dozing late at night, we were suddenly halted near the gates of a hedge-enclosed field. A scout car had led us to this place and it was now looking for a sheltered spot where we could settle for the night. The scout car entered the dark field, while our truck hung close to a hedge, as we waited for it to return with the OK for us to enter.

Suddenly the field became alive with machine-gun fire, with what was all too apparently a scrap in the field between two scout cars — reconnaissance armoured vehicles — one being ours and British, the other being theirs and German! Both were charging and chasing each other around the field, with bullets rattling against the armour-plated sides of both vehicles.

The driver of the German vehicle must have been the first

to become giddy from making frantic and frenzied circles inside the field, because he then bolted through the gateway and went off in the opposite direction to where we were hidden in the hedge.

We now had the field to ourselves since it was obvious the Germans had no intention of hosting our visit. They did, however, treat us to some entertainment before they disappeared into the dark, because we certainly had a good few chuckles in thinking about the way the contestants were firing bullets up each other's backsides as they hammered and careered around the field.

We knew well enough that at this particular time in the campaign, the Germans were on the run backwards almost everywhere in France, and we were sure that we had seen the last of these particular tail-enders for some time.

We quickly settled into the field for a few hours' 'shut-eye' before the dawn of the new day arrived.

I was awakened early in the morning by the sounds of laughter, shouting, singing and the clapping of a great crowd of French civilians who had gathered around in obvious delight to celebrate their 'liberation.'

It was, of all places, the town of Armentières where we suddenly found ourselves being hugged and kissed by hordes of French men, women and children.

We had been joined earlier by the rest of our platoon, who had been in radio contact, and we were now all responding happily to the fantastic mood and welcome by the citizens of Armentières.

Into the centre of the town we went, to be further greeted in the most amazing fashion. The entire population of the town was out on the streets and every one of them, it seemed, trying to get near to embrace me and my colleagues, truly a great sight and experience — never before or since experienced, and unlikely ever to happen again!

There were many people in Armentières who still cherished fond memories of 'Tommy' from the First World War, and it was clear that their feeling, friendship and welcome was sincere, honest and true.

I was also profoundly struck by the fact that the language difference was no difference at all, because of the joyous mood of the time — more the ecstasy of the moment — that transcended verbal communication of the two peoples into a single body language of love. Never before had I kissed so many pretty girls — or Frenchmen for that matter, who also seemed to know a thing or two about kissing. Marvellous, truly marvellous. . .!

I am sure that our OC was also in love with the place because he somehow managed to grant his soldiers' fervent wish to dally a while among these grand and friendly people. Whether it had already been planned or whether it was a trumped up excuse I was not in a position to know, but I do know there was a big cheer from all of us when we learned that we were to build a Bailey bridge in the area. It would allow us to remain at Armentières for at least a couple of days or so — we should see to that!

Everywhere people wanted to take us into their homes and there was opportunity galore to make friends by the hundreds if only the time and pleasure were allowed to us.

The following day saw us hard at work on the construction of our Bailey bridge. The scene at the site of the bridge looked as if a regatta or other great public event was taking place, because of the spectator crowds that had gathered.

For many folk of Armentières it was, however, not entirely a day for celebration, because the day was also a day for mourning and funeral for some of their dead heroes. The story was that a short time before we arrived, a small group of French resistance fighters were trapped in the town hall of Armentières. They held out for some time against the Germans who surrounded the building. The resistance men were killed when shells from the German guns were directed at the building.

It occurred to me that perhaps the Germans we had earlier encountered in the field incident might well have played a part in killing the brave Frenchmen.

The bridge we were engaged on was being built at much less than record speed, not least because of the presence and celebratory good humour of the local people who crowded around on all sides. There were, for example, many pretty girls and lovely women who were much too distracting for our concentration towards speedier pace and progress.

It really was a change from our past bridging tasks, when urgency and speed were paramount. Here we had a wonderful gallery we could leisurely play to and thoroughly enjoy.

It was here in the midst of this marvellous throng of people where I saw her. Even among so many other pretty females she seemed to stand out a mile. Her delicious beauty struck me in an instant, and even at quite some distance away I saw and felt a magic that somehow had me hypnotized from the start — although she had in no way singled me out.

She was small and petite, about sixteen years of age and, considering the austere times, dressed in a surprisingly chic red costume. Her hair was a colour that was raven blue/black. It was long to her shoulders and fell smoothly on either side of a small fairy-like face. She had, in striking contrast to her hair, light blue eyes and a creamy white complexion that really did have the lustre of a flawless pearl. She was for me an exquisite china doll and undoubtedly the loveliest creature I had ever seen.

I worked away impatiently, afraid that she would cease her wide-eyed wonderment at what we were doing, and perhaps at any minute disappear into the crowd to be lost to me forever.

By normal standards I could, I suppose, be considered a shy person. I was a young soldier, having just reached a twenty-third birthday, with nineteen of them spent in my little Welsh village back home. A natural reserve therefore had to be overcome before I could muster enough courage and cheek to do something about meeting this lovely person. My increasing resolve and determination to speak to her at all costs, saw me suddenly throw down the tools and equipment I worked with to dash impulsively through the crowd to make my way to where she stood.

I had little idea of what I should say until I actually said it. The catchy little tune I learned as a small boy came to my mind and I remembered some words, 'Bonjour . . . Mademoiselle from Armentières . . . parlez vous . . . English!' I think that my compulsion to meet her must have been in obedience to some divine directive, because I knew then that we were fated to meet. It was as if I were expected and that she waited for me. Or was it perhaps simply confirmation that a faint heart never won a fair lady!

After just a short while I found myself walking and talking — my few words of French and about the same from her in English — in more secluded surroundings where, for my stolen hour or two, we got to know each other better.

I had, however, to get back quickly to my squad before my absence became too obvious.

Before we parted we arranged that as soon as I could manage it I would visit her at her home to meet her parents. She gave me good instructions how to get there and I was sure that all the king's horses, officers, NCOs and men wouldn't stop me from seeing my little angel again!

On my way back to join my squad I found it difficult not to spend more time making more friends because of the number of people who continued to hail and greet me like a long lost brother.

My few hours of absence were unnoticed, or if it had been noticed it was not bothered with because — so I was told — of delay in obtaining sufficient bridging equipment.

It was for this reason, also, that we were given the rest of the day off, as a rest period and a well deserved break.

I spruced myself up and was off like a greyhound in the direction I knew would take me again in the company of the loveliest, sweetest, most refined and sophisticated girl I had ever met. Her name was Micheline.

In the short time I had spent with her I also found her to be a shy person, with a wistful kind of sadness that somehow reflected the sadness of the times. France was indeed at this time having a hard time of it, with most of her people starving or nearly starving to death. Food was everywhere a desperate shortage, with even the rationing system in many areas broken down totally. It was not unusual to see hungry people begging for food. Even though we had arrived, it was — and was likely to be for some time — a desperate struggle for survival for the people of France.

In the circumstances, a Tommy with a packet of 'hard tack' biscuits or a tin of bully beef to spare, was a lord and master who could command the 'highest lady in the land.' Indeed, 'beef (flesh) for beef' was no corny joke but a commonplace reality. Those were days when a bar or two of chocolate was sufficient wealth and payment to satisfy the most lustful soldier.

But there were — even in those degrading times — some people who somehow managed a dignity and good grace that would not be surrendered. We were the conquering heroes who could all too easily take advantage of people who had suffered humiliation, oppression and hardship for years. In the circumstances it was easy to become oppressors ourselves — or a kind of lesser of two evils!

I went on my way following the instructions Micheline had given me. I felt excited about my invitation to visit her and her parents at home, but excited also because I knew in my heart that she was as suddenly in love with me as I was in love with her.

Although like most soldiers in such a situation I was all too aware that I was a 'here today and gone tomorrow' character with a 'live today for tomorrow we may die' outlook, I felt strongly that this was one relationship I wanted to be permanent or long lasting.

Micheline was not to be trifled with or despoiled in any way — and the bottle of Camp coffee, sugar, tea, chocolate and sweet biscuits I carried with me were to be gifts from the heart, and not to be selfishly offered in barter or exchange. My occasional parcel from Wales somehow always had a timely arrival!

I found the house to be a nice one, in a pleasant middle-class surrounding and was generally as described to me by Micheline earlier.

I liked both her parents, with her father in particular giving me the heartiest of greeting, endorsing it with the usual warm-hearted Frenchman's kiss. He was a short, balding, middle-aged man who did most of the talking and gesturing, while mother, a kind looking woman with motherly reserve and politeness, sat obediently and quietly.

We were none of us very conversant in each other's language, but we managed somehow to get along fairly well with rather more signs than words. I gathered that Micheline's dad was — or had been since there was for some time a state of suspension or collapse of local Government affairs — a superintending chief clerk at the town hall.

We enjoyed some of the coffee and biscuits I had brought, while we persevered without too much of a language problem to know more about each other, our concerns and happenings, etc. I was given a good account of the fight put up by the freedom fighters before they were killed at the town hall. But I was not at all surprised to be told that there had been also as much cowardice, treachery and German collaboration in the town as there had been resistance, sacrifice and heroism etc. My thoughts were that it was no different from other places I encountered. People everywhere can be like so many straws in the tide. I had seen for myself on earlier occasions how everyone vied with one another in quickly rigging up an armband with their own printed letters 'FFI', meaning Free French or Freedom Fighters, or something or other. It was often laughable and farcical the way one Frenchman with FFI armband would whisper aside to me about another standing close who would also wear an armband, 'Today FFI — yesterday *collaborateur!*' with the other whispering exactly the same about the first. In the circumstances it was never easy to distinguish the sincere from the false, and I took a philosophic view about it all. Resistance or collaboration, with the who's and the why's would, I was sure, continue well into the future, with the war's victors being the eventual deciders.

Micheline had an older sister who made an appearance later in the evening. She was about twenty years of age and was also a lovely looking person. She was, however, rather silent and subdued. This I found rather strange until I learned later that she and her father were not on speaking terms. It appeared they had quarrelled because she mostly lived and worked as a hostess at the 'Black Cat' night-club in Armentières. The father was later to explain, rather ashamedly, his difference with his daughter by saying he thought that the 'Black Cat' was more of a brothel which in the past had been frequented by Germans. Micheline was also to tell me later that it was her sister — who she was sure was no prostitute — who had kept the family from suffering hardship and hunger because of her earnings at the 'Black Cat.' In any case, Micheline explained, there was little else she could do in order to survive herself.

I had seen, all too plainly, a sadness on that lovely face also. She departed after an hour or so and I, too, had a feeling of sadness that I had managed no real communication with her. I was left feeling that I should have done more to show her that I was on her side, that I understood the wartime predicament and behaviour of people and that I could forgive and forget the faults of most people in such circumstances. I was sure, however, she had left feeling lonely and unhappy because she felt awfully guilty in some way.

I spent a few hours alone with Micheline in her own room, which she had tactfully requested of her parents she ought to show me.

Micheline had a childlike innocence and sweetness that captivated me completely, and she was, according to every part of me, the girl I would marry. She, too, was all mine as we kissed and cuddled for some time. My great passions must have been overwhelming for her, for she trembled like a quivering little bird as she urged me to make love to her. My own desire for her was too great to be repressed, and we were soon carried away on a passionate wave of love for each other.

The following evening, though later than previously, again saw me getting ready for another visit to the home of Micheline. I had made a sincere promise that I would do so if at all possible. On this occasion, however, I took with me a good friend hoping that perhaps Micheline's sister would be at the house and could therefore make up a foursome. I intended that she would not be left out of affairs as she unhappily seemed to be earlier.

Micheline's delight was plain to see when I arrived. There was also sincere warmth and welcome for us both by her parents. Unfortunately we learned that Micheline's sister had come and gone before we arrived. It was for both of us a disappointment, but more so for my army friend, Eddie, who stayed for an hour or two before he, too, went on his way. Before he went, however, we were both requested by Micheline's father to write down our names and addresses — which for me was an address in Carmarthenshire, Wales, with Plymouth, England, for Eddie.

A short time afterwards Micheline and I were alone again for the little time now remaining for us to be together. We already knew that I should be leaving Armentières on the following morning. Our bridging task was done and my unit was due to move out then.

We both therefore wanted everything that was lovingly possible between us before cruel time and circumstances forced us apart. We again made love, with Micheline sighing, clinging, quivering and with whispered pleadings expressing a desire for my child. It was a gentle demand for a souvenir of our meeting and love. She seemed to be but a child herself, but her embrace was irresistible.

I left after being overwhelmed with kisses, tears and the blessings of Micheline's good and kindly parents. Micheline herself promised that she would come around to see me off at our unit location from where we would depart after breakfast at around nine am.

True to her word, the beautiful Micheline arrived early in the morning, to be joined by several other mademoiselles, who were also around to see other soldier friends and sweethearts depart likewise.

As we moved away I was left with a vision that was to remain always with me. My last picture was of Micheline — my sweet angelic Micheline and my own divine mademoiselle from Armentières — sadly weeping, her long black hair around head and shoulders shaking with sobs. I saw her as she looked up with tears running down her cheeks as she waved me a final goodbye. I remember I waved and shouted, 'Wait for me Micheline. I want to marry you. I'll come back to you!'

Alas, it was never to be so, for I never saw Micheline again.

The story however does not end here for it had an interesting, if not strange sequel, which is as follows.

Over the next few months my craving to get back somehow or anyhow to Armentières was sheer Hell. I could not get Micheline out of my mind, and the only thing that stopped me deserting was knowing that I would only burden her and her parents with my fugitive presence which could only add to their difficulties and hardships.

Time went on, as did the war, for the many months later when I received the usual weekly letter from my old dad back in Wales. In it he said that a 'mysterious letter' had been received which was handwritten in the French language. Having no knowledge of French, my parents had no idea of what it was about except that my Christian name was mentioned. A nearby neighbour claimed to have knowledge of French and volunteered to attempt a translation. The result of it all was that the letter was never translated by the 'good neighbour' who failed to return the letter, claiming it to be lost or mislaid. Consequently I never did receive the letter.

For my part I did not know, or remember, Micheline's surname or correct address, and I was therefore sadly at a loss to know how to communicate or do something about the matter. Communication with 'aliens' was not at all easy in those days.

It was some considerable time later when a chance meeting with Eddie — whom I had not seen for some time because of his absence through injury or sickness — revealed a strange turn of affairs, which at least threw some light on the matter of the letter.

Eddie's story was that some time after we had moved out of Armentières a Polish airman crashed with his plane somewhere in that area and was treated at a medical establishment or unit in Armentières. Because of, at that particular time, a strict censorship of mail and lack of mailing/postal facilities for Continental civilians in battle/war zones, etc., Micheline or her father had somehow managed to smuggle two letters to the Polish airman who was to be flown back to England. By a strange coincidence the airman was flown to a station in, or near, Plymouth where he posted one of his letters addressed to Wales. The other letter, being addressed to Plymouth, he decided to deliver personally himself.

It was Eddie's sister — whose photograph I had been shown in our earlier days by her very proud brother — who came to the door as a personal recipient of the letter.

Eddie's remarkable story was that as a result of the meeting Eddie's sister and the airman fell in love and were quickly married.

Eddie's letter came from Micheline's father, but I understood that mine came from Micheline, my mademoiselle from Armentières, whom I have never forgotten.

Who knows I may go back one day, but perhaps too much water has passed under the bridge we left behind!

10

A Rough Time At St Michel-Gestel

I had long been aware that military briefings, at any level of chain of command in a theatre of war, were perhaps more occasioned, effective and significant according to the circumstances of chance than to deliberate strategic planning and intelligent organization. It seemed to me that instruction, information and news concerning past, present and future service disciplines were relative to several factors — not least to the combatant heat of the moment and whether your position in the rank structure qualified you for any such information at all.

For the guys at the bottom of the heap it was usually a snappy order and command that accorded well with the old dictum 'Yours is not to reason why. . .' etc.

So far as I could remember, the only briefing we got concerning our important forthcoming piece of action was a quick few words passed around to the men of Nos. 1 and 2 Platoon. The words were that we were about to go on a dangerous operation. We were to move that night to a position believed to be well behind the German lines to prepare the way for a major surprise attack which, if successful, would crack the German forces in Holland.

I understood that the 51st (Highland) and 53rd (Welsh) Divisions were ready to strike deep in a sweeping direction towards S'Hertogenbosch. Two great fighting divisions, but they did, however, require our Engineer skills, equipment and 'sapper guts' to ensure that anticipated obstacle points, blown bridges, mines, etc., in advanced positions were cleared, or reduced, to allow the armoured columns etc., the speed and momentum critically necessary for surprise attack and penetration.

We set off under cover of darkness, travelling as usual in

our section three-tonners, our accustomed 'home from home' by now. There were new faces on the truck — a couple of reinforcements from yesterday's batch of new arrivals.

The unit had been continually in the front line for as long as I could remember in the NWE Campaign which was, of course, from the very beginning, considering I landed D-hour on D-day. We were truly a unit of the 'first in, last out' brigade in the best RE tradition! Casualties had been high in many of our operations and, being a forward unit, the heat of our particular war was such that casualties were an everyday occurrence and expectation. As a somewhat veteran soldier by now, I had a sort of resigned fatalism or acceptance that if I didn't get 'it' today, it was sure to be 'up' tomorrow. It may be truly said that some battled — to fight to live another day!

The fighting strength and efficiency of a unit in these circumstances were obviously dependent on rear echelon organization for finding skilled and trained replacements for those who were killed and seriously wounded. Sometimes, unfortunately, it was clear that our providers of reinforcements were having no easy time of it because so often a batch would arrive who were mostly unskilled, poorly trained and just green in the extreme. Engineers, it should be said, were unlike most other troops in action in that sappers were the most individual of operators in the field. More often than not they worked alone or in small groups, with too little time and too often too much to do, to know or worry about who to throw in at the deep end! Sadly inevitable that for many of them it would simply and ingloriously be a case of 'gun fodder.'

The chap who sat next to me in the truck was one of the new intake. He was a nice fellow, but a rather frightened one whose nervousness appeared rather more in evidence because of a peculiar twitch — or was it more of a slow blink or wink? — of his left eye. A long scar along his eyebrow indicated an accident and injury, at some time earlier in his life, which had caused his slight affliction.

We had time enough to talk and I gathered that it was a car accident which had caused the injury that had since given him a deal of embarrassment. It seemed that he had been slapped on more than one occasion by 'offended' females, in dance halls and such places, for 'winking' at them. More seriously he

also said that he was an only child and that his father had died
before he was born — a result of wounds in the first Great
War. I understood that his mother was now terrified of a
similar fate for her son.

I could well understand the fellow's apprehension and fear
in his present predicament, which really was as nasty a one as
could be. His name was Phillip.

I had a feeling — born of some experience — that before
the night was over Phillip would have a baptism of fire which
could be the horror his mother feared most!

As our truck moved behind the leading armoured recce
vehicle, my view from the back of the truck was one that
became more eerie and ominous. We were now moving with
some difficulty through places which had earlier been bombed
and shelled, the vehicle gingerly trundling its way between
burning buildings and piles of rubble; abandoned homes and
deserted villages blazing away in the dark of night; the crackle
of flames and flickering shadows on falling and fallen debris.
This together with a dread and fear that something worse lay
ahead was all too weird for words!

We somehow got to the task area where, for me anyway, it
was of some doubtful relief to get my feet on *terra firma*. If
and when the flak starts to fly, a three-ton truck is not the
safest place to be — but then some other places are not either!

We first had to clear away some large wire barriers which
had been placed between concrete road blocks that were well
arranged around and about the approach to a demolished
river bridge.

The demolition of the bridge must have occurred a short
time before we arrived. This was evidenced by the fact that
close to the bridge I had, in the dark, come across the dead
body of the person who obviously had detonated the explosive
charge, a strange and peculiar circumstance of death, indeed,
because he was in an upright position with the lower half of
his body jammed and crushed between two large concrete
blocks which appeared to be parts or sections of the larger
road obstacle blocks. I could only wonder whether the story
was one of suicide, bravery, treachery, stupidity or just one of
an explosion that somehow went wrong. The body was found
to be warm when a gold watch was removed by a soldier
who always swooped with a vulture-like habit of cleaning

up such bodies.

Our task was to throw a Bailey bridge structure at the same river crossing point, thereby making use of the good road approaches of the old bridge. Here were surface-sound roads, uncratered and unmined — a most unusual circumstance considering German thoroughness and standards in such matters of defence.

Our signals vehicle, armoured car, was placed between a block of houses and behind a thick wall to ensure for ourselves a communication and control point. Radio messages were then passed back to somewhere in the rear for the vehicles carrying the bridging equipment to be brought forward in secure and controlled order, so that our operation might be carried out as quietly and efficiently as possible.

Thus far we had been given little trouble by the enemy; things appeared to be going well despite fears that we were on another trip to Hell.

An advance into enemy territory is a test of nerves at any time, but at night-time the same nerves are often pitched to the impossible high key of trying to protect the body from all the menaces, threats and dangers posed by an infinite variety of forms, shapes, figures that lurch and loom in the dark. I am sure that a nervous 'high' of this kind can endure only for relatively short periods. Concentration weakens, and a natural desire creeps in to be relieved of the tension and strain of long fearful moments. With awareness, familiarity and relief of seeing no immediate danger in the emerging foreground, come moments of lowering guard, a time even for some kind of show and pretence that we are unafraid, perhaps even brave. Such are the real moments of danger — when suddenly you live no more, except maybe in a more heavenly abode!

St Michel-Gestel is a place somewhere in Holland. Here we found it to be a small silent village — deserted even by the village cats. We had scouted around and now had a better feel or grasp of our dark surroundings. Here again, familiarity began to breed a contempt that became more evident with more noise, more a relaxed and casual attitude, more strolling than hurrying, perhaps worst of all in striking up matches to light up cigarettes for habitual smoking. It was, I suppose, all too easy to believe that the enemy had scarpered.

The construction of an assault type of Bailey bridge is

normally started on the home bank of the river, canal ditch, etc., and is gradually pushed out, either manually or by winch truck, to the bank on the opposite, enemy, side by stages of additional building or equipment on to the tail-end. A skeleton frame or launching nose is first pushed across, on rocking rollers with stout base plates, until it touches down on the opposite side. As it moves across the gap to be bridged it is counterbalanced and followed by the heavier class load structure used in the bridge proper. 'Class loads', in bridging terms, are calculated on weight to be safely carried and the design of the structure. A 'BB' is perhaps best described as a kind of giant Meccano set, with girders and panels that can be multiplied and fixed to give greater strength and class load design.

The launching nose of our Bailey was under way and gradually moving to the opposite bank. A certain L/Cpl 'Mac' and myself were having a free ride by sitting on the front part of the framework with rollers, etc., ready for positioning when the far bank was reached. Mac was a good pal of mine. I was, after all, the matchmaker who saw him get married shortly before embarking for Normandy. We had already gone through tough times together and we often worked closely, as we were doing here.

The nose of the structure was still many yards from the opposite bank, and we waited for the pinning of more panels at the rear before our next push forward a couple of yards or so.

We were, just then, perhaps a little too relaxed and I cannot say that I was particularly disturbed to hear the whirring approach of a vehicle coming from the direction I was facing. I knew that there had been signal and scout vehicles somewhere in the region behind me, and it was possible that they could somehow have found their way around to the other side of the river. It was an armoured half-track vehicle that loomed out of the darkness and came to a stop at the edge of the river bank, about five yards from where I was perched. It stayed for a moment or two before turning to disappear back into the darkness. When it turned, however, I clearly saw on the side of the vehicle the white and black cross markings of the German Army!

I asked Mac if he, too, had seen what I had just seen. He

confirmed with a nod of his head.

It seemed only a minute or two after I had expressed a fear that we could now expect trouble, that we did in fact get the first nasty dose of it. It was the scream and explosion of a shell (88 mm) that appeared to strike, with great accuracy, the very framework we were precariously perched on. The skeleton structure shuddered, shivered and swung wildly as Mac and I clambered back over sparse steelwork to find more protective cover. Another shell whistled and fell and I was to see no more of my old friend Mac. His death was something of a mystery to be told in a subsequent chapter.

The first crashes of shells were the opening notes of a symphony of death which was to be heard for several hours.

Our task and location was known to the Germans, but we had little idea of where they were. One thing sure enough was that a battery of 88 mm guns was out there in the darkness, well fixed on to a target of sitting ducks — us! Our task was specific — to build a bridge at this point and no other. Our time, too, was limited to a working period of a number of hours, after which the attack from our side was planned to start. Certainly an awful dilemma for the Commander of the working party, who could, after all, decide only that there was no alternative but to face the music and get on with the job.

Deadly accurate shelling from 88 mm guns — surely one of the most deadly weapons in World War Two — was not the kind of music that could be easily faced and, as shells fell fast and furiously, the bodies and limbs were sent scattering.

Like some scared rabbit dodging the blast of a shotgun at close range, I bolted a couple of times into a nearby building, discovered later to be a cloister, nunnery or convent of some kind. I soon learned, however, that it was as deadly and dangerous inside as it was outside. I remember trying to crawl behind the stout frame of a piano for shelter against shells that penetrated the roof and were also blasting the building from inside. Flying shrapnel and falling masonry played notes of a peculiar tune as it whined, thumped and struck the keys of the 'old joanna.' I scooted from one end of the floor to the other like a puck piece on ice, while desperately clutching at my steel helmet. I soon became well-acquainted with the fact that the concentration of blast, flying steel and stonework etc., in enclosed areas could be more destructive of life and limb than being in open shelled areas. But really, wasn't it all a providential matter of being in the right or wrong place at the right or wrong time? I had known people to be killed cowering in trenches while others close by survived by standing openly defying the enemy to do his worst.

The shelling which had earlier been heavy and concentrated, became more intermittent with lulls of several minutes between bombardments. The Germans were now playing a cat and mouse game by conserving their shells and delivering them when it was perhaps guessed (or known even!) that we would continue to remuster at the site for further attempts to complete the bridge.

It was now, indeed, a nightmarish game of blind man's bluff, when we would move to pick up equipment which would suddenly explode with another shellburst of deadly timing, a game well-directed to bring death and destruction was being played most cunningly by the clever enemy.

I saw many a good man fall that night as they made sustained and gallant efforts to make progress towards completing the bridge task. I saw, during one such effort, the decapitation of my old cardsharper friend, little Jock, who was always lucky at playing card games. His head and lower body lay about four yards apart on the roadside. Some other bodies nearby, also, could hardly be described as being in one piece.

The night was a mixture of brave and intense working spells in between spasmodic bursts of shelling; the dispersal and re-assembly of working groups; of tending the wounded; of roll-calls and in looking for the 'lost sheep' who were mostly found to be dead, many hours of the real nastiness of war which for many of the lads was also a lifetime of sad consequence.

Phillip — the fellow I most feared for because of our earlier conversation on the truck — had indeed been unfortunate in having the worst kind of introduction to war up front. Some time during the night when shelling was heavy, I had come across him when I discovered a pair of legs sticking out from between the wheels of a damaged bridging vehicle which had been abandoned and left in a side road. I pulled at the legs to find the still body of Phil. He looked dead enough, yet he was alive according to the strong pulsing heartbeats I felt. I checked for wounds but found none. I looked closely into the wide staring eyes and was astounded to see the two centre dots spinning like small cartwheels. I slapped him several times hoping for some kind of response. It was after several minutes of puzzled endeavour that I got the reaction of an amazing outburst of non-stop stuttering. There was no meaningful utterance from him at all and I could only conclude that the ceaseless blabbering and stuttering was that of a person in a deep and dangerous state of shellshock. I went in search of a stretcher and, with a little assistance, saw him safely away to a position of greater safety. In doing so I suppose I was subconsciously thinking more about the fellow's mother. I understood later that his condition persisted despite good medical attention.

With the first light of dawn came the completion of an assault bridge which had cost more than enough in the blood and lives of fine soldiers.

The enemy guns appeared to be more subdued, except when the odd shell or two came over to serve as a vicious reminder that the enemy was still on target. It was, however, comforting to know that their share of the receiving end was about to be delivered in good measure. They were about to find the dogs of war at their own throats in a very short time when our big push was likely to begin. Their chances of coming out best in any battle with the men of the 51st and 53rd Divs were the absolutes of nils and zeros. 'For what they are about to receive may the Lord have mercy on their souls!' was not the kind of benevolent benediction I had for them just then!

With early dawn and the easing of our own perils and labours, I could see rather more of the destruction done by the night's bombardments to the little village. The rubble of ruined buildings, the bits and pieces of household goods were strewn around as if blown about by a mighty tempest. In the dim and misty early morning light I could also make out the figures of nuns picking their way through litter and rubble, carrying what appeared to be bowls, bandages and sheets. They were amazingly indifferent to the dangers still around and I wondered if some civilians, perhaps sheltering or trapped in some of the houses, were also casualties, I have but scant knowledge of the extent of the merciful work that must have been bravely done by those good ladies, but our later knowledge gave reasons to believe that one or two of them somewhere around at the time were German soldiers dressed as nuns! Two of them had indeed been caught and held later in the day when they tried to bluff their way past RPs at a traffic control point. There was also a funny incident concerning one of our lads who was known — because of his refined way of speaking — as 'Duke.' It seems that Duke, at some later time in the morning, was pressed somewhat by the call of nature. It wasn't just the small field with angled hedge that saw him with his trousers down, because as he was in the crouching position he was suddenly aware of a face and head in nun's garb peering through the hedge at him. Duke hopped quickly and awkwardly to find a less undignified posture, only to see the 'nun' bolting like mad across the field showing trouser bottoms and boots in so doing. Duke explained that his predicament was such that he was unable to give chase!

There was a strange occurrence, also, when another L/Cpl — always a rather gluttonous soldier — went wandering into the nearby cloistered convent building in search of food. He had in the past always been able somehow to ferret out a jar of bottled fruit or something for himself. He found his way to the basement larder and was more than a little surprised when he opened the door, to find two German soldiers inside, one with a walkie-talkie radio set. They came quietly with their hands up. I saw them both when they were brought out of the same building where I had previously taken cover a couple of times during the night's heavy shelling. I wondered just how close I came to them then! The German with the radio set could well have been responsible for pinpointing the location, directing the accuracy of the shelling from which we suffered so badly.

When I thought more about the two Germans and their improperly dressed military comrades, the more I considered it likely that our first arrival on the scene must have caught them by surprise and somehow they became trapped on the wrong side of the river. It could also perhaps explain some of the mystery of the strange death of the person crushed by the concrete blocks, mentioned earlier, when the old bridge was destroyed. Circumstances seemed to indicate a panic situation to blow up the bridge at any cost!

The disguised Germans must also have taken refuge, some time in the night, in the convent building where they probably found the nuns' garments for their disguise, certainly an old trick but always a most effective one — and one indeed I should have played myself in a similar situation. Who, after all, could possibly shoot at a nun?

Which takes me on to the mystery of my old friend Mac. It was known early in the night when a roll call was made that Mac was missing, as were also others from the same troop. In the hours that passed, all missing persons were accounted for, with the exception of Mac. We could find no trace of his body.

Missing persons on active service are always matters of concern for a number of good reasons, and efforts are usually strenuously made to find the missing person, his body or remains, as quickly as possible.

So it was that a young lieutenant and myself searched around for some time rechecking identities of fallen soldiers. In a few cases we had even to uncover bodies that had been buried in back gardens by Dutch civilians returning to their homes. Drawing a blank here, we began asking questions around the troop, and eventually gathered that someone had seen Mac, in the first period of shelling, fast making for somewhere towards the rear of the convent building. The same person also said that he heard shouts and screams from the garden area of the same building shortly afterwards. We decided, therefore, to search that area more thoroughly.

We found the well-hidden body of my old friend Mac in the convent garden. His death was due to multiple stab wounds with a bayonet or knife. He had, most likely, bumped into the hiding Germans — the 'nuns' - in all probability when he sought shelter.

There was, I suppose, more that I should wish to forget than to remember about our bridge at St Michel-Gestel, but one particular incident I remember well enough as being truly part of the story.

It was at the height of the worst action when a severe burst of shelling had scattered the troop. I waited in the dark and in the lull that followed, expecting more of the shellbursting at any moment. Suddenly I hear a strong Geordie voice ring out from the direction of the bridge — which clearly was the target bull's-eye for the German guns — 'Come on, lads, let's have youse! Let's build the bridge!' I think what a gallant NCO the Geordie is, and I am inspired to believe that if he has the guts to face up to such danger, then so have I. I move towards the bridge and the Geordie voice, but in the darkness I cannot find him although his voice, strangely enough, is coming from where my feet are. I look down and see a manhole cover beside a manhole — with a man in the hole. Geordie, with the exception of his mouth which was slightly raised above the line of road surface to give better voice projection, was well and truly ensconced in the ground below!

A classic case of the mind being willing but not so the body. Hardly a brave example, one might think, except that here it was something that worked extraordinarily well in that it served somehow to inject some discipline at the right time. It served also to inspire and remuster men for the critical task that had to be done — for other men in the troop had responded as I had done. We followed a brave voice in the hour of darkness!

The history of the Royal Engineers is a glorious one that sparkles with many accounts of gallant tasks and brave deeds. There can, however, be few that can outshine this little gem of almost unknown military history of the bridge at St Michel-Gestel.

11

On The Deck Of A Railway Bridge

It was easy enough to become familiar with peculiar tasks if you were in the battlefield ranks of the REs, the British army's Jacks of all trades! It was, I understand, the sappers who were the true originators of the saying 'the improbable will be done immediately, but the impossible will take a little longer!.'

The task here was not an unduly tough one if it was not for the fact that it was to be done within view and range of heavy enemy guns.

A railway bridge, carrying a single railtrack, was the point of our interest in that our planned task was to resurface the bridge by redecking over the track lines with boards and timbers. The purpose was to prepare a way for wheeled and light tracked vehicles in support of an attacking thrust by Canadian Infantry, waiting somewhere to the left in some strength.

The bridge was on well elevated ground and could be seen for miles around. Except for a couple of farmhouses nearby, and woods in the far distance, it was mostly good open countryside which swept low into valley-like landscape to the left of the bridge which ran west-east. As I understood the military situation, it was somewhere down there that the Canadian Force (Cdn Inf Bde?) were facing a strong German force — with the scrap about to begin. Perhaps it had already started?

We were soon moving around the bridge, sizing up what had to be done. Shells soon came screaming over, to cause early moments of terror, but then it became clear that the guns were finding the bridge a very difficult target to hit. Shells were dropping short or overshooting to drop ineffectually on to the lower safer ground. Seeing the continual failure of shells to strike the immediate vicinity of

133

the bridge was, after a while, temptation to stand or stroll on the bridge, watching shells whistling by, with a contempt which was in effect, 'Ah-eh-you-can't-catch-me!' kind of attitude. Almost 'cocking-a-snook', you might say.

Up front, the guns of war were seldom at rest, and if it was not the whistle of nearby shells that you heard, then it was the thunder of more distant artillery — or sometimes even the thunderous sound of our own artillery at our shoulders, blasting our ear-drums with incessant booming.

I was aware that the guns of the Royal Artillery had moved up and were now in a position not far behind us. I had, in fact, talked to the RA reconnaissance officer who had been scouting around on the lookout for vantage-ground that might be used as an observation post. He seemed to be well satisfied that the nearby farmhouse would serve for the purpose. He was a friendly fellow and I volunteered to go with him, in view of his anxieties, to ensure that the place was not mined or booby-trapped — which was all too often the case with isolated buildings in battle zones.

The farmhouse was deserted except for a couple of old horses and a few pigs that looked hungry and in poor condition. A familiar enough scene, seeing cattle penned up, deserted and neglected in some war-torn district farm. As often as not they would be dead or dying. The dilemma with live animals was whether or not to release them from their pen prisons, knowing that they could be in more danger outside from blast, shrapnel, flying bullets, etc. Better policy was always to concentrate on the two-legged creatures in grey uniforms!

I saw the RA officer safely settled in a high loft position where he had a most commanding view of the ground extending to enemy held territory and positions. I proceeded to examine the rest of the building in the likelihood of it being used as a billet.

It was about ten minutes or so later that I went up to the loft, to find the officer in radio contact with his battery unit somewhere to the rear. He peered through an opening in the loft with a pair of strong binoculars while in rapid dialogue with instructions and commands to direct his battery's fire on to enemy positions. I also peered into the distance trying to figure out what was happening. I was only able to see blurred outlines and shapes until the officer passed me a second smaller pair of binoculars.

It was certainly a new and quite exciting experience being around to see a bit of what went on with the Gunners. It was even more exciting when I focused the powerful lenses on the distant objects to find the scene and action before me viewed and played like some military chess-board game. A fairly large concentration of German infantry and armour were gathering for what was obviously attack formation, infantry following up behind advancing armour. The RA Gunners had considerable fire power at their disposal, and this they were bringing to bear like magic at the almost instant command of their observation post officer. The fire was directed with pin-point accuracy, to break up the neat geometry of enemy formation. From the left, they tried reforming away to the right, but again the Gunners' fire was directed with deadly efficiency to break them up and wreak havoc in their ranks. I watched in amazement as they tried several times to obtain some kind of coherence and discipline for their attacking move, only to be thwarted and hammered by the RA Gunnery. They then appeared to melt away back into the distant wooded areas.

As I left the farmhouse to return to the bridge I wondered whether the Canadians would ever know of the contribution made by the RA officer and his remote controlled artillery.

Back on the bridge the enemy shelling appeared to have ceased. The decking was completed, though hardly in good cabinet-making style. Some Canadian vehicles had already crossed, on timbers loose and jumpy, in the direction of the enemy. Things had hotted up considerably and the battle appeared to be in full swing.

As with vehicles crossing the bridge first in one direction, so it was that before long some vehicles carrying wounded soldiers and prisoners were crossing back in the opposite direction.

I was in the process of battening down loose decking timbers when I spotted a Canadian jeep approaching fast from the enemy side. As I looked at the jeep belting towards me like a scalded cat out of Hell, I could hardly believe my eyes. Many a sad sight I had seen before, but for me this must surely be the most sad of all. There, tied and bound to the vehicle, was a German soldier in a forced sitting position on the bonnet of the jeep. His posture was like a rag doll or puppet that rolled and jerked grotesquely as the jeep struck and bounced on the loose decking boards. The blood-spattered face and swollen lacerated head lolled and spun on the roped body like some Guy Fawkes dummy on fireworks day. I thought at first that it might be a rather peculiar transportation of some dead body, until the head spun round to show that the eyes were alive — even though it was mostly the whites of the eyes that showed.

I always had the greatest respect for the Canadian soldiers who for me were in the same mould as the Aussies in being some of the finest soldiers in the world. However, my thoughts on seeing this kind of 'Canook' (Cdn) barbarism was anything but complimentary — unless 'cruel bastards' might be so in the circumstances!

I was so sickened by that truly hideous sight that I resolved I should find out what it was about, and to report the matter for possible disciplinary action against the two Canadians I saw in the jeep.

For me it was one thing to fight in defence of self and country, but quite another to perpetrate this kind of act. To humiliate and torture anyone in this mad crazy way was, I felt, the height of depravity and evil.

I continued with the task in hand, but I thought hard about the brutalities of war, the reasons for them.

War itself, I reckoned, was the biggest and most monstrous brutality of all. We were all victims of it because it was so compulsive in the way it removed the humanity from humans, the way it took away man's dignity and respect to reduce him all too often to a state more bestial than animals. In the severe conditions of war few of us are without hate, revengeful feelings, without propaganda and without reasons for vicious and violently cruel acts. What are atrocities in times of peace are simply the norm — even the heroic deeds — of wartime. Emotions, reasons, conduct were altogether a mixture in all of us, given the right conditions, to do anything as bad as that done by the two Canadians.

Such were my thoughts. A few recollections of personal experience were also with me to serve as a reminder that I was in no position to pass harsh judgement on the Canadians until I knew what the whole story was.

Indeed, who was I to judge when I remembered that my own murderous feelings had been aroused often enough too? There was, I recalled, one occasion — already referred to in another chapter — when for half an hour or so I was gripped by a feeling of hate so intense that it was surely the ultimate in hate — a peak perhaps experienced by relatively few of us. It happened back in Normandy when I had crossed to a position on the enemy side of the river to give protection and covering fire to a bridging party, Pegasus bridges at Benouville/Renville. I had found for myself a vacated German foxhole which was partly fortified by loose metal German duckboards. I was in the process of leaning across — perhaps a bit openly — to fry some bully beef using a small tommy cooker. A sudden burst of fire from a German Spandau MG took my bully beef and cooker away, viciously kicked up the dirt in my face and savagely rattled away at the duckboards. For half an hour or so I was pinned down by a German machine-gunner who had me spotted. My slightest movement to seek out the location of my enemy brought a hail of bullets that smashed and ricocheted around the duckboards and my foxhole. The reality of being trapped, of being shot at by someone out there who was deliberately and intensely concerned with tearing out my heart, riddling my skull and blasting my belly, is a reality that brings with it an indescribable hate, of wanting somehow to tear the other fellow's eyes out, to cut out his tongue and to hack him up into small pieces.

But so much for that kind of anger of war.

I remembered also another kind of hate and cruelty, which again unfortunately is little affected by Geneva Conventions, edicts etc., which by the very nature of things in a battle zone can somehow seem to be excusable. For example, it was, I think, somewhere on the outskirts of a Dutch town near to the Belgian border where I was forced, late at night, by heavy enemy mortar fire, to take cover — under the guidance of an infantry patrolman — in a nearby air raid shelter. The bunker was dark except for a small glowing red light of something burning at the far end of a fairly large chamber. There were a number of shadowy figures moving around in the semi-dark interior of the bunker. Someone was moaning, crying and roaring as if in considerable pain. I naturally thought that it was another case of a wounded Tommy until I looked closely to discover it wasn't a Tommy at all. It was a German corporal whose moans and cries were the result of being scorched by a heated iron bar, while being held by some of our infantrymen. He was, it seemed, being tortured for information.

The atmosphere of the place gave me the creeps, and I moved out of the damned place after having the situation explained to me by a lookout guard at the exit. It appeared that the section patrol had already lost a couple of their party on a mission to sound out the enemy strength up ahead. Having taken a prisoner the NCO i/c patrol had decided to lessen the risk of losing more of his party by forcing information from the prisoner on the danger and strength of the enemy on and around the patrol road ahead.

I moved away wondering where my sympathies should lie. I could only reasonably conclude that in truth the cruelties of war were being suffered on both sides. Both were forced into vile predicaments as to what to do for the best.

A further incident should also be told since it brings together examples from my own experience of the angers, cruelties and conducts that can with grim reality be associated with the bloody awful business of war.

It happened when, together with another battle-hardened character, I was called upon to remove the German 'S'-mine booby-trap which had been placed on the dead body of one of our own Despatch Riders. The body was face down with a trip wire attached to the hidden underside of his belt. The wire was fixed to a concealed 'S'-mine (the jumping-jack mine with 360 ball-bearings). Anyone turning the body over for identification, burial, etc., would obviously trip the wire to initiate the mine. Fortunately the wire had been spotted by someone rather more observant and cautious than most. He did the sensible thing in getting us REs to remove that particular danger and snare for anyone else.

Strangely there were two bodies in close proximity, the British DR being one, and the half incinerated remains of a German soldier. The dead German was lying near the burned-out shell of his vehicle, and was now putrifying in the sun.

I proceeded with the task of removing the booby trap from the British DR, and also the task of burying him. My RE workmate in the meantime was to check the wrecked vehicle and German corpse for further booby traps, and to bury the German.

My unpleasant task completed, I went over to find my colleague involved in something I felt was a great deal more unpleasant. Although well hardened by much of what war's grisliness could offer, I was still not quite able to stomach the way the other fellow handled his shovel when I moved to his patch. He had, it seemed, decided on cremating instead of burying the German. He had poured petrol — taken from our vehicle — over the body and was 'stoking up' with prods and digs of his shovel to make it burn better. I succeeded in converting him to having better respect for the dead — whether enemy or not — and together we buried the remains, and marked the grave.

There was no anger or cruelty here, only perhaps crude and detestable wartime conduct of a brutalized soldier.

So much for examples of anger, cruelty and conduct in war. How then, I wondered, would the seemingly deplorable behaviour of the Canadians figure in such an unholy state of battlefield madness and confusion?

I was to know the answer within an hour or so. It was an answer not at all unexpected, one indeed which could hardly give rise to any more questions on the matter — for me anyway.

A Canadian vehicle with some Canadians aboard had come up to the bridge from the home side. They were hanging around for some time, apparently waiting for another vehicle to catch up before crossing the river. I therefore had the opportunity to talk to them about the puppet-like figure I saw tied to the bonnet of the Canadian jeep. It turned out that the persons I spoke to were of the same command unit as the 'guilty ones' and they knew enough of the incident to offer the following explanation.

Three Canadians were originally in the jeep, being somewhat more forward in the line of battle than they realized. They came suddenly under rifle fire and quickly dispersed, one of the trio hiding behind the jeep as the other two moved in opposite directions under cover of hedgerows to locate the source of the rifle fire. One of the Canadians fired several rounds into a suspiciously obscure spot and was surprised to see a German arise holding a white handkerchief or flag. The Canadian moved forward to take his prisoner totally unaware that another German was lying crouched behind his rifle. The other Canadians hidden close by watched with horror as their colleague was shot down as he made his approach. They, in turn, seeing such treachery, immediately let fly at the exposed German with the flag, cutting him down. They then succeeded in pinning down the killer German to his hole in the ground. They also succeeded somehow in taking their prey alive with a vengeance all too clearly shown in the way they first beat him up and tied him on to the jeep.

For me it was the one explanation that well accounted for the treatment and sight I had seen when on the deck of the railway bridge.

Perhaps here again we have, as with the other instances, a further example and manifestation of yet another ingredient of brutal war, that of terrible feelings of revenge.

I somehow, though, formed one line of thought which was not to be dismissed so readily. It was that perhaps the deed done by the Germans was not so much a nasty trick as more a spontaneous difference of opinion — perhaps of guts too! Was one German soldier all too ready to surrender against the wishes of the other, who perhaps had more courage and heart for the fight.

Justice, however, is all too absent in times of war — particularly on the battlefield.

12

Somewhere Near The River Maas

The approach of winter 1944-45 saw my unit in the Dutch coal-mining district of Sittard-Geleen. We were, indeed, close to being miners ourselves because it was decided that being encamped within the enclosure of one of the mines was, in the circumstances, as good a place as any for the unit to find shelter in the increasingly sharp temperatures of what was to become an extremely cold winter.

I recall that the encampment was a mining complex surrounded by a high wall and having a gate entrance. It was rumoured that some German soldiers were trapped within the compound and that it was therefore unsafe to wander around the area too freely — particularly since sniping shots had already been reported.

Christmas was still some time away but with many, if not most, of the British forward troops taking a hard-earned breather after their magnificent speedy advance that did much to sweep the enemy out of France.

Belgium, too, had been liberated, and I had already enjoyed a brief visit to the capital city of Brussels almost within hours of its liberation by our own Guards Brigade. It was a visit I remembered well because it was an occasion when I foolishly threw a few small cans and packets of foodstuffs to some hungry-looking bystanders and was almost mobbed to death by a riotous crowd for doing so. I had underestimated the degree of hunger those poor people had undergone prior to our arrival. Many were close to the point of starving to death and it was no wonder that they fought like dogs for a scrap of food. It was, however, a city I found fascinating in many ways and it was a place I was to return to later on a few more pleasurable visits.

We were, however, here in Holland, near to the River Maas

and quite close to the German border, having something of a
rare treat with a lull in military operations and activity. Even
so, I was soon to discover that it was quite easy to get killed
at any time — and not only by the enemy either! It really is
strange sometimes the way in which a course of events can take
you into a bad unlucky patch and then somehow bring the
good luck of getting you out of it. Often the other way round,
too, when it's a bit like winning the football pools and then
having an almighty crash with the new Rolls Royce you
bought. For some people I suppose life is generally like that
— full of incident and never a dull moment.

In my case it was just an unlucky little slip that almost cost
me a supremely high price, and I was in the event extremely
lucky to get away with it.

I had ventured to go out for a local scout around. It was late
afternoon and I had been warned to go careful because some
bodies had been found along the riverside a short time earlier.
They were the bodies of a couple of British soldiers who had
been knifed to death. This, together with talk of a number of
Germans having infiltrated the area wearing British uniforms,
were obviously reasons enough to indeed be wary.

I cannot remember how it was that we met, but it was some
time later in the evening when I found myself with female
company. She was a pleasant enough Dutch girl but, as I was
to find out later, she was concerned most of all in getting me
to escort her to wherever it was she wanted to go.
Understandable at such dangerous times and places and I was
happy to oblige up to a point. It was quite a crisp evening and
I went walking along with her, going a good deal further than
I had expected to go. It was when I found myself walking
along the riverside with her, near the spot where the knifed
bodies had been found, that I began to ask myself whether my
journey was really necessary.

I hesitated about going along with her further, although I
disliked the thought of ditching her in such a lonely spot. She
had, though, already misled me about how far she had to go,
and I now made it plain that I would accompany her only for
another few hundred yards or so. It was at this point that I also
decided to take my rifle from its slung position, push a round
into the breach, release the safety catch and carry the weapon
in my right hand at the ready. It was also a gesture against a

possibility of being 'led up the garden path.'

We parted company soon afterwards and with light failing fast I felt a lot easier at making the return trip — although I was by no means relaxed or off guard. I eventually got on to the long straight road that led directly to the main gate of the mine-surface enclosure, where I would be identified and admitted by a couple of unit sentries. As I plodded back along the road I could hear the echoing sounds of other army boots also plodding along at some distance behind me. They were clearly the resounding footsteps of other members of my unit who were, like myself, heading back to the more secure precinct of our coal-mine 'home sweet home.'

Clearly, also, there was now less reason for having my rifle primed and held at the ready. I therefore stopped momentarily to clear my weapon by withdrawing the bolt of the gun and with it the bullet which I had earlier kept in the breach for possible quick action. Just a simple safety operation which — as I had done often enough before — was to push the withdrawn round back down into the attached magazine with the thumb of the left hand, ensuring that the bolt was over and above the round when pushed forward, locked and uncocked with a trigger release. It would then be a matter of applying the rifle's safety catch so that an accident was unlikely to happen.

But — horror of horrors! — despite the well-practiced drill, I had somehow not forced the round down far enough into the magazine before pushing the bolt home, although I felt so sure I had done so. Certainly the last thing I wanted just then was to let off a loose accidental rifle shot. I was at that moment some twenty or thirty yards from the armed sentries at the main entrance to the mine. To them I was an approaching figure or outline clutching a rifle. To those who were following behind me I was also a figure or outline who was also moving towards the sentries, swinging a rifle. The last thing I expected as I pressed the trigger in order to clear the gun was a live round up the spout. It went off with a blast and a flash that left me gormlessly standing for a second or two amazed that such a damned silly thing could happen to a clever guy like me!

I then realized that I was in deadly danger, my war experience instinctively telling me to get to Hell out of it, fast!

The wall on both sides of the entrance gates were some thirty yards away and it was towards the wall base to the left of the gates that I galloped, swerving and bent low to avoid being hit if shot at. It was the kind of quick thinking that undoubtedly saved my life because even before I got to the half way mark the bullets came at me fast and furiously from both directions. I miraculously dodged the line of fire pumped out by the two sentries I momentarily glimpsed crouching low behind their MG.

The firing coming from behind me was now the most deadly because I had no way of defending myself except to fall flat on my face. As I did so — hugging the ground closer than a snake's belly — I could hear the vicious thud of single rifle shots against the wall behind me. I had indeed stirred up the deadliest hornets' nest imaginable and all I could do now was scream and shout like Hell. 'Help! — Accidental shot! — It's me! Don't shoot! Don't shoot! Accident!' My position gave me some advantage over the sentries and I crawled along the wall to get as close as I could so as to get myself heard, to shout my name and explain the daft situation. My yelling, shouting and shrieking was mercifully followed by a cessation of the shooting when a more comprehensible verbal exchange prevailed, with me on the outside of the wall explaining matters to the sentries on the other side at the gateway entrance. The guys behind me — my would-be assassins — must have also got the message because they also moved up nervously and tense to my position.

Gradually the grim misunderstandings were put right after explanations on all sides. It appeared that in the closing darkness the two soldiers following behind me were alarmed to see — as they saw it — the figure ahead of them stop and fire at the sentries at the open gate entrance. They then saw movement of what appeared to be the sentries falling to the ground. Being convinced that the figure before them had fired and shot at the sentries — a figure that could possibly be a German in the situation — they decided to shoot first and ask questions afterwards, particularly when they saw the figure run and move suspiciously to the cover of the wall. They fired about five or six rounds each. The sentries on the other hand were also convinced that the approaching figure had deliberately opened fire upon them. They immediately dropped to the ground and began firing with their MG weapon. They were truly convinced that an attack on them was being made, particularly when they saw the figure run, followed by more shots coming from what they thought were snipers following up from somewhere behind.

I was to reflect that such a shot like the one I let off that night was one bloody great way of starting a war between Allied Forces. It was, however, an incident when and where there was plenty of shooting and panicking, but mercifully no killing. I was, however, left with a nick in my left shoulder — a flesh wound that was little more than a graze by what might have been a flying chip of brickwork, a ricocheting bullet or a near miss from one of the directly aimed shots.

But having got out of that particular scrape reasonably well, my fate was soon to push me straight into another — only this time it was a scrape that was also a crush and a grind that was to leave me feeling more than just a little weak at the knees.

It happened when a few days later that I found myself on a detail on which I was to carry out a simple and straightforward task of Bailey bridge maintenance inspection. The bridge in question was a smaller type of class 40, having a double/single arrangement of panel linkage for its construction, extended panel pairings in single tier on both sides.

The bridge was sited at some remote spot in the network of military communications, the road being a poor secondary one which appeared little used, if at all. I am unsure about its exact geographical point and can only guess that it may have been somewhere in the Dutch Weert/Roermond region. The layout was a 'Z' kind of situation, with the bridge diagonally placed to the approach roads at both ends, which obviously meant a sharp turn to the right to get on to the bridge for any vehicle travelling from either direction. Except for the roadway, the whole area around the bridge was strewn with German mines — surprisingly a few warning signs '*Achtung! Minen!*' still to be seen.

The task would take an hour or two and involved a close check on the equipment of the bridge to ensure panel pins, nuts, bolts, etc., had not worked loose, that bracing bars were properly adjusted, bearing plates and bank seats were properly secure and that the ribands were tight and properly fastening down the decking of the bridge. It was a usual tendency for the nuts on the riband bolts to work loose, given a fair amount of traffic, resulting in the loosening of the decking boards. It was the ribands therefore that usually required most attention.

It had been sometime in the afternoon when I was dropped off from a vehicle, with the tools for the job such as spanners, hammer, etc. A DR had followed behind and had been detailed to hold himself available at the bridge for liaison duty and to give assistance should I require it. However, it was not long after I proceeded with the job in hand that my DR companion felt he had an opportunity to attend to some other matter on his mind and, after explaining that he would be back within the half hour or so, he rode off in the direction of our own rear lines.

I was therefore alone, but fairly well occupied with the bridge maintenance task. I had no idea just then of what the military situation was concerning the enemy, his territory or his positions. I somehow had it in mind that the situation at this spot was one involving little or no danger from the Germans.

The road leading away from the bridge on the eastern side turned sharply to the left and dropped considerably, thereby making the approach road poorly visible to me as I worked away in a stooped position on the ribands fixed along the edges of the decking boards. Completely alone and apparently with nothing to disturb me, I progressed steadily and leisurely until I was made aware of the noise and sight of a large vehicle arriving on to the bridge from the eastern side. I had worked on many Bailey bridges and knew by experience that I could safely keep clear of any crossing vehicle by standing back against the panels and on top of the ribands whilst allowing it to pass. In this case I stood up and quite casually — almost absent-mindedly as I remember — stood back to allow the moving vehicle to pass me by. The vehicle was almost upon me before I realized that I was looking into the faces of German soldiers high in the cab of their German vehicle. . .!

I was suddenly trapped, the vehicle appearing to mount the riband baulk on which I stood in an obvious murderous attempt to crush me against the steel panels. The next few moments were some of the most horrific and agonizing of my life as I found myself squeezed and spun like a top between the side of the moving vehicle and the steel ribs of the bridge panels behind me. They really were viciously cruel moments of whirling, crushing confusion when I thought surely I was a goner. But suddenly — at a point which must surely have been the ultimate before crossing the threshold for the next world — I was released and freed of the crushing pain and revolving dizzy confusion. I had spun the entire length of the long vehicle and had come out of it like something thrown out of a mangle. I found myself uncontrollably whimpering and groaning in pain and shock as I clung with arms and elbows to a panel-top in a desperate attempt to keep myself upright. I was paralysed from the waist down — totally without feeling or control in my legs. It was that lower part of my body which had suffered most because of the single panel height of the bridge, and also because of the fact that my hips took the greatest amount of pressure and walloping in the spinning process. My pelvis had obviously taken quite a hammering.

The German vehicle disappeared, leaving behind what must have been a very pathetic-looking figure indeed — one which hung like a limp rag to the side of the bridge. It was as much a mental blow as a physical one, for I was sure that the attack had left me crippled for life. I remember hanging on for some time crying and sobbing in an emotional and physical mixture of pain, self-pity and anger that 'the bastards got me after all.' I was all too ready to believe that my guardian angel had finally deserted me — that is until it came to my rescue again when my brain and survival instinct began working again. I wasn't dead yet, though if I didn't somehow get clear of the bridge it was likely that I soon would be. The Germans could return back across the bridge at any time. It was such a thought that got me moving — for what dear life I still had left — on arms and elbows along the side panelling as fast as I could, which really wasn't very fast at all.

It took time and a thoroughly painful struggle to drag myself to somewhere near the end of the home side of the bridge, from where I could hear the least fearful sound of the returning DR's motor cycle. I was in no condition to jump for joy, however, upon the fellow's arrival, nor was I very receptive to his clumsy, though well-intentioned, attempt to manhandle me when he realized I was injured and unable to walk. I was able to gasp out some kind of brief explanation as to what had happened. Having got the message he then lost no time in getting on his motor cycle again, departing all too quickly while shouting something about fetching help.

With the DR disappearing again, I was left to ponder my dilemma. There was every likelihood of the Germans returning in their vehicle. They may well have made the mistake of overrunning their own lines and, unless there was another way to get back, they would be forced to return via the bridge. They had perhaps been as greatly surprised at seeing me as I was at seeing them and were now in ignorance of military strengths, etc., lying low somewhere waiting for clear signs to dash back. It somehow seemed to me less likely that they were on some special mission, reconnaissance, or that their vehicle was a front runner in a planned enemy attack. Perhaps they were already somewhere around on foot?

Speculation about the enemy left me in no doubt that I should have to get clear of the bridge and find somewhere to hide. It could well be a long time before help came via the DR — particularly if he was to run up against those I already had the misfortune to meet!

My rifle had been left with other items of gear on ground near the home side of the bridge — left because of encumbrance otherwise in moving around, and under the bridge, to carry out whatever maintenance tasks were necessary. My intention was clear, since I had nothing better in the way of a personal security plan, and was that I would move, with rifle and bayonet, on 'all twos', since propulsion on 'all fours' was out of the question with me being down to a kind of half-manpower drive, to just about the safest place I could think of — the middle of the nearby minefield! What better, in the circumstances, than a concealed position surrounded by a good protective belt of mines — the one place unlikely to be traversed by unwelcome visitors?

Together with my bits and pieces I dragged myself along for a good hundred and fifty yards before entering a section of the mined area offering what indeed seemed to be an ideal spot of cover. Set well back from the road was what appeared to be a small partly hedgerowed enclosure in which stood a dilapidated and derelict wagon hut of a kind used by road-workers. I had encountered too many minefields in the past to have fears about this one, and anyway those as well indicated with warning signs, as this one appeared to be, were always a darned sight better than the unmarked ones, to be sure! As an experienced RE and minefield campaigner, all I required here was my good eyesight to examine closely the ground, and my bayonet to search out the disturbed soil and hidden mines. But also it occurred to me that for this particular little journey of a couple of dozen yards or so, it would be sensible to mark my trail into the minefield so as to facilitate my return when getting out again. This I did by a series of little digs with my bayonet, the holes and little heaps of loose soil marking my track as I elbowed myself forward. I moved around and avoided a couple of likely volatile ground spots and was therefore untroubled by mines in reaching my place of intended sanctuary — a place for resting, hiding and licking my wounds perhaps.

The shelter was an old cabin of a sort which had a door hanging loose on broken hinges. Inside were a number of empty sacks, which suggested the place had been used at some time for storing potatoes or animal foodstuff.

I was weary to the point of exhaustion and with a numbing bodily pain which left me in no doubt that my snake-like crawl and journey had done little by way of recovery for a very bruised and battered body. I wondered whether it was a body that was soon to become a carcass as I lay down in a corner of the cabin with a few sacks above and below me. I was soon asleep — or perhaps mercifully unconscious in some blissful kind of way.

My guardian angel, however, must have been carefully watching over me for what — as I was to discover later — was a deep slumber, trance or coma for two and a half days. I remember that I awoke with a puzzled and lost feeling until I was reminded by my pains that I had been in a nasty kind of collision. But remarkably, and most importantly, I soon realized that I had recovered the use of my lower limbs and although I felt as if I had been run over by a bus, I was able to stand and walk even if it was with some difficulty.

So by the grace of God I had managed to survive yet another of war's little nasties — perhaps as close an encounter with death as I could possibly have experienced.

Within the next day or so I was able — due mainly to the help, information and transport of a friendly Infantry Troop Commander who had found me hobbling on sticks along some country lane — to rejoin my own squad again. I was to learn that following upon the DR's report, the C/Sgt Major had taken a search party to look for me while also proceeding in search for the infiltrated enemy truck which had also been separately reported and sighted.

I was allowed to get 'holed up' for a few days in order to recuperate and recover fully from the knocks and bruises received. But I am not at all sure that I ever did.

13

Luckier Than Some

Early January 1945, with a Continental winter at its worst, was a time and occasion when I was to find myself in the peculiar state of being happy and miserable at the same time — a kind of not knowing whether to laugh or cry situation! I was happy at being one of the soldiers taken by chance out of the front line of battle for a spell of leave in the UK. Earlier a sudden military decision had been made because of the favourable turning of the war tide, that a small percentage, at any one time, of the troops of certain combatant units in the field, be allowed or granted periods of UK leave at OC's discretion.

An adopted system, in the case of my own unit, was to pick out a few names at a time by lucky draw, and I was fortunate therefore in being one of the early privileged few. Such luck could indeed be a providential life-saver since the fighting at the front was nonetheless furious and with yet more battles to come. But escaping the shot and shell at the front line to run the risk of freezing to death behind the lines was something I had not reckoned with and I was miserable therefore because — although moving happily in the right direction — I was travelling on a slow war-damaged train and feeling intensely cold. I sat on a hard wooden seat by a very draughty broken window and watched the ice form from the powdery snow which blew into my compartment. There was no heating, comfort or speed to be had from an old German (?) locomotive that seemed ancient enough to have been an early successor to Stevenson's *Rocket*. I wrapped up, curled up, shivered and cursed during the long cooped-up hours of travelling — which as I was to learn later resulted in a number of fellow passengers having varying degrees of frostbite.

But cruelly painful though the journey was, its purpose for me was the best of all reasons — to get back again to Wales

if only for a short stay. My year of absence had been a long,
long time because so much had happened in the meantime.
I had for the most part given up hope of ever seeing Wales
again because seeing the war at first hand had made me more
of a fatalist than optimist. But, unbelievably, it was about to
happen!

I had always thought a great deal about the old folk back
home, as they did about me, and we corresponded regularly.
My old dad especially was painstakingly diligent and faithful
with his usual weekly two long, witty and informative letters.
He was a scholarly man whose beautiful handwriting was a
matter of admiration and pride to me. A great morale
booster, to be sure, and never once did he let me down in the
three and a half years up to that time. I knew, too, that he
was equally consistent and loyal with my elder brother who
was also an overseas campaign soldier like myself. In this way
dear old dad was able to keep us both informed about each
other's circumstance and situation. James, my brother, was a
longer serving soldier than I, and almost certainly, as one of
'Wingates chindits' in Burma, had suffered a much tougher
time than myself in the war. Because of our different theatres
of war, James and myself never communicated direct and were
therefore totally reliant on the old fellow back at home for
news of each other. I had not seen my brother since late 1940
but I knew that he had done exceptionally well to have made
the rank of Company Sergeant Major (WOII) in the South
Wales Borderers. Considering that he was a Militiaman and
barely two years older than myself, such rapid promotion
meant, at one time, that he was one of the youngest, if not the
youngest, infantry CSMs in the British Army. But I knew, too,
that he was already paying a high price for such distinction.
In the jungle warfare against the Japanese he had already
overcome a couple of lesser wounds only to fall victim to a
third which was most serious. I remembered getting the sad
news a few months earlier that he was fighting for his life with
a bullet in his heart, and, because of the difficulty of removing
the bullet at some ill-equipped military hospital, it was
thought that he might not survive. Because of my own combat
situation in the field there was little I could do except hope
and pray for his recovery.

Perhaps it may have helped because in the later news I

received I learned that he had miraculously pulled through his dangerously ill condition, but was still listed as critical.

As I sat on the train I wondered about my brother's complete recovery or whether he would be seriously disabled for life. I also tried to imagine the kind of jungle situation in which he caught such a 'Nip packet.' He and I had always been close and I knew from my days of sparring with him, a set of boxing gloves were always around then to sort out our differences in the good old-fashioned Welsh style, that in a scrap he was a tough terrier type. Perhaps this time he had stuck his neck out too far? One day, maybe, I should know all about it. . .

As I endured more of the painful journey, I sought comfort in thinking about my approaching reunion with the other members of my family. My parents especially must have gone through a period of great anxiety since I last saw them over a year ago and I wondered if they had changed much as a result. Maybe they would find a change in me? I thought also about the one peaceful little spot in the globe which was the destination I yearned for, and which was my home village in Wales. Living close to death in war has a sentimentality all of its own and I had dreamt often enough of arriving at the village station, to cross over the quaint little bridge as I had done so often before. I had a clear picture in my mind as I recalled and anticipated the details of the little bridge, and I determined that when I got there I would stand, in wonderful reality, at its centre and offer a prayer of thanksgiving for having made it after all. . .

The following day saw me looking and feeling less like a traveller in Siberia and more as one who was on good old British soil again — back for the first time since leaving for the initial assault landings in Normandy on D-day. I was back and sadly aware that there were those of us then who went off together and would never return.

It was late evening when I neared the end of a long and wearying journey. A few miles beyond Llanelly — the once so-familiar place-name was somehow different and strange — and my destination was at last reached.

A short time later and it could have been that I was not without a lump in my throat as I stood on the little bridge and thanked my guardian angel for my deliverance thus far.

From the bridge where I stood I could see the platforms below and the dimly lit street alongside the railway station. I expected and hoped that nothing had happened to change the much yearned for simplicity and tranquillity of the little village. But alas! Already I could see and hear something that disappointed and displeased me greatly. The noisy, staggering figures and groups I could see were American soldiers, some with local girls obviously the worse for drink.

I was angry... my village was contaminated! Polluted! Violated! At that moment I hated not only American soldiers but all soldiers, all uniforms and, for that matter, all and everything associated with war. Yet, I could have readily charged with a machine-gun to rid them from my most cherished, almost personal, piece of Welsh homeland.

It was at that moment, too, that I had some real understanding of the German fanaticism — young and old persons alike — in defending their German homeland.

As I sped homewards, my anger and disappointment soon gave way to more reasonable thoughts that there were few, if any, places left in Europe totally untouched by World War Two — so many places destroyed, in fact, and so many people killed. I had, indeed, much to be thankful for and a lot to be pleased about! As for the Yanks, well, it was good to know they were on our side since it seemed unlikely that I would have survived if they were not.

In the days that followed I was to discover that there was a particular problem with furlough as a fortuitous respite from the front line of a war theatre. It was that it starts to end almost as soon as it begins to start simply because the thought of going back into action again is a weighty and unpleasant one. Indeed, those who have had experience in such matters would surely agree that, bad enough though it is to be constantly forward with the guns of war, how much worse it is to be pushed back after a spell and lapse in the rear. Then it is that the first scream and crash of an enemy shell does something nasty to a nervous system which has been lulled for a time into a sense of false security. One can then feel the hair stand on end, the belly turn over and the skin crawl — all down to experience and intimate knowledge of death-dealing weapons of war.

But as sometimes there are the big wars up front on foreign

fields, so there are often the little wars on the soil of our own backyards. So, too, are there the bad and good guys who make the war or keep the peace — all seeming to be part of life's dynamics to create a confusion of incidence or pattern of coincidence of relative size and significance.

Which leads me on to relate the peculiar circumstances towards the end of my leave which gave rise to a very strange encounter at the very end of my leave, an umpteen million to one chance, one might say!

It was during an evening visit to the nearby town of Llanelly that things began to happen. My leave period was running out fast and may have been a good enough reason for me to want to drown my sorrows in booze. But the only trouble with wanting to drown your sorrows in such days of wartime rationing etc., was that beer, whisky and the like were in short supply, and anyway my capacity and liking for the stuff did not usually extend beyond a small bottle or two of Welsh ale as and when obtainable.

It was early evening when I entered a certain pub which I had visited with two pals of mine in earlier pre-service days, the two friends mentioned in my introductory chapter. I was saddened to think that of the three of us who joked so light-heartedly about each other's call-up and fate in the war, one was already dead — having died of typhus in India after only a short period of service in the RAF. For him to be struck down by a killer disease, without seeing any real action at all, was surely the most cruel fate of all for a splendid young man who had been, as I remembered him, a handsome and dashing 'Clark Gable' type. His death was part of a double tragedy for his mother who was also notified of the death of a second son — torpedoed merchant navyman — on the same day.

I gave a thought also to my other absent friend who, although alive and kicking somewhere in Asia with the 'forgotten 14th Army', had also more than a fair share of misfortune. His repatriation, I knew, would be anything but a joyous one, because in the few years he had been abroad a strange quick succession of deaths in his family group of six meant that he would be coming back to a tragically vacated house and home, leaving him the sole possessor, a sad homecoming indeed for a young returning soldier.

Such facts I knew for some time, and my visit to the pub was perhaps a subconscious desire to turn the clock back. I suppose I was looking more for company than booze.

Sometimes, depending on demand, stock, supply, etc., some pubs would, or could, only serve their regular customers. Whereas beer was but an occasional problem, whisky and such spirits were seldom obtainable by non-regulars. For Britishers accustomed to general wartime rationing and shortages, irritating and frustrating though it may be, it was an acceptable fact of life. It was not quite so, however, for a good many American servicemen, based in Britain, who often misunderstood and interpreted the situation as unfair discrimination.

And it was perhaps a feeling of this kind that led to a disturbance of the peace just a few minutes after I entered the place and sat down with my glass of beer. The bar room was empty except for the elderly guy behind the bar as I sat at a dimly lit corner table. As I did so, I was soon to observe the unsteady entrance of two burly American soldiers, who perhaps were too drunk to be aware of my own presence in the place. I watched as they staggered up to the bar and saw them thump out a demand for whisky. The barman replied that he had no whisky, whereupon they then demanded rum, and got the same negative answer.

I found myself becoming increasingly angry as they began abusing the barman and accused him of lying. But it was when they started shoving and pushing the old fellow around, to hunt and search behind the bar and under the counter, that I could contain myself no longer. I strode forward to make some kind of protest and to at least offer some protection to the old barman whose objections were putting him in danger of being knocked around. The reception I got from the Americans, however, was anything but friendly and showed itself as a swinging blow to the side of my head from the fist of one of them. I would, I suppose, have had a few more blows had I not possessed a trained and powerful left hook well capable of exacting more than a fair poundage of bruised flesh in any such exchange. I also had the advantage of boxing experience and of being sober to enable me to execute quick KOs of the two inebriated louts. Together they made a nice heap in the small area behind the bar.

But I also had enough sense and experience to know how and when to beat a hasty retreat. The barman had, in his moments of hectic botheration, phoned for the American Military Police. I felt that to await their arrival would be a most foolish thing to do regardless of rights and wrongs in the matter. Better by far to make a quick exit by the back door and find another pub to keep me out of the way of American soldiers for a while.

I found the sanctuary of another public house just a short time later, but as it happened, and as fate would have it, I had got away from a couple of nasty Yanks only to fall foul of an even nastier Welshman — another incident in the sequence of events which was to lead to a remarkable coincidence!

My left hand was painfully swollen as I sat down on a long upholstered seat which faced the bar. Some other persons also sat on the same seat, and I noticed the one nearest to me was the unfortunate associate of the two wooden crutches placed nearby. He was a crippled, misshapen little man who, a short time later, I was to see and hear remonstrating against the approach of a Salvation Army girl selling her *Warcry* magazines. The point of his objection was that as a 'pitifully poor war wounded cripple' it was he who should be on the receiving end of charity money and should not be asked to give it. He questioned as to who needed it more than such as himself. The surprised young SA girl quickly offered the shilling in her hand and apologized by saying that she hadn't realized his condition and circumstance. The little man's response, however, was a rejection of the offering, and — playing to the gallery somewhat — saying that he was merely making a point of principle. The incident appeared to be an opportunity for the crippled man to move close to me to tell me how hard life had been for him 'ever since he was wounded at Dunkirk.' He went on to say that it was only by dabbling and fiddling on the black market that he was able to scrape a living for himself. He lowered his voice when he said that he was off to Swansea Docks in the morning to pick up some choice black market goods, and he could even obtain for me a couple of bottles of Scotch whisky and a few pairs of ladies silk/nylon stockings on the cheap. He could deliver them in the afternoon of the same day.

It was, I suppose, a mixture of the fellow's hard luck story, a glib tongue and the temptation to obtain scarce wartime luxury items on the cheap which caused me to nod my head. The unfortunate result of the gesture was that I was persuaded to part with a fair amount of money because of his further tale of woe that he couldn't afford to lay out money in advance, etc. So, as far as I was then concerned, the deal was on and I would collect the items around midday, at a certain pub near my home.

But alas! I was unaware, until the following day when the man with my money failed to turn up, that I was another victim of a particularly evil little con man who, pretending to be war wounded at Dunkirk, was in fact a born cripple. I discovered that he was a cunning character who played on his deformity and the sympathy of people to cheat them out of money. I gathered that he was a person with a bad police record, having had several spells in jail.

I was, however, determined that he should not get away with his con-trick on me and, following upon information received about his whereabouts, I went after him to get the goods as promised or my money back. I found him within the hour at the place where I was told I was likely to find him. It was a dingy little pub very close to where he lived. When I confronted him he made some excuse about not being able to find me etc., but then said he would go to his house close by to fetch some of the goods, since he had not the money to return to me. I threatened him with the police if he was not back soon. I still had hopes of whisky and stockings as parting gifts for my parents before going back overseas on the following day.

The man returned soon enough, but with just one whisky bottle in his hand. He could, he said, only manage to get one bottle of whisky and would therefore have to square up the other items in due course. Obviously an audacious rogue, and I could only shake my head in astonishment and disgust as I held up the 'large bottle of whisky.' I saw that the colour was unlike that of genuine whisky and was in any case several inches short of full measure. He watched rat-like as I took a suspicious sniff and sip of the stuff. The beginnings of a mocking grin on the rascal's face was quickly removed when I grabbed him firmly to pour the cold tea content of the bottle over his head. There was nothing else I could do except remark as I turned away that I was sorry for a creature such as he who was more twisted in his mind than in his body. I did, however, make the mistake of setting down the bottle close to him and it was the handy weapon he used to strike me with as I turned my back to him. The bottle caught me a hefty glancing blow to the side of my head and also dealt me a further heavy blow to my hand before I managed to wrest the bottle from him.

It was easy and tempting to set about the wretched man with his own crutches, but I decided it was wiser to get away from a conflict in which the odds were perhaps more in favour of the cripple.

I left the premises nursing injuries which quite remarkably had been inflicted on the same parts of my body, viz the side of my head and my left hand, received less than twenty-four hours earlier with the Americans. My head was gashed and my hand badly bruised and swollen, with both areas of punishment much more painful than before. I wondered about my bad luck in meeting such nasty people and whether perhaps it was after all safer up in the front line against the Germans! I wondered also about my peculiar luck in receiving dual injuries in precisely the same dual parts of me. Strange coincidence indeed, but I was soon to discover that it was to be followed by a more remarkable one...

The following day saw me more as a soldier coming out of the battle front of war rather than one returning to it after leave of absence. My head wound was well padded and plastered, with my bruised and swollen left hand eased and protected by an arm sling. My injuries could well have been a reason and excuse to overstay my leave, but we 'leavers' had been unit warned to play the game by the other lads awaiting their turn for leave. The efficiency and fighting strength of a unit up front could be maintained only by having the smallest possible number of absentees. Extended leave therefore, for whatever reason, could only be at the expense of some other poor blighter. There were those back there who could make life — and death even — hard enough without giving reasons for making it so. Also there were more than enough dirty jobs in the fighting line 'for the dishing out of' and I had no wish to be the one out of line at the line, so to speak. Discipline was never lacking in my unit.

I was at the railway station for the start of my long return journey and also for the privilege of a further share of the war action. For despite the dangers and hardships ahead, I was well aware that I was luckier than some who would never have such a privilege — fine comrade soldiers buried in distant fields.

My train was the Fishguard/Paddington Express and was already full of passengers — as it usually was on the much earlier travels I made — when it pulled up at the platform. The best a soldier like myself could hope for, in the way of travel comfort, was standing room and breathing space somewhere along the corridor of the train. They were those wartime days of large-scale troop movements, etc., when packs, kitbags, rifles, gas masks and military gear of all kinds were dumped and stacked in most available corners. I could therefore expect little comfort on a four hour journey which meant standing around, with my injured limb in an arm sling, being buffeted by the burdened, squeezing, pushing bodies moving along the narrow corridors of the train. But I knew all too well that there were worse things in life, and I was prepared and content to make the least of any discomfort to come my way.

It happened, however, that I had not long been on the train when mysterious forces began working to ensure that my journey was to be more than just a comfortable one. I had stood for the ten minutes or so in the corridor of the train, during which time several persons had squeezed past. One particular person, however, having passed by once, appeared to go out of his way to thread his way back a second time to grasp my unslung arm in order to direct me to his compartment where, he said, he had a vacant seat for me. I could not help wondering why he had selected me rather than one of the others who were closer. Perhaps he had noticed my slight incapacity or maybe thought he knew me? Anyway, I was of course happy at having the comfort of a seat for the long journey ahead, and was most grateful to the obliging gentleman whose own seat was next to mine. He was, I observed, an elderly man, but fine-looking and smart, with a stamp of authority about him somehow. His clipped grey moustache, bearing and speech clearly indicated a retired military officer — which indeed was the case from what I gathered from our conversation later.

He was a friendly man who, as we chatted about things in general for the first hour or so, was to share his tea and sandwiches with me. His face was vaguely familiar as if I had seen him somewhere before, although I couldn't think how, where or when.

He was in every way a real gentleman, and it saddened me to suddenly discover that he had a thick built-up sole on one of his well polished brown boots — an obvious affliction which perhaps was a club foot, or more likely a shortened leg as a result of war or accident. I had somehow failed to notice it earlier.

Our conversation touched on the subject of war, and I was further saddened when he happened to mention that he was, in fact, returning from a visit to his seriously war-wounded son. He explained that he was gravely concerned about his son who had been blinded by enemy action in Burma and was since suffering deep bouts of depression. His son, he said, had always been a very fit and active person and was therefore taking the tragedy of his sightlessness rather badly. He went on to say that he had hoped his son would become a General Staff Officer as he himself had been, and that it was particularly shattering that such a promising career had been so prematurely and tragically ended.

As we conversed I was interested to learn that his son had not only served in the same war theatre and campaign as my brother James, but also in the same regiment of the South Wales Borderers. It was even of greater interest when our conversation revealed that both his son and my brother had actually served in the same battalion — my brother as CSM and his son as a Company Major. We agreed that the circumstances were such that both would be known to each other and an account of our coincidental meeting be passed to each of them as the opportunity arose. It might be of interest to them also. . .

But the coincidence, however, as I shall explain later, was to be more fully realized when I was to pursue the matter further.

Meanwhile, my fellow traveller was even better company for the rest of the journey because of what we now had in common. We had got along together extremely well, but even so, I was still surprised when at the end of our journey he pulled out his wallet to offer a thick wad of paper money, 'As one old soldier to another, can I help you in some way — you'll need some extra money perhaps to see you OK on the other side?' I rejected his generous offer by explaining that to where I was going British money was non-currency (it was a point of time in the war, on my part of the front, where a state of currency confusion existed, when Dutch Gilders, German Marks and British Forces Voucher money (BAFVs) were either used or considered) and that even with valid money there was little or nothing that could be purchased at the battle-front.

It was when I was about to help a truly fine British gentleman off the train with his cases that he raised the question, 'By the way, where in 1941 did you have to attend for your call-up medical examination?' I replied that it was at the Masonic Hall in Swansea. 'Ah, well then,' said he with a twinkle in his eye, 'you may remember seeing me there. I was the President of the Board.' It dawned on me that he was indeed the Brass hat on that all important day. We shook hands and he went off leaving me wondering whether he had, in fact, remembered me — a nobody in particular — after what seemed to have been for me a lifetime.

I had made a mental note of the name of Major L, the wounded officer, but it was some time before I was able to inform my brother, and in turn be informed by him, the details of what was to become a remarkable connection.

The story that emerged was that the Major and my CSM brother were together in the jungle on a reconnaissance or offensive situation when they were both struck almost simultaneously by enemy fire. My brother's account was that he and the Major had gone ahead of their troops and were discussing the tactics of approach for attack on enemy positions when suddenly he received what he felt to be 'a sledgehammer blow to his chest.' He fell to the ground and began crawling in the direction of his own lines. Weak and unable to proceed very far, he could only wait and watch helplessly the nearby movements of enemy soldiers in the dusk of the jungle. He covered himself with foliage and was fortunately unseen by the Japs who passed within yards of his position. Then, because of the seriousness of his wounds, he went into deep unconsciousness.

He regained consciousness in a British Military Hospital, and was later to learn that he had been saved by a combination of luck and more than a little courage on the part of one of his sergeants who had somehow managed to recover and carry the unconscious body of his Sergeant-Major away from the danger zone for critical medical attention.

The situation concerning the Major was similar except that several bullets were pumped into his body as he lay on more open ground, with one of the bullets cutting across the eyes of the unfortunate officer. The Major's life, apparently, was saved by the bravery of a certain NCO who dashed forward to pull out his Major in defiance of raking enemy fire in the area.

So it was that my brother's account of the sad fate that befell himself and the Major, was one that struck me as being of amazing coincidence — particularly in the way I was somehow singled out to meet the one person who was so closely connected with this particular drama. Such a gentleman, whose son, I hoped, recovered to better health and mental adjustment.

14

We Move Into Germany

We were now up to the Dutch/German border. Like so many of the British and Allied troops who had fought the Germans in France, Belgium and Holland I, too, was somehow relishing the thought that at last the battlefield was now the German Homeland itself. Deutschland was now to be the host nation to the host of missiles and ground attacks which in the past had been the rampant and unwelcome visitors in other lands. The shells, mortars and bullets would now be humming a different tune, and not at all in harmony with the strains of *Deutschland über Alles*. Indeed that particular song was losing much of its popularity as the fortunes of war changed dramatically for the Germans. Despite their erstwhile military superiority, genius, discipline and courage they had — almost unbelievably — failed to keep the Allied Wolf from getting to their front door where we now stood. The Russian Bear was also moving fast towards the back door!

Our next step would be the realization of a military dream for those of us who fought and hunted the foe determinedly along many a blitzed and blazing road from Normandy. We had left behind a trail of dead and mutilated friends and we now vengefully wanted to smash the door down. We were anxious and ready for the final thrust of the sword to kill off the evil two-headed demon and monster — Germany and the Germans. For us it was a St George and all that!

Certainly this was the way war and its agents of propaganda worked. I was not alone in believing that all Germans were atheists, square-headed beasts, masochists who tortured, terrorized and raped. Indeed, being a good soldier was all too clearly a standard set by the amount of hate you had for your enemy-in-war. How could you possibly entertain thoughts of dignity, kindness, humanity attributable to the enemy and still be a good soldier? He who did would not only be a bad soldier, he would more likely be a dead one! Too many warriors on all sides are trained to shoot first and ask questions afterwards — and if you knew it you did it.

We were, though, not quite ready to smash the door down yet, which could only really be done by the crossing of the River Rhine. But we were, so to speak, very much on the doorstep where we could in our vengeance kill Germans on their own soil, bury them and triumphantly dance upon their graves. A dose of their own poison for a change.

I was to discover, however, that the brunt of the anger and initial venom of accumulated bad feeling of British troops were in fact taken by the least of all military and politically minded of the Germans — the Rhinelanders. They were mostly hard-working agricultural (Bauern) types who were as religiously God-fearing as any people could be.

I remember my first incursion into Germany from somewhere near the Dutch border. I was more than a little surprised, in view of the atheistic picture I had of those we called 'Huns', to see so much evidence of Christian belief. Religious pictures, shrines, altars, carvings, etc., were to be seen in houses, villages and fields everywhere and not at all consistent with what our propagandists had told us.

It was on the first of my many forays into shell-torn, often burning, German houses and villages where I saw and found more than enough tragedy and pathos to dissipate much of my hate — to make way for a little compassion even. It was sad to see, on a number of occasions during our reconnoitres and house-to-house searches, the stillness of an old person's body or that of an invalid lying cold and stiff on some rubble-covered bed. They were the helpless people who were unable to flee or take shelter from the horrors of war. Sometimes a body could be found clutching at a crucifix or at rosary beads. So many stricken bodies I found in what were, or had been, very religious homesteads.

I suppose it was for me a hate anti-climax. Maybe it was that for the first time I was seeing not just the combatant German soldiers, but also defenceless German women, children and infirm civilians — not the participants of battle but the victims of war.

There was also about this time a fairly lively trade — more

of a bartering kind — springing up and operating along the border points. It was a rather one-sided form of trading since most of the goods, loot would be a more correct description, came from the German side. The Dutch were certainly not slow — who could blame them? — in directly obtaining the goods themselves or via scavenging Tommies. One could only wonder whether it was altogether a question of retribution — perhaps even of restoration. In any case a steady flow of household goods, bicycles, even cattle could be observed changing ownership from Deutsch to Dutch.

Since time immemorial invading troops of all nationalities have helped themselves in more ways than one in the countries they overran. In this respect British troops were also not indifferent to opportunities for plundering themselves. Indeed, if all the stories and rumours were true, then it really was a situation and fact that the higher the rank the greater the booty. Some officers, it was said, had even managed somehow to get thoroughbred racehorses back to England.

Diversion there had to be from the bloody awful business of constant battle. Looking for, and finding, valuable loot in any theatre of war was just about the best possible diversion — next, that is, to ravishing women which was also done often enough if the truth of the matter could ever be known. How many victims in this Second World War will never be known, that's for sure. I myself was certainly no saint although up to this point I had survived all the crudities and obscenities that war and military service could put to me without — strange and surprising though it may seem — need or habit of using swear-words. It is true to say that I had never once in my life used swear-words or cursed in the way soldiers usually do, and I had often to take some ribaldry from fellow soldiers because of it. I was therefore no forcible ravisher of women. But I must admit, however, that when it came to cracking a safe or two I was, if anything, as good as or perhaps better than most. I really did find excitement and sport in this kind of diversionary activity, and when the opportunity arose I was as ready as anyone else in seeking a fortune for myself.

As a trained sapper engineer I had used explosives extensively. I knew just about all there was to know about blasting anything, from the simple 'one primer job' to stun a fish or two in the river, to the more complicated one of simultaneously blowing up a four or five bridge series job involving hundreds of separate charges. I worked and lived with explosives for a good part of my military service. I had, in fact, become so familiar with the darned stuff that I found it convenient and useful to actually carry around with me my own personal small pack loaded with explosives. I found a surprising number of uses for it, not least for blowing up mines *in situ* and for use in other awkward situations.

But best of all I found it handy for blasting open the tough metal safes I somehow had the habit of coming across from time to time. Great fun, but alas no great fortune since most of the safes I cracked were stacked with piles of paper money all of which was worthless and useless. Circumstances were such that we were unable to spend or buy with such currency. It did, however, come in handy sometimes as a most satisfying kind of toilet paper — particularly the notes of high denomination!

One of my most profitable safe-blowing operations was when I cracked one that contained a fine collection of about forty or so guns of different type and date. They were soon disposed of and well dispersed because of the impossibility of keeping possession of the entire collection.

The problem for any front line soldier in war-ravaged towns and villages was not so much finding valuable loot, but rather in keeping possession of it. His mobility and safety when the flak flies is all too often more important than grabbing a fur coat or bagging a silver tea-set!

Safe-breaking I found to be great fun and good excitement. Seldom was it disappointing since the best part of the game was the actual operation and anticipation.

I remember one particular occasion when I really did have a fortune within my grasp. It happened at a time — just about the only time over a very long period — when my explosives kit and I were separated. My old faithful 'banger pack' was left on the section truck when I was dropped off to carry out a reconnaissance of a deserted factory somewhere in Holland. Such recces were an important part of Royal Engineer activity since it helped to gather and provide information about local resources etc., which could be made available, utilized and exploited as the circumstances of war demanded.

As I was dropped off the truck — my pack under the

wooden seat on the truck — I was told by the driver that he would return to pick me up an hour or two later.

I entered the factory, which turned out to be a very large mill for spinning cloth. The factory was silent and still as if some giant hand had somehow intervened to stop everything suddenly, all within a magic moment. Rolls of cloth, finished and unfinished fabrics, materials wound on bobbins and spindles lay all around on motionless machinery. Offices with cups and glasses neatly arranged on tables showed unfinished liquid content and biscuits, all plenty of evidence to make me think that there was nothing like a shell or two to make people disappear rather quickly.

My reconnaissance was completed rapidly enough and consisted merely of making a few notes about the machinery and materials I saw around the place. There were a great number of huge rolls of cloth, some of which looked like real silk. A sly and crafty truckload or two could make a fortune on the black market... if only!

I found myself with quite some time to kill before the arrival of the truck which was to pick me up. As I walked around the main administrative block of the building, I observed in one of the offices a very large metal safe. It was a good six feet across and reached up to the ceiling. I cursed my luck for not having the explosives which would have enabled me to quickly learn the secret of its innards. I was about to walk away from its formidable security and casement when I remembered seeing a heavy crowbar and sledgehammer in another room. I had time to spare and a stout six-foot crowbar could give me a great deal of leverage if somehow I could get some wedging action going between the two doors.

I set to work with a vengeance and for the first half hour I worked like a Trojan without making much of an impression. Gradually, however, I succeeded in getting a nice little hole going which enabled me to get the spike end of the bar levering away at the metal casing. It was hard going, but I gradually managed to tear back a good section of metal. The operation was a bit like trying to open a sardine can with a table fork. Unfortunately I was to discover that the first part of the job was by no means the hardest, since there were three separate layers of steel held together by rivets and packed between with fireproof material.

My progress, however, was steady and relentless. I had somehow succeeded against the odds in having made a fairly big tear in the outer casing, a lesser one in the middle and a considerably smaller one on the inside.

I was able, after a while, to squint inside and with a few glimpses was just able to make out what appeared to be leather bags and metal boxes inside on the facing shelf. I succeeded in making a final hole the size of my fist, which enabled me to feel around for the possible release of inside locking bars in an endeavour to open the safe doors.

I was in this precise position with my head turned towards a window which faced the main driveway approach to the factory. I could see that a furtive figure was moving in the distance and was, as I observed, hesitant and dodgy in the way it was making its approach by moving and sneaking behind cover alongside the driveway.

I kept out of sight but I saw that the figure was that of a not-so-young female, dressed all in black and that she was intent on making her way in my direction.

I quickly dumped the implements I had been using into another room. We were, after all, not at war with the Dutch, and I certainly had no wish to be caught red-handed even though her own game might be no different to mine. I was sure she had not seen me as I hid and waited silently behind the door. It was not long before I heard the shuffling and nervous panting as the woman in black came through the door. A small thin woman of middle age. I saw that she carried a bunch of keys, and I heard her cry out as she moved towards the safe. She stood gazing at the busted and battered safe in dismay and puzzlement. She was obviously at a loss as to what to do since she was unable to use a key because of the damage. Her mutterings were in Dutch — or even double Dutch — but it was clear enough to me that she was cursing the scoundrel who was responsible for the outrage.

I made my presence known and in doing so saw the poor woman almost jump out of her skin in fright. I succeeded with friendly gestures and words in calming the lady down, and I was quite surprised that she was able to put some English words of her own together fairly well. I gathered that she was something of a chief secretary or director and that she was very concerned about whatever was in the safe. I told her that

Germans had been spotted in the area some time earlier and that it must have been they who were responsible for the damage. I also said it was important to know what was in the safe so that we could offer some protection if the content was of great value.

It was only after a friendly bit of conversation that she told me the safe — among other things of value — contained twelve thousand golden gulders held as a gold reserve and hedge against the less trustworthy paper money. She would, however, have none of it when I craftily suggested she should come back some hours later when I would do her the favour of using explosives. Her firm refusal to leave the place spoilt any plan I had to successfully complete the job I had started and had slogged so hard at.

It was but a short time later that I heard my vehicle hooting away to let me know it had arrived to pick me up. As I mounted the section truck I felt pretty sore about 'the one that got away' - so much so indeed that I could not restrain myself from aiming a hefty kick at the wooden seat below which was my darned explosive pack. Fortunately it was only my temper that exploded!

But yet again a further tale of another 'one that got away', only this time a rather comical one for the telling.

It was at one of the German border towns, perhaps it was München Gladbach or somewhere thereabouts. Whatever town it was, it could in the prevailing circumstances only be described as a place where there were tons-upon-heaps-upon-piles-upon-mountains of rubble and rubbish. Roads were hardly roads, streets were anything but streets since blockage, damage, ruin and debris were everywhere. Difficult to imagine just how much tonnage of high explosive had been pumped into the area over a period of time. Surprisingly, however, here and there a house or shop — sometimes even a row of them — could be seen standing in splendid isolation, seemingly proud at being the selected and privileged few.

Shells were still hammering away around and about the place as I sought cover in one of the buildings. I found myself in a sturdy shop enclosure which, judging by the number of sign-boards littering the area, was situated on what had been, or was, a main street or shopping precinct.

Seeing signs, cabinets, empty jewellery boxes, etc.,

indicated that I was sheltering in what was, or had been, a jeweller's shop. There was little evidence of any real jewellery about the place although I did sample a handful of what could have been — and what later turned out to be — real gold frames for optical lenses. A keener look around the place revealed a stout iron safe in one of the back rooms. It was locked and had somehow become detached from its main bearings and supports. It was as if someone had failed somehow to make off with it. Transportation was all too obviously a problem for Germans everywhere in such hard times. There were more empty jewellery cases, labels, etc., lying around the safe. I was left wondering and looking for clues which might indicate whether the 'goodies' had been put into the safe, or taken out of it. With a little reasoning I supposed and concluded that a locked safe would have to be presumed to have something to hide and protect. I reckoned that a safe should, with sense, be left open for all to see that nothing was contained. In this way no one was likely to damage or tamper around with what for some people was a costly and essential piece of furniture or equipment.

Anyway I somehow had the feeling that something was hidden inside.

It was not easy in a battlefield situation to know exactly where you were at all times — particularly when you were in a maze of environmental features that were all around one moment and gone the next. Here, however, there were landmarks which could with justification be considered as likely permanent ones. I carefully took bearings so as to know the exact bearing of where both myself and the safe were because I intended to return. I was always one to follow a good hunch, or satisfy a craving curiosity. But I would have to choose a better time however. Getting away from shelling and whistling shrapnel was rather more important just then!

It was on the following morning that I was able, with a couple of other guys, to find my way back to where the safe was. The battered town was a great deal more peaceful. The shelling had ceased and our army bulldozers were moving in to make way for anxious troops waiting to press ahead.

The two who were with me were two rough and tough fellows, seasoned campaigners who had been around long enough to know quite a few tricks and games themselves. I had brought enough explosives with me to ensure that there would be no resistance to the kind of wallop I had in mind for the black steel box which was the kind of container that people like us were always anxious to see the inside of.

I observed that the morning after the day before was something of a calm after the storm. Now there appeared to be lively military activity with quite a few soldiers and military vehicles moving around. Already a good deal of road clearance had been made to allow armoured vehicles to push forward. Altogether it was now quite different to when there was, naturally I suppose, a complete absence of human activity at the time when the shelling was around. So much to be said for speedy troop infiltration when the firing stops — a time for the crowds of army 'heroes' to make their appearance!

My colleagues, whom I knew as Buster and Big Toby, and myself were on course and making our way towards the building where I knew the safe was located.

It was with quite a bit of amazement and not a little disappointment that we saw, as we moved closer to the building, that an army scout car was parked immediately outside.

We entered the building from the opposite rear entrance to find a Major — from a particular infantry regiment — and two of his sergeants well engaged in working out ways and means of opening the safe. Their only problem, as I could see it, was that all they had were a couple of hand grenades, a primer and were lacking any apparent sensible means of initiation and detonation.

Royal Engineers have always had the respect of most other regiments when it comes to the subject of explosives, and I had little or no difficulty in explaining that I was better equipped in training and material to do the job properly. It was, I suggested, a reasonable arrangement for me to lay a simple, quick and effective charge and for all of us to have equal shares in the spoils of anything of value that was found.

The other three went off for a quiet whispering session amongst themselves before agreeing to the proposal. It never crossed my mind for a moment that they could play the dirty on us if they were so inclined by pulling rank.

I prepared the charge using 808 HE, a kind of powerful

gelignite explosive, and ensured that enough was enough. It had to be just right.

It was decided for safety's sake that the Major and his two sergeant henchmen should keep a look-out at the front of the building whilst we three RE 'musketeers' kept watch at the rear. There was of course, because of increasing troop movement, the possibility of other persons moving around at the wrong time. I suggested we should all wait for a few moments or so after the explosion before entering the building because of the danger of collapsing masonry, etc. I gave warning also that there would be a fair amount of dust and filth flying around immediately after the explosion and that this should be allowed to settle.

I had cut two foot or so of safety fuse, burning time rate of two feet per minute, which allowed us time enough to get outside and wait anxiously for the big bang.

The explosion went off with a muffled crack that thankfully and mercifully left the building apparently unmoved. I had some difficulty in restraining my colleagues who instantly made a dash to enter the building. I reminded them that it was safer to hold back for a minute or so before entering. Buster was the first to dash impatiently before the minute was up, which to my mind was a bit rash. I was to discover, however, that Buster was, if anything, a bit more clever than I, in that he was more aware and much less trusting of the guys who were at the front of the house.

Big Toby and myself entered a few moments later. The atmosphere inside the place was as thick and murky as an overcooked pea soup with the safe's powderish fire-proof packing material falling like black snow.

I could just about make out a pair of scuffling figures near the safe which now had open doors. Buster was yelling away and grappling with a sergeant who suddenly lashed out viciously and felled Buster to the floor. The sergeant then bolted away through the front door whilst clutching a bag or case of some kind.

It then became all too evident that the Major and his sergeants had beaten us to the contents of the safe. They had obviously moved in quickly to help themselves immediately following the explosion while we had foolishly and trustingly waited just that little too long for the dust to settle. I got to the front door to see their vehicle speeding away like mad.

Buster recovered to say that he had got to the safe to see the Major and his sergeants moving away from the safe with several attaché-type cases. He succeeded, until struck down, in holding on to one of the sergeants in an attempt to relieve him of some of our share of the loot.

We spent more time laughing than crying about the matter and we soon discovered that a little something had been left behind after all because a closer inspection of the safe revealed that two sets of diamond pendants — obviously genuine — had somehow fallen loose to the back of the safe. These we drew lots for and which ended up with me losing out yet again!

15

Crossing The River Rhine

The German forces, having been driven back, squeezed and contracted like a battered tin can, were now furiously and feverishly preparing a final defensive line against the advance from the west by the Allies. The River Rhine was indeed a formidable natural obstacle, but the Germans were sadly and painfully aware that it was but a temporary barrier to the Allied thrust aimed at the very heart of their nation.

It was clearly a losing battle, as every German must have known, which would result in much futile loss of life. Unfortunately all that was on offer for them was 'unconditional surrender' which was too bitter a pill for any proud military nation to swallow, particularly since it also obviously demanded total and complete submission to the Russian hordes whom they regarded as primitive barbarians.

A fight to the death was perhaps the best choice for many Germans. For others, a battle to the bitter end for the sake of honour, self-respect and the imagined further glory of the Fatherland. There were those also who would continue to hold out tenaciously with faith and hope of being saved by some kind of 'last ditch' miracle. A question, too, of how many fanatics or morons had been produced by training, discipline and brainwashing over a long period of time.

But courage was never in doubt, the German soldiers basically being little changed or in any way different since the time a British General Officer (commanding a brigade) wrote to *The Times* newspaper in 1914. 'I am disgusted by accounts I see in the papers of the inferiority of Germans as soldiers; don't believe one word of it. They are quite splendid in every way. Their courage, efficiency, organization, equipment and leading are all of the very best, and never were surpassed by any troops ever raised. They come on in masses against our trenches and machine-guns time after time; and they are never quiescent, but always on the offensive.'

The Germans would therefore see to it that even though they were unable to stop the Allies crossing the Rhine, they were certain to make them pay dearly for doing so.

The Allied troops, on the other hand, were consolidating and preparing a thorough military build up and layout, within a few miles of the Rhine river, to ensure successful launch and crossing when opportunity and time was right and proper.

That time was fast approaching, for already the guns of both sides had for many weeks kept up a ceaseless barrage in an exchange that daily sent thousands of missiles in both directions across the river.

It was expected that our unit would have some good part to play in the assault river crossing campaign. We were a unit with a good deal of experience and expertise in Bailey bridging — our unit being one of the first to carry out tests and trials of the bridge's innovative equipment under the supervision of Professor Bailey (designer and inventor) himself, way back in 1942 in the lovely English county of Kent.

It was no surprise therefore to find ourselves — a sapper threesome — moving with some apprehension into the smoke-screen area of the Rhine for the first of our river-related tasks and missions.

The smoke canisters were placed about a half a mile or so from the river bank creating an eerie kind of no-man's-land behind a smoke screen intended to conceal military movements within the British sector. It was a good half mile or so of the no-man's-land before reaching the water on our side of the river, with a likely similar stretch of land on the enemy side. Observation posts or patrols on both sides were keeping a watchful eye on the Rhine and its ground approach.

Our task was a peculiar and dangerous daylight one in that we were to recce and prepare a travel route or path across the rough open ground leading to the river so as to allow our intended attacking amphibian crafts (Dukws) to reach the water safely and without damage. Because of the heavy infantry loads and the low and soft belly of the craft when moving on wheels, deep ruts and rocky projections, etc., posed considerable danger for night attack across river. It would

indeed be a sad state of affairs if Dukws took in water as they
took to the water!

Because of the danger of being spotted by the ever alert
enemy across the way — who might so easily bring fire to bear
upon us — we moved around inside the no-man's-land on
foot. A vehicle was out of the question. Fortunately the
enemy's view at ground level from across the river was blocked
by the fairly high barriers of the flood embankment and river
banks. We had, however, no way of knowing whether a good
pair of binoculars from some distant German observation post
could watch our little game.

The picks and shovels we carried would help to even out the
nasty bumps and projections on the ground and our supply of
sandbags could, where necessary, level up any potholes, shell-
holes and ditches. The ground we had to cover was long and
broad which meant, if we were to do the job properly,
spending an uncomfortably long time in a situation where we
might be spotted and fired upon by the enemy at any moment.

To the left of us were what appeared to be a desolate group
of farm buildings, and to these we directed our early
attention. They could perhaps offer something in the way of
cover in an emergency. In any case we had to satisfy ourselves
that there was no great danger from that particular
blind spot.

My two sapper colleagues were two rough and tough
characters. Both were Northerners, one a Mancunian who
had seen the inside of a couple of UK prisons before enjoying
the active service freedom of HM Forces. The other, a lanky
Glaswegian, was a guy with normally just three interests in life
— women, booze and gambling. Here in such a situation,
however, they were as good a company as could be had, or
wished for.

We approached the farm structures carefully, but without
much fear or suspicion. It would be difficult to imagine
anybody holding on to such a position considering the terrific
non-stop thunder of the guns from both sides. Anyone staying
at such a place would indeed have to be deaf or daft!

It was no surprise to see a number of starved pigs inside a
pen, but we were surprised, on looking around further, to find
a fine looking horse alive and well inside a small paddock
area. Close by was a cart, which in turn suggested that the

harness might also be found. This again suggested that altogether they might be a useful combination which could greatly assist us in our task. We could, for instance, fill up dozens of sandbags with earth, load them onto the cart and then offload them as necessary when finding holes, ditches and rutted ground, etc. Our tools and ourselves could also be trundled around by horse and cart and more importantly we could, from the enemy's distant point of view, be taken for farmhands performing a task relative to the farm.

The harness we soon found, but we decided before harnessing and hitching up — just in case the horse bolted with the cart as the three of us worked — to fill up a good number of sandbags with loose earth from a nearby vegetable patch and then load them onto the cart. The filled sandbags we arranged wall-like on the cart so as to serve as a bullet-proof barrier if things got nasty as we moved closer to the river. A bullet travelling from a rifle or machine-gun can be lethal up to 1000 yards and we could be well within range if the bullets did begin to fly from across the water.

After putting together the horse, cart and harness, we soon found out that the theory of our plan was a lot easier than the practice which really wasn't easy at all. In fact it turned out to be damn nigh impossible. From the start the horse was a brute — a thoroughly German animal that seemed resolute and determined not to work for the British. A half hour of coaxing, bullying, tugging etc., only served to move us out onto the open ground by a couple of hundred yards or so, when and where the creature positively refused to budge an inch.

Despite my own endeavours to prevent it, the horse was given rather harsh treatment by my fellow 'non-travellers', who could hardly be described as merciful types at the best of times. Considerable time and effort had been wasted because the animal refused to be their four-legged friend, and so they showed the creature just how bad they felt about it all with more wallopings than I cared to witness. All to no avail, and the horse stayed put!

The animal's total stubbornness made me wonder whether perhaps horses, too, suffered shell-shock, whether perhaps it was a racehorse or hunter type that had never been between cart shafts before, or was it perhaps some kind of horsey ESP that warned against doing what we wanted it to do. My own reasoning told me that by finding one horse, one cart and one harness-set at the farm, a close connection of the three was surely sound and conclusive. Why then such obstinacy?

Perhaps the reason had something to do with what followed some ten minutes later when we were forced, without the services of horse and cart, to carry out our task by trudging around on foot to examine and repair the ground.

It was an extraordinary piece of good luck that caused me to look more closely at the ground to spot a trip wire in the high rough grass. As RE sappers trained in such matters, we were soon acquainted with the fact that we were at the edge of a belt of ground that had been mined.

It was not for the first time in our military service that we found ourselves on all fours feeling and prodding the ground with our bayonets; the eventual result of our labours being a haul of seventeen Teller mines and four 'S' mines.

It took a good few hours to make a clean sweep and do a good tidy up of the area, having fortunately no problems from across the water.

In the meantime the horse had remained where we had left it — no longer 'that damned horse' but more of a blessed one that had refused, despite a bad beating, to convey us into what would have been almost certain death for us all.

I unshackled the animal and was glad to see it move back in the direction to where we originally found it. Before it went I think we all felt like kneeling before it to ask for its forgiveness!

So another tricky job was done, one we were happy to get away with so very lightly.

But with one job done there was as always another in the offing, and for the 'PBS' in front line of battle the next one was always going to be the worst. A psycho-analysis for each and every individual, at such times, most likely would be the same except perhaps for intensity in the degree of fear of the job to be done and relief when the job was done. A kind of stop and start mentality registering and recording either fear or relief. Scars of battle are all too often mental ones caused by terror of what lies ahead. Life, after all, is all about not getting killed. Yet with man's survival instincts at odds with the sacrificial demands of war and country, make it a kind of conflict without and a conflict within to make them both the crippling agonies of war.

It was but a short time interval before I received fresh instructions and orders concerning, this time, a midnight visit to the water's edge of the River Rhine. The purpose of the visit for this occasion was to prepare the way for an assault Bailey pontoon bridge. I was to be in a party of four consisting of a reconnaissance officer, a corporal to assist the RO, a signals radio operator and myself as Bren-gunner. The RO was detailed to make a close examination of the given riverside area, and to find a suitable launching site for our pontoon bridge. Measurements would have to be taken and a check made on the approach and support ground, the water level etc., so as to ensure speedy and efficient bridge building across the Rhine. Perhaps finding the snags, handicaps and opposition was also part of the reconnaissance mission as much as anything else.

As we set off, the night sky was just about the right one for the job, cloudy and dark enough to hide us from the enemy at reasonable distance, but not too much of a blackout to prevent our recce ops being carried out with some degree of visibility.

We left the armoured vehicle we travelled in, together with its driver/operator, at safe and secure distance from the immediate danger zone to which we were now approaching. First we should have to move quietly and steadily a couple of hundred yards or so before reaching the rise of the flood wall embankment. This we should have to negotiate with the possible danger of being seen against the skyline of scattered cloud. We should then have to crouch forward for another fifty yards or so before reaching the river bank which was also a fairly high embankment — a rise of some eight to ten feet or so of quite steep slope. We should then finally have to make our way up and over the bank to get to the water's edge to search out the best conditions for the intended bridge site.

My own earlier daytime experience of moving around almost openly near the river, being untroubled by the enemy, made me somewhat bolder than the others and rather more ready to push forward to get the job done with. I gave little thought to the possibility that considerably more activity was likely by both sides operating close to the river under cover of darkness — a time for patrols to probe and reconnoitre.

I had moved to the nearside base of the river bank and was, as I remember, feeling impatient and scornful at what I felt to be undue caution on the part of those with me. I must have been facing the wrong way when it happened. My back was turned to the bank as I was awaiting and searching out the figures following stealthily behind. I was suddenly aware, not so much of the explosion of a machine-gun behind me from the top of the bank, but of the thud of bullets which was a distinct 'pop-pop-pop' striking the ground in front of me. I was momentarily ignorant of what it was until I heard a warning yelp. A charmed life was indeed mine because I was most fortunately able to tumble into one of the many holes and trenches peppering the river bank, probably dug by Germans while awaiting transportation across the river during earlier retreat. As I did so I spun around to find I had the perfect silhouetted figure on the bank above me to fire at. The advantage was mine; a lone German soldier high against the skyline peering downwards at the dark indistinguishable features of the ground below. It took a short sharp burst of my Bren gun to instantly silence and remove the outlined figure firing wildly above me.

There followed a long fearful stillness and, except for the distant thunder of guns, an eerie silence around us. I had no idea of what was now on the other side of the bank. It seemed likely that we were two parties — that of my own and the German one — surprising each other by strangely coming into contact by converging at the same time and spot on the river bank. It was possible that the Germans were also as still and silent on the other side of the bank as we were on our side. With the bank between us we knew as much about their strength as they knew about ours. I couldn't tell if the lieutenant and corporal had been hit by the German's spray of bullets. We were all, in any case, remaining silent, with myself hardly daring to breathe, straining and staring in the dark for the slightest sound or movement which could be the deadly danger I was any moment expecting in such a situation. Could it be that the first to move, or make a sound, would be the loser? The Germans now had the advantage since our task lay on their side of the bank and was a task that had to be done. They on the other hand could quietly withdraw without us knowing much about it.

It seemed to be a long period of hush before the whispered voices of my companions and that of my own brought us together. Miraculously no one had been hit despite the spray of bullets by the German gunner who could have been no more than a few yards away when firing. It was likely that when coming to the top of the bank from the riverside he had spotted some of our movement in the grass below and fired wildly, mercifully missing us.

When we eventually moved away from the positions which had held us like statues, it was to move and creep quietly away to the right following along the bottom of the embankment.

At some distance away we moved up and over the bank. We did so cautiously to say the least, but surprisingly we encountered nothing to interfere further with our task.

Flares could often be seen to light up the night sky on some earlier occasions and as we had no wish to be caught and lit up by one of these our job was very quickly done. Nor did we loiter in any way, either, before getting away from the danger zone back to our unit base.

It was some time on the following day that a start was made on our Rhine pontoon bridge. At some early stage in the task our operations were held up for some time because of enemy artillery fire coming from a concrete gun emplacement almost directly in line with our bridge. OC unit had sensibly requested RAF support for an air strike to be made to knock out the position rather than risk the danger of the bridge equipment being blown out of the water. It was mentioned that a bulldozer operator working his machine on the far bank had been hit and killed already.

I used the break in the proceedings to walk the short distance back to the scene of the shootings on the occasion of our earlier night's excursion. I wanted to satisfy my curiosity by finding the exact spot where the shooting occurred, and I wondered also about the German I shot at from close range.

I soon found the evidence I was looking for close to the water's edge. It was the body of a sandy-haired German Army Corporal in his late twenties. His face, unmarked, was of clear cut and good-looking features. I experienced a strange and sad feeling as I looked, gazed and looked again at the lifeless body with face turned upwards towards the sky. I had seen too many corpses to shed any tears, having usually a philosophical attitude that any of them might have been me but thankfully wasn't.

Here, however, things were different because of the relationship and closeness brought about by a fateful and deadly meeting at the midnight hour.

It was perhaps for some subconscious reason that I wanted to know more about the poor fellow, and I wished I could somehow find the time to give the body a proper burial. It seemed likely that his grave would be a watery one if the river's water level rose a little higher. I gave way to the impulse to check his identity by extracting and examining papers from his jacket. Strangely, as if it was something I knew I should find, the first thing I found myself looking at was a photograph of what was obviously the person himself, his lovely-looking wife and beautiful child. I somehow had no wish to look further, and I then replaced the items carefully and respectfully while at the same time I found myself talking to the body, 'Sorry old chap. Didn't want to do it, you know, but you made me.' All real enough, but altogether like something that could only happen in those old films like *All Quiet On The Western Front* or *Journey's End* while you sat in a cosy cinema seat.

The reality was that I managed even to find the empty cartridge cases — eight of mine and 'unlucky thirteen' in respect of the other fellow. But such souvenirs were not for keeping, and these I threw far out into the river.

As I walked back I wondered about the circumstances that brought the German across the river. Had he somehow crossed alone on a spying expedition or had he been on lonely guard and outpost duty? Had he led a patrol or was he a lone volunteer? I knew only that he was now just another one of the countless casualties of war and that I for some inexplicable reason was not.

When I rejoined my working party, it was with a feeling of gratitude to the RAF as I observed their air strike against the troublesome gun position. The attack was apparently successful except for one particular piece of enemy artillery which remained and continued to play a part in a hopeless kind of way. It was peculiar in the manner you first saw the flash of the distant gun and then to watch a certain exact spot in the middle of the river — to the left of the line of the bridge — where the shell would fall and explode harmlessly. I watched fascinated as it happened with predictable repetition. It was as if the gun was fixed or locked precisely in range and traverse bearings.

I wondered about the gun that kept firing in such a despairingly strange and hopeless way, as I wondered earlier about the dead German corporal, just questions with no answers, but obviously there was a story of a sort behind both. Perhaps it was only the Lord master of the universe — popping away at the buttons of his Heavenly computer — who was privileged to see the whole picture, which really and truly I wouldn't want to see.

The bridge went ahead and was completed, as far as I knew, without further incident. We were across the Rhine at surprisingly little cost in casualties.

16

We Cross The River Elbe

We were somewhere on the River Elbe on a bridging task which seemed likely to be the very last Bailey bridge operation of any military significance in the Second World War. Strange indeed, and fortunate, considering my perilous existence and journey since advancing from Normandy after the initial assault on D-day. Then I had helped to construct the very first of the Bailey bridges in the European Campaign (the River Orne and canal bridges at Benouville/Ranville). In between these apparent phases of beginning and end, I had somehow miraculously survived the many battle involvements of most, if not all, of the major river crossings using assault Bailey bridges. There had been, of course, other engineer unit tasks, often even more dangerous and deadly, such as mine-lifting, bomb disposal, demolition and road-making, etc. There had been tight situations, too, when our role in the war game was more that of Infantry than Engineers. Now, sadly, only but a few faces were the familiar ones of the early days, few of them without some scar of battle — all of them with an awful sickness and weariness of war.

We had already made contact with a few small groups of Russian soldiers, whose main formations were moving rapidly from the east to slice through the tenacious but doomed German forces, many of whom could now have only been overcome in their own back garden. There were few other places left for them to retreat.

It was just a short time earlier that I had my first glimpse of a Russian soldier. I remember that both he and I had entered a small German village from different ends of the street and it was obvious to me, even at some distance away, that he was well and truly loaded with vodka — or whatever that was similarly strongly alcoholic. He was a lone figure,

185

staggering from one side of the road to the other, shouting out what were obviously Russian obscenities and shaking his fist at the houses alongside. He moved thus, stopping occasionally to pick up stones to throw at windows in passing — somewhat differently 'stoned' himself.

An old German Frau emerged from a house where the windows had just been shattered and began to plead with him. I went forward feeling that the old Frau would be struck down if I didn't move quickly. As I approached him, the 'blotto Ivan' stared at me sheepishly for a moment or two and then with the biggest of big drunken grins he came up to throw his arms around me, to hug me and to tug away in friendly handshake. He gave me a few more hugs, muttering something like 'Komrad' before I finally shook him off, with a somewhat forced smile, for him to move off as before — proceeding on his fist-shaking, shouting, stone-throwing way!

My encounter here was surely evidence enough that the great link-up of the main British, American and Russian troops was fast approaching and with it, perhaps at last, the end of a terrible war.

But the war, however, was not yet over even though we knew that the once mighty Wehrmacht was now a crushed and broken force. There was still another bridge to be built, another strategic thrust forward to kill off the final spasms of resistance.

The Elbe bridge was completed with little opposition from the enemy, although a few dead bodies lay scattered around the area. I remember also that I had to let fly a couple of times with a Bren gun at solitary German aircraft that flew overhead on what were probably the last few reconnaissance flights made by the now almost non-existent Luftwaffe.

Our bridge task done, we could now take it easy and await the columns preparing and waiting somewhere to the rear of the site, like some coiled spring to burst forward to overcome yet another river and natural obstacle.

There was little for me to do until the crossing of the armoured vehicles, etc., was made. I therefore wandered around to the east side of the river doing my own reconnaissance and hoping for something perhaps more exciting than humping heavy bridging equipment.

There was a wooded area, on hilly ground overlooking the

bridge, through which a small road track ran extending to some place beyond. Another road, or track, ran to the left on the lower ground almost at right angles to the other. I had gathered from someone who had earlier been on stealthy patrol of the area that a Russian labour camp (slave labour or Ukranian volunteers?) was known to be somewhere in the woods over the hill.

I followed the track into the wood with the intention of finding the camp, to meet up with the Russians and to tell them that the British were now here in strength and so to liberate them. From my position up the hill I could, and did, look down through the trees at the Bailey bridge now neatly straddling the river. I was fairly sure that there were no enemy troops around, or they would surely have shown themselves during our many hours of bridging.

I was wrong, indeed, because from my view of gazing down at the bridge I saw movements in the trees well below me to the right. I could see German uniforms by the dozen, then by the hundred moving in the direction of the lower road. I watched in amazement as they began to line up on the road and, much to my relief, saw someone move to the front carrying a large white flag. I then knew it was safe for me to close in their direction, accept their surrender and direct them to a more secure captive zone. I had dealt with surrendering or surrendered prisoners before. As I approached I could see the column growing massively as more and more figures spilled out of the woods. They were a truly pathetic sight. Surely Napoleon's retreat from Moscow could have presented no sadder picture. There were badly wounded soldiers on wheelbarrows and carts pushed along by soldiers who were themselves bloodily bandaged. Soldiers with clothing tattered, tottering along with crutches or hobbling painfully on legs strapped with sticks, uniforms more red than grey. The leader with the flag spoke to me in good English, obviously a high-ranking officer but with insignia removed and discarded.

I was unable to see the end of the column which had swelled to become numbers more in thousands than in hundreds. I took them slowly but surely in the direction of the bridge, where, having arrived, I handed them over to some RE Captain. He refused to allow the prisoners to proceed across the bridge until the crossing of our own forces had been made.

He was, I suppose, quite right to do so, but it was sad indeed for the army of prisoners, many of whom must have died unattended and neglected for the twenty-four hours or so — sprawling in great numbers along the river bank in obvious defeat and misery.

After handing over as I did to the Captain, I resumed my intention to visit the Russian labour camp. This time I found a pal who would come along with me. After walking a couple of miles or so from the river, we came eventually to the main entrance gates of a wooden hutted camp. This was the camp we had been looking for. Standing alongside what was clearly the guardroom were two hefty-looking civilian guards, one of whom looked distinctly Mongolian. Perhaps the usual German guards had disappeared some time ago and now the Russians — allegedly forced to work from such camps — were their own bosses? They appeared somehow to have some kind of camp discipline.

I approached them, my hands held high in friendly gesture, my Sten gun well slung behind me, and shouting 'English — we are British.' They were friendly enough but suspiciously reserved — or maybe shy? I indicated that I would like to go inside to look around with my friend. My gesture, at least, seemed to be well understood and inside we went with the Mongolian-faced character as our guide.

It turned out to be a peculiar sort of tour because the camp huts seemed to be made up mostly of dozens of little cells or cubicles measuring no more than a yard or so across for each. Two or more people of both sexes were apparently living in each cubicle where the only item of furniture appeared to be the bunks, one above the other. Our visit became more of a peep show than anything else as our guide pushed open the door of each little living quarter where the occupants appeared to be living in each other's laps or on top of each other's bellies. Many couples were in a love-making situation since there was, I suppose, little else to do in such cramped conditions.

The women were surprisingly huge and beefy. They were definitely the rough and tough types and I saw none that matched up to my idea of a dream girl! As our guide in turn pointed us out and introduced us in their own tongue, we were treated to many a toothless grin from plenty of muscular females.

There appeared to be a fair balance of both sexes at the camp though, strangely, I saw no children. The smell in some of the cubicles was anything but the wafting of Eau de Cologne and I was glad to get out into the large open yard around which the huts were grouped.

People started congregating around us in small groups and some began to clap and sing. Then the groups got together to become a fairly large crowd to form a circle around us. It was obviously turning into a 'liberation' celebration as many people were joining in with concertinas, tambourines and balalaikas. In what seemed to be no time at all there were people in Cossack dress leaping into the centre of the circle expertly showing the skills of Russian dancing. The clapping and singing kept time with the music as one dancer after another performed his or her piece in the middle.

I enjoyed it all, but as people became more excited I found myself being pushed further back into the crowd. I lost contact with my pal and found myself being badly jostled by strangers and newcomers — some with bottles — who had no notion of who or what I was. I felt it was time to get out since I could well be taken for a soldier on the wrong side. I had also heard it said some time ago that a Russian when sober was the most quiet and inoffensive of people — but the maddest and baddest of all when drunk.

There were signs of confusion, for me anyway, and I was beginning to feel that it was unsafe for me to be around much longer. I moved my Sten gun to my front and took some comfort with a firm grasp of it. I managed somehow to get out on the fairly long road that led back to the main entrance gate. I had given up hope of seeing my colleague in the packed crowd and it was just possible that he was outside the camp already. I hoped to move out without involvement again as I had spent more time away from my working party than I had intended.

As I moved steadily in the right direction I was aware of people hurrying behind me. I walked on quickly trying to ignore the three rough-looking Russians who came up to me gesturing wildly. They stood in front of me to bring me to a halt. I was, of course, unable to understand their gibberish except that I heard the sound 'Ess-Ess' being spat out a few times. At first I thought that they were apprehending me and accusing me of being a German SS soldier. I stood back and brought my gun to the 'on guard' position. I certainly had the advantage of a very effective rapid firing defender in the weapon I always carried. It was only after more sensible sign-making and gesturing that I gathered they were holding on to some SS guy in their guardroom, and they wanted me to go with them. I pointed with my gun to indicate that they should walk in front of me — in case of misunderstanding — to lead me to SS or 'Ess-Ess.' I suspected that they had somehow gone out of their way to show me that they were now very much on our side and, as always, ready and willing to jump on the bandwagon of victory and success when it came around. I had seen it before in France, Belgium and Holland all too often — but then who could blame them, considering the ravages and savages of war?

Sure enough, when I got into their guardroom, I observed in some dark corner a slumped figure with head drooped forward on to one of his arms as if hiding his face. The Russian who stood guarding him was now in his moment of glory, and this he demonstrated by grabbing the hair of the unfortunate man's head, pulling it back violently with an awful bang against the wall to show me the man's face. I looked hard but it was hardly a face that I saw. It was more a bruised, broken and bloody mass of raw flesh — all too obvious that he had been beaten up with punches and kicks. But I knew too well that the SS were hardly the most popular members of the human species; with a reputation for being merciless themselves, it should not be surprising therefore to find mercy in short supply for their own captivity. The battered face, forcibly turned upwards, cried out several times a word unintelligible to me, but which sounded like 'Bruder' or 'Bruter.' His captors pushed photographs in front of me which I presumed they had taken from him earlier. 'Ess-Ess' said someone excitedly pointing to a proud and strutting figure in full SS uniform. A good photograph, indeed, of the uniformed figure walking down the Wilhelme Strasse, Berlin. There was no doubt about the uniform, but I was unable to relate resemblance in faces. It hardly seemed possible that the pathetic creature in the corner was the same person as the elegant, military, proud figure in the photo. I gazed again at the face held upwards. He was thin and weak-looking, shabbily dressed in a tattered bare old army jacket which differed from his own civvy trousers. I noticed an old leather bag near the brown shoes he was wearing which seemed to be well-heeled and soled. Red stitching on his leather bag seemed to match the red stitching on his shoes — which I thought peculiar.

However, I was anything but convinced about it all and would have much preferred to see the blighter disappear out of sight somewhere way beyond. It seemed, however, that I was expected to be duty bound to relieve them of their prime catch for the purpose of allowing us, the Brits, the pleasure of hanging, shooting or further torturing the wretch!

The light of day was falling fast as I stepped out of the guardroom with my miserable stumbling prisoner. I ensured that he walked a good couple of yards in front of me, for I could not be absolutely sure that the Russians were wrong about him being SS. He walked in front of me in a kind of half-demented way, holding on to his battered leather bag, stopping every few yards or so to shout the same-sounding word as before. I still had some distance to travel and I tried to hurry him along. He continued to falter, shout and fiddle around with his leather bag. I wondered about his bag and what might be in it. Lengthening shadows of the trees across the track and the way he stopped to gaze into the woods made me wonder whether he was up to something. Perhaps there was after all a hidden gun in his bag? You never could tell with SS. I gestured to him to halt and open up his bag for my inspection. It seemed to me that he took more than enough time to prise open his precious bag. I stepped close and gazed inside while motioning him to stand back.

I had seen enough and, as I gazed at the swollen face and bloodshot eyes, I felt a great sorrow and pity, for here again was yet another of war's little tragedies, too numerous and unimportant for the history books. The bag contained nothing more than the bits and pieces of a cobbler. Amongst the scraps of leather, shoe-tacks, hammer and boot-last, I also saw a ball of red twine — no doubt shortened by the stitching I had contemplated earlier on his shoes and bag.

Just then, I was pleased to see British vehicles carrying infantry, come rumbling by. I stopped one and explained that my prisoner was suspected of being SS, but that I had no evidence of it. I said his head injuries were bad and needed medical treatment.

I helped the man aboard the vehicle before telling the corporal that I was almost sure that the fellow was just a simple-minded, abused and misunderstood little cobbler.

As the truck drove off I thought about his yelping out the word that sounded like 'Bruder' or 'Bruter.' Perhaps, after all, that was what he had been trying to explain — that it was his brother in the photograph, not himself.

But somehow I still had my doubts.

As I walked back to the bridge I was certain of only one thing, which was that in war you cannot be sure of anything — least of all your own survival.

17

At The End Of The European Campaign

When VE day came, it seemed that it was a great day for everybody except myself. I remember it well as a day when Providence's hierarchy ordained that it was not to be a day for me to be celebrating and rejoicing like all the other European souls around at that time. Ironically it was destined that on that particular day I should find myself being marched under escort on charges of serious breach of military conduct and discipline.

Altogether a funny business since I had no recollection of anything that occurred which constituted the charges, for me all was total oblivion when and where the alleged misconduct was committed, and I therefore had no defence for the case laid against me.

So on this great historic day somewhere in Hamburg, in one of the few large villas that survived the innumerable Allied bombing attacks in and around that great city, I found myself well and truly on the carpet and brought before my CRE (Commander Royal Engineers). I had, I think, reason to feel sorry for myself on that day!

The beginning of this particular piece of misfortune began a number of weeks earlier when my platoon positioned itself among the timber stacks of an old sawmill. It was afternoon and we were resting in preparation for another Bailey bridge river-crossing scheduled to start early next day. I remember that we were strafed a couple of times by the machine-guns of an enemy plane, and they were times when I was indeed thankful for the shelter and protection of the close stacks of timber. I remember also that it was some time later in the afternoon when my timbered den was visited by two of my less genteel colleagues — in fact they were two noted military ruffians. They brought with them a number of unlabelled bottles of what they called for want of a proper name 'Hootch', which they said they got from a bargee whose barge was anchored somewhere along a nearby river or canal.

It should be said that any unlabelled 'hootch' found anywhere in those spiritually austere days was indeed suspect and might be any kind of concoction, from being almost pure wood alcohol to a mixture of meths and fruit juice. I was, however, no expert in sampling alcoholic drink, and when I was offered a great mugful of whatever it was that came out of the bottle I accepted with gratitude to the rough guys who came generously to share their spoils with me. Nothing like a liberal drop of the 'hard stuff' for a soldier's morale in the field — morale being anything but high after months of slog and battle without break. I was easily persuaded to gulp down the vile liquid and I did so with pretended relish and gusto.

Alas! one of the last things I was to remember for some time was a small group briefing about our forthcoming bridge task, and of my asking a couple of good relevant questions. I was to think of those questions many times later because they were the final point of departure before entering a state of oblivion wherein certain actions, held to be mine, had later to be accounted for by me.

The big void had descended, and it must have been some eighteen hours later when I became aware of being in a strange small room, and of being aware also of an extremely loud ticking of a clock close by. The clock was on a chair near to my head and close to the chair I saw a bucket together with a bowl of water, around which were some first-aid kit with towelling and bandages. Waking up to find these peculiar objects around and about me gave me a rather strange feeling, perhaps made more so when I realized that one of the objects in the room was a stretcher upon which I was lying. All was quiet except for the ticking of the clock, and I had some dazed and puzzled moments before it dawned on me that the likely circumstance of it all was that I had been hit during the sleeping hours of the night and that I was now lying in a wounded or injured state. The thought had me convinced that if I felt along my body I should discover the reason for my predicament. Thoughts of a missing lower limb or large shrapnel hole caused me to hesitate before searching myself with tentative hands below the blanket coverage. Perhaps the damned plane at the timber yard got me drilled with a bullet hole after all?

I was, if anything, surprised at finding no outward evidence of wounding or injury, and I began to wonder what the Hell I was doing in such a place and in such a situation. Apparently finding nothing wrong, I made to get to the upright position, but as I did so it was then that I was overcome by an awful dizziness and nausea. I fell back sick, confused and bewildered. I was unable to explain the situation and all I could do was to wait for somebody else to come and do so for me.

The ticking clock indicated a time around 10.30 am, and it was perhaps just a short time later when a soldier I knew came into the room. I knew him as the batman to the 2 I/C of our unit. I waited to find out what the score was as he came close with a long searching look before asking me how I felt. I replied that I didn't quite know how I felt but that I would be pleased if he could fill me in as to what had happened to me.

It appeared that his knowledge of the matter was limited to the fact that I was in one Hell of a state throughout the night, and that a medical officer and an assistant medic had been fighting for my life for most of the time. It was, I was told, believed that I had actually 'died' at some time during the night, but that the doctor had performed a near miracle in somehow getting me back to life again. It appeared that I had been brought in unconscious and in a pretty awful state with head swollen to almost twice normal size, frothing and convulsive. It was a serious and near fatal case of poisoning, believed to be caused by a noxious mixture of alcoholic substances. I was also told that I had earlier been in some kind of trouble involving confrontation with members of the RMP — who had also appeared on the scene a few times during the course of the night.

I had absolutely no recollection of the happenings so described and I was therefore saddened by the news that I had somehow been the cause of such fuss and bother.

It was sad news also to learn from the batman that the unit had moved off just about an hour earlier to commence the scheduled bridging operation. I had always played my part fully on every major operation in the field by our unit and I was proud of the fact that most, if not all, were critically important in helping to win the war. I certainly did not wish to lose out now when it was almost sure to be one of our last bridging ops of the war in Europe.

I understood that the 2 I/C was shortly to return to check on my recovery, and possibly to have something to say and to ask about what went wrong?

Considering that I had as fine a record as anyone for good military conduct and discipline, it came as a shock to discover that I had in some unconscious way fallen below my generally high standard of behaviour.

My wristwatch and signet ring — both gold and quite valuable — I found to be missing from my left hand. The batman orderly could not account for them since they were not among my other possessions. I could only ponder on why they had been removed and concluded that they must have been stolen during my stupefied state. I wondered whether the two guys in the timber yard had something to do with it, perhaps by 'fixing' my drink in some way?

Only a short period of time elapsed before the appearance of the Captain 2 I/C. He was a good officer and friendly fellow who concerned himself very much with the welfare of his subordinates, no stiff upper lip Guards type but more in keeping properly with the kind of approachable down-to-earth sapper officer. He was, he said, very pleased at my recovery particularly since — as he put it — I had almost 'kicked the bucket' during the night. He confirmed that it was the skill of the medical officer, who had worked hard almost continually throughout the night, whom I had to thank for still being alive.

The story of my missing hours was even more of a surprise when I had the 2 I/C's account of what was supposed to have happened. There was nothing I could confirm or deny, and was as follows.

An evening reconnaissance was being made by a small group of RMPs with a view to planning an attack and traffic route through an enemy occupied small village. From a high ground observation position the RMPs had their field glasses focused on a road junction at the village centre. Having seen the movement of German enemy just a short time earlier they were suddenly surprised to see a lone British soldier — without helmet or weapon — strolling casually from another direction and sit down at the road junction. The RMPs were, according to their own statement, concerned about the safety and condition of the soldier and decided on a rescue operation. They moved speedily and bravely in an armoured car only to discover that the soldier in question was not so willing and ready to be rescued and manhandled commando-style. The soldier, an erstwhile Regimental boxer back in England, had something to say about the matter to such an extent that it was the rescuers who also needed rescuing, with two of them being hurt — one rather badly with a suspected broken neck.

Somehow the situation was brought under control, by what means is not known but which may well have accounted for the soldier's amnesia, with the services of the MO being involved and the soldier being stretchered off to his own lines.

Such was the picture given by the 2 I/C, about the events concerning my predicament which I was to confirm later. In the eyes of the Captain I had been a bad boy and had therefore some explaining to do. I could, of course, only explain the truth of the matter that I was normally a non-drinker who had little or no experience of heavy alcoholic drinking. I said I was caught in an off moment without knowing the potency or poison of the drink I was given. I therefore could only apologize to the Captain and ask that, in view of my hitherto good record, would he please allow me to join my section on their operational task.

The Captain, however, took a good amount of persuasion, during which I stressed the point about having never missed out on any other vital operation, before he gave way to my request.

I was duly conveyed, feeling more than a little weak and wobbly, to the bridging site. The construction of the bridge was well under way when I joined up with my usual squad. My involvement and labour with familiar faces and equipment was perhaps the mental and physical tonic I needed for my somewhat speedy recovery, considering my moments of near death — or perhaps a kind of death itself — less than twenty-four hours earlier.

The bridge task became what was yet another good job done and it was, I suppose, a couple or so days later — just when I began to hope all was forgotten or forgiven — I was called in to see my OC. The Major was a kindly man, truly a great officer and OC — DSO, MC — with later, I believe, a bar.

I was surprised to receive what turned out to be little more than a mild rocketing, mainly about foolishly rendering myself incapable of carrying out military service, also a bit of fatherly advice about the evils of alcohol. I was, however, still left with a feeling that I would have to wait a while yet before knowing whether I had got off that lightly. The OC explained that for his part as OC and Acting CRE, in the temporary absence of the Colonel, he would let the matter rest. But he reminded me that the war was almost over and that his power and influence was not quite the same as it was in the earlier battlefield conditions when it was much easier to turn a blind eye to the often errant ways of otherwise good combat soldiers. It was in this case also unfortunate that RMPs sustained injuries which could possibly result in matters not easily laid to rest. . .

Time passed by for another week or two with me again beginning to think that the incident was past and forgotten in the prevailing spirit of anticipation with the closing end of the European war.

My own anticipation was hardly a consideration that the time was fast approaching when the circumstance and condition of battlefield blood and guts was giving way to flag waving pomp and ceremony, the spit and polish brigades and reappearance of the Colonel Blimps of the British Army.

It was therefore more than disappointing to be sent for one afternoon to be told, almost apologetically by the Major, that unfortunately a full report had just been forwarded to the CRE — now back in command — by the RMPs. They were, I was told, pressing charges because of the serious injury sustained by one of the policemen involved.

So it was that on VE day, a day to be celebrated and enjoyed by everyone — not least surely by myself — I was instead to have the humiliation and indignity of being marched under escort to face a serious military charge — although I had little idea of what section of the Manual of Military Law I was being charged under.

As the proceedings got under way I felt myself to be more of an impartial observer than the accused principal, since I still had no recollection of anything that was alleged to have happened. It was as if I had gone to sleep one night to awake in the morning to be told of my responsibility for some dastardly crime done in the unconscious hours of the night. My case was just that exactly except that I had rashly imbibed liquid of doubtful content before getting into a state of insensibility.

The witnesses for or against me were present in good number, with one in particular being pushed around in a wheelchair and wearing a stout surgical collar — a witness unlikely to be in my favour to be sure!

I found it almost impossible to relate myself to the evidence, testimony and statements of the proceedings. I was hopelessly at a loss to recognize that I was in the picture at all... that is until the last witness made his appearance. I saw that he was a mature person who appeared kind, wise and experienced, and that his rank was that of Major, RAMC. It was the statements of this medical officer that made me feel more positively in the picture and made me aware that fate and my own fortunes of war were still playing a few remarkable tricks. It was as if my guardian angel had chosen the very last day of the war, through the medium of the medical officer, to somehow give a sign that his, her or its guardian duty to me was well done — perhaps finally with the conclusion of the war! The officer's evidence was a rather grim account of my desperately critical medical condition and treatment: how he had almost lost the battle for my life when my heart stopped beating on two separate occasions; the miraculous effort and success in getting it pumping back to life again. The officer observed somewhat wryly that 'it was indeed miraculously good fortune for the accused to be standing here accused on this day.'   Strange indeed that after a journey along a war path that brought me perilously close to death a few times — almost shot, shelled, mined, drowned, crushed — I should now at the end of it all hear a factual detailed account of how I 'died' of poisoning (alcoholic?).

But, however, whether resuscitation or resurrection, I was to find myself later listening to the strictures of the CRE who said sternly that drink or drunkenness was no excuse... but that — less seriously — some matters had to be taken into consideration not least my previous good record. He would, he said, take time to deliberate the matter further before passing judgement.

Surprisingly, we were then all dismissed, the reason perhaps being — as I was to reason later — to avoid an embarrassing leniency in front of those who might expect something more harsh. The OC had obviously discussed the matter earlier with the Colonel and would, I guessed, have made merciful recommendations on my behalf.

Whether the fact that it was VE day had something to do with it I will never know, but I found myself unexpectedly at liberty to carry on as usual and in the circumstances to enjoy the rest of the day, like everyone else seemed intent on doing.

But fate continued to twist and turn in mysterious ways because it so happened that the misery of the first half of the day was to be well compensated for by a most blissfully enjoyable second half of the day. It was but a short time and distance after getting away from my ordeal of 'being on the carpet' that we — myself and another soldier who was the driver of the vehicle I had earlier made the journey with — chanced on a meeting with a couple of extremely pretty girls.

Chatting up the girls anywhere in Germany was not an easy thing to do in those difficult early days of peace, not only because of hostility and language problems but also because fraternization with the Germans by British troops was forbidden by order of the British High Command. It was a somewhat ridiculous order, made to be broken a million times over — not least by those of high command themselves!

Love, however, knows but few barriers, and with good sign language, the right hungry kind of look and plenty of bombed and empty buildings to hide away in, was to see me, in particular, well set for a couple of love sessions which — as I was to remember and dream of later — were of the highest order of sweet, sweet bliss.

The Fräulein was a shy, dainty seventeen year old, with whom I shared some of my packed lunch while we both sat among the rubble strewn around inside an empty bombed building. We sat close on lumps of rock or masonry as we endeavoured with signs, gestures and some recognizable words to know each other better. I soon understood that she had lost her family in some way — how and when she did not say — except for her war-wounded and crippled older brother. He was a discharged Wehrmacht Fighter Pilot who would, she said, be very angry if he knew she was with a British soldier. He was apparently her very strict guardian, and she gave a little sob as she tried to convey her sad feelings of somehow letting him down. But she also made it clear to me that she wanted peace, freedom, fun and love, not more of the horror or war, hate and hardship she had experienced too much of in her young life.

As if to demonstrate her feelings in rather more personal and intimate terms, she came and sat on my lap, and cuddled up to me. As I did my own bit of cuddling and caressing I was enchanted and surprised, considering the austerity and primitive roughness of the times, at the silky elegance of her underclothes, some items of which she removed. She trembled and quivered a good deal as she faced me and spread herself along my eager thighs as I squatted amongst the lumps of debris.

I had never before experienced making love in the sitting position, especially with a lovely girl whose bare, firm young breasts were pressed against my face and mouth. It was her quivering excitement and the loud moans, sighs and cries of her ecstatic moments which for me were visions, sounds, and sensations set more in a heavenly paradise than the Hell of war-torn Hamburg.

I, too, wanted the comforts of love and peace, and I would have been well content to have remained forever with such a delectably compatible body and soul. We stayed together long enough to indulge gloriously our passion a second time, but then in the lying down position. We sought and obtained a truly marvellous fulfilment because we knew we were soon to part.

We then went our different ways, sadly never to meet again.

For me then VE day was, it may be said, a day of mixed blessings.

As for the CRE's deliberation and judgement, all I can say is that I never did get to know what was decided. Some mention was made some time later about a stoppage of three weeks' pay, but I never did see the evidence or suffer the hardship of it, if it ever happened!

18

In And Around Hamburg

My first journey into the devastated city of Hamburg was made at some time in the final stage at the war's end in Europe. I was well familiar with war scenes of destruction but, even so, I was appalled at the extent and scale one could see here — enough, as it were, to put any 'Sodom and Gomorrah to shame'! The picture was of a vast city laid bare by the flame and blast of bombs, a wilderness of rubble and ashes which combined to conglomerate into a complex of tangled steel and broken buildings, much of which stood out against the skyline like monuments or tombs of some vast graveyard. A graveyard it certainly was for the great number of human bodies that still remained beneath the mountainous heaps and piles of debris, bodies to remain buried for quite a long time.

I remember my long ride in a vehicle not only to see a tragic landscape of material damage but also to see a pathetic trail of human wreckage and suffering. Because there was no other place to call 'Home', many if not most of the surviving families having dug themselves out of collapsed buildings, were having to dig themselves back in again to burrow and live like rabbits.

Our unit had a particular and rather satisfying task to perform in the area of Hamburg, which was to destroy the submarine pens at the Hamburg Naval Base. To this end we later proceeded with a vengeance considering the war's history of deadly missions originating here which decided the sad fate of so many British ships and crews.

Myself and a fellow soldier were perhaps the first of British troops to enter the main German Naval Headquarters building. Our entrance to the place was not without incident because as I proceeded to move around from one room to another — separated from my colleague — I was suddenly surprised by the appearance of a German Naval officer pointing a gun at me. It was so totally unexpected because the many days past had seen the almost complete collapse of German hostility and opposition and I really expected the place to be deserted. I was therefore caught completely off guard and greatly alarmed — only to find to my great relief the German officer turning his weapon around and holding it out to me in open surrender. I was quick to take it from him and I was more than a little shaken to see that it was a fully loaded weapon, which would indeed have ended my young life had he not had his second thoughts about pulling the trigger. Or was it perhaps a calculated gesture done for his own protection and possible future well-being?

I was to discover, however, that having surrendered his weapon, he was not so willing to surrender or subordinate his feelings of hate and bitterness about the war. He appeared rather old for a serving officer, having white hair and a bushy grey beard. I guessed that his braided uniform and medals would suggest his rank was that of a vice admiral or ship's commander at least. I really did not know what to do with the old guy, particularly since I felt obliged to him for not having put a bullet into me, which he could so easily have done. He seemed proud of the fact that he could speak a little English, and because of it I soon found out what a pompous old Bosche the fellow was. He acted as if somehow he was on trial to defend the honour and glory of the German Navy. They had, he said, been betrayed by the treachery and stupidity of the other services of the German Armed Forces, in particular by the Luftwaffe and that nincompoop *Schweinhund* Goering.

He continued ranting and raving against what he felt to be the big let-down of his branch of the Service and, if I was to believe all he said, I should be convinced that such an élite were not so much well and truly defeated as unfairly conquered. He had obviously been in his Ivory Tower HQ for too long to know much about humble pie and was clearly a German diehard if ever there was — a damned foolish one who thought he could still wave the German flag around even at the critical time of Germany's unconditional surrender. His air of authority and superiority, together with his denigration of those others who had surely given their all, annoyed me so much I could have gladly shot him with his own pistol. Instead I took him to the front of the building and told him to go to wherever his home was. I explained that the war was well and truly over and finished for him and his kind, that his views and uniform might not be so kindly tolerated by other war veterans of the British side and that he was well advised to get rid of them and quietly disappear somewhere. He went on his way, but appearing somewhat reluctant to do so. Perhaps he was disappointed at such an inglorious end, thinking perhaps that it was hardly in accordance with the heroic picture of a brave captain going down with his ship!

As I went back into the big building I had little or no idea of where my soldier pal had got to, since it was easy enough to go astray in the maze of ghostly corridors of slain power.

I wandered around to find much of interest. One room I entered must at one time have been truly the centre point of command being, as I could see, the main conference room. Great framed portraits lined the walls on all sides of long conference tables. Many photograph portraits were signed with original signatures and all were great names of the Fatherland. I had no qualms about cutting away the signatures with my jack-knife — a collection of German VIP autographs which I managed to hold for some time before they too became part of the dust and debris of war. Ironically, the signature that outlasted the others was that of Admiral Doenitz who was the final German figure-piece on the checkmate chess-board of World War Two. He it was who signed the surrender terms for and on behalf of what remained of the German Nation.

My continued search of the place took me into a section which was evidently the photo processing department. Photographic equipment and material were stacked around everywhere. Here I filled a fair-sized suede leather bag with camera lenses of all kinds — an intended present for a young officer I knew whose civilian occupation was commercial photographer, a most delighted recipient later. Hardly loot, it might be argued, more a motive and instinct for sabotage!

I expected to find my fellow soldier somewhere close around in the main building and I therefore proceeded from one room to another to seek him out. I shouted his name to let him know that I was near. As I did so I heard the clattering sound of something falling behind the door of an adjoining room. Thinking I should find my colleague I pushed the door to find it opened into what obviously was a telephone exchange. A telephone was lying on the floor and was all too clearly the cause of the clatter and distinctive sound I had just heard. There was no one I could see at first sight and I wondered if my pal was having me on with some little game he was playing. I was, however, a little wary after my earlier experience with the 'Gross Kapitan' and I was now well armed and ready for any trouble. I was sure that somebody or something was around the place somewhere, and it was but a moment or two later that I saw the cowering figures of two young females hiding behind a stationery storage cupboard. They shivered and whimpered with fright as I motioned them to come away from their hiding place. They were two quite good-looking girls, a blonde and brunette, both about nineteen years of age. It took a good few minutes to convince them that I had no intention of shooting them or raping them, and their relief when they realized that I was, after all, quite a friendly fellow was something somebody in my position could thoroughly enjoy. They were, they said, telephone switchboard operators who were Polish, not German, something I very much doubted. Later in a more relaxed and friendly atmosphere they indicated as best they could, considering the language problem, that they were fearful of the treatment they really were expecting from the Russians and even the less feared British and American troops, of whom they heard enough tales of attributed atrocities.

I was indeed fast becoming a very popular guy with the two ladies, particularly as they smoked English cigarettes for the first time. All fair enough I suppose since I was hardly the bestial invader or intruder they so feared earlier. So friendly, in fact, did I become with both girls that in a very short time our giggles, laughter and kissing led to a very intimate threesome on the floor, with the girls volunteering everything they could give to make it a gloriously exciting encounter, all very much a setting and circumstance to thrill, enjoy and remember.

One of the girls gave me an additional treat as she made me understand that, by way of appreciation, she wished to present me with a special gift which she kept secreted away in a gap under the stationery cupboard. She brought out a package which opened to reveal a sparkling ornate pair of naval daggers — or what I took to be more properly a pair of admiral's ceremonial dress dirks complete with sheaths and tassels, worthwhile souvenirs, to be sure, which I was happy to accept without asking too many questions!

The girls appeared to be genuinely sad when I took my leave of them. I was sad also in knowing that their situation was just another instance of the confused predicament suffered by countless casualties of war — the 'Where do we go from here?' or 'What do we do now then?' syndrome. I left them by saying I would perhaps have an early opportunity of revisiting the place and therefore perhaps meeting up with them again. But unfortunately I was never to see those exciting sweeties again. I was, however, consoled with the thought that such providers of comfort and joy were likely to meet with good and kind treatment themselves at any time and place in the future.

19

In The Aftermath Of War

It seems certain that in the entire history of man and his world, no nation or race of people suffered such a grand scale disaster as did Germany and the Germans in World War Two. Sadly, too, the end of the war was not the end of the misery for most of the Germans who had suffered and survived so much of the horror of war.

In the months following VE day I was to see much of the continuing pain, anguish and hardship for so many people, in an aftermath of war too full of chaos, tragedy and problems for quick or easy solutions.

No doubt future records and history books would show with data and statistics enough information about the collapse and bankruptcy of the nation in material terms, but collapse and bankruptcy in human terms was another matter, not so easily documented or case-filed. Only those eye-witnesses of happenings in the early post-war period could possibly have feeling and understanding of what things were really like for the German people at that time.

To me it seemed that, for them, the humiliation of defeat, the devastation of their homeland, the disintegration of organization, the loss of families or relatives, the famine of goods and the prospect of a fearfully bleak future were all too much by far. For most it was a calamitous situation too total and final to make possible a counting of the cost. For the average older German, recovery of the nation was very much like some stricken creature licking the wounds left by recent amputation of limbs — too much suffered and too much lost to be ever put right again.

I was of the victorious and they of the defeated, yet both of an epoch and struggle in which so much of the end product was weariness, deprivation, dreams of youthful pre-war days and a wistful hunger for those indefinable nice and good things that for so long had been absent in our lives.

I was later to think often about attitudes and the psychological tenor of the times because I think that I too was affected by the continuing fatalistic mood which prevailed in an environment of depression, sadness and a barrenness of everything essential and basic to civilized life and living. I wondered how I should feel as a German whose country was overrun by hordes of foreign troops all pressing to exploit the victory and defeat situation. Not easy for proud and courageous people to cringe and beg for mercy.

In the course of time I was to see things happen which would have driven me insane or to suicide if positions had somehow been reversed.

Cringing and begging was a way of life for many, however, and I remember one incident in particular as an incident which perhaps bordered on the ultimate in pathos and tragedy, yet somehow was part of the general picture as I saw it.

It was, I remember, a cold blustery winter's night when a few of us soldiers found the bright lights of a club or restaurant. It was unusual in those days to find a German establishment able and willing to provide even the most meagre service in the way of food and drink. But here at this place we found orchestral music, a waitress service and a reasonably good imitation of a meal — even if the centre-piece or *pièce de résistance*, was a chunk of undercooked horseflesh! Perhaps some enterprising Germans had got together to get things going again and maybe profit by pandering to the British who could trade with something better than useless money — things like cigarettes, coffee, etc.

It was a nice evening if only for the music and cosy atmosphere. I always had a liking for Continental tunes, and three of my favourites — *Berliner Luft, Fascination Waltz* and *Die Fledermaus* overture — were played for me on request (greasing palms by staining fingers, so to speak).

An unusually pleasant evening that left me flushed with the enjoyment of it all, and in generous spirit as we left to go on our way. The night was cold and the wind whistled as I got out of the door and on to the road to turn right.

Strung along in the shadow of the building outside were

about a dozen or so miserable-looking figures, some of whom
I could just make out were holding out caps or hats. As I
walked by I could also hear a chorus of '*Bitte* — *Bitte.*' They
were begging, which was no unusual thing for me to come
across in those grim days. Usually we Tommies, of the war-
hardened kind, passed such beggars by with thoughts that it
could so easily have been us doing the begging. On this
occasion, however, because I was in a good and generous
mood I went across to pass on a few cigarettes, starting at the
front of the queue. Into the first outstretched hat went two of
my cigarettes, only to be met with a somewhat negative and
disappointing response in the way of appreciation. I could see
why when I looked up into the man's terribly disfigured face.
His eyes had been shot away and because he was totally blind
he was unaware that cigarettes had been put into the hat. I
had a mixed feeling of revulsion and pity as I looked closer at
that awful scar in a frozen white face. He stood shivering in
the cold, unaware that I was putting in a few extra cigarettes
for him. I tapped his hat and murmured '*Cigaretten*', to
which he responded by giving me my overdue '*Danke.*' I was
to discover that there were two more who were blind, and
some others who were limbless, as I went along the line of
outstretched hats, exchanging '*Bitte schon*' '*Danke schon*' as I
doled out a few cigs to each in turn.

I walked away feeling very sad for the poor beggars,
particularly so as I saw that most of them wore tattered old
greatcoats of the late annihilated German Army. I wondered
how much less than any one of them I had of war experience
and suffering, or being one of them how I should feel at being
one of the war games' broken toys and thrown onto such a vile
scrap-heap. For me the end of the war meant I was a proud
and victorious soldier. I was one of us who had fought and won
the good and just fight, was celebrated by an organized and
appreciative society in a homeland almost untouched by war
damage. But for those poor devils it was all so different. For
them, for all their service, courage and sacrifice, only chaos
and devastation, rejection and blame, destitution, neglect and
the ultimate degradation of begging in the cold of a winter's
night, while hearing the strains of nostalgic music played for
the alien conquering heroes.

As I went on my way I could see the waters of the River

Weser and realized that it was somewhere at this place where music of a different kind was once played by a legendary piper — also a tragedy.

Although sad and sorry as I was for such tragic military casualties of war — and there were more than enough of them — my profound pity was somehow always reserved for those whom I considered to be the real victims of man's savage acts of war — the innocent women and children.

Profound pity it really was with an earlier experience of mine, which should also be mentioned as yet another example and variation of the human torment I found along the misery trail of war.

It was during a spell of patrol boat duty, which I had been detailed for as a kind of watch on the River Rhine. The duty consisted of ensuring that the traffic of barges, etc., up and down river ceased when darkness or poor visibility prevented safe navigation of the river. We had also to look out for anything untoward or sinister. A short time earlier an accident had occurred when a pier of a military bridge had been struck by a carelessly navigated barge, causing the collapse of the bridge and the death of several British soldiers who were being transported across in a vehicle at the time. So many bridges had been destroyed by the defensive war action of the Germans that routes across the River Rhine at that time were hopelessly inadequate. The few military improvised structures — complete and incomplete — had therefore to be carefully watched and protected against the increasing frenzy of river traffic. Obviously with so much damage to overland road and rail routes, pressure became intense for bargees and the like to over-extend their activity and capacity to dangerous limits. Generally though, I had little trouble with the river people, and I often spent a cosy hour or two with many a bargee on his craft.

My river patrol duty was a four hour on and four hour off arrangement, operating from a base point somewhere along the river at a place called Wesel, at the site of a demolished bridge.

I was to become rather well-acquainted with this devastated little West German town, on three counts. I had already been to the place at some earlier time, a time which followed soon after an Allied air and ground attack which left the place in ruins. It was, or had been, a small garrison town which, as I recall, was almost completely wiped off the map and suffering something like a ninety per cent casualty rate among its inhabitants. I remember seeing then the anguish of a few returning citizens who, in looking for their houses, were at a loss in finding any recognizable part of the town at all remaining. Wesel was also to be a place where much later I would find myself coming back to for a fairly long spell of post-war service to assist in building, what I understood to be, the greatest Bailey bridge construction ever made — a great engineering task and a structure of paramount importance as a major crossing point across the Rhine for many years to come.

But during the period and at the time of my boating duties, however, there was no bridge at Wesel — the nearest crossing point over the Rhine being somewhere near Dusseldorf. It was also a period when a distinct lack of everything else for the war afflicted population of Germany was, ironically, a reason for moving around *en masse* in searching for better means of survival as, for example, to seek out a farmer relative, perhaps a hundred miles away, who might supply a bag or two of vegetables. With bridges destroyed, the migrant hordes would often find themselves moving around in circles, totally unable to reach destinations because of river barriers, etc.

So it was that on one cold night, close to midnight, I came across a wretched family group waiting at the side of the river near the dead-end road which led to the destroyed bridge. Their condition was sad in the extreme. A mother and two of her children had come to the end of their tether in more ways than one and were huddled together in despair and exhaustion around an old pram on which hung the bits and pieces of their worldly possessions. Inside the pram I glimpsed the pallid face of a third younger child.

The two older children — a girl aged about ten and a boy a couple of years younger — were bare-footed and in rags, both with their feet covered in sores, blistered and bleeding. The mother, a shabby dishevelled woman in her mid-thirties, was moaning and wailing in her dejection and disappointment at her dead-end situation.

For her and her little ones there was nowhere else to go — except into the dark swirling waters of the Rhine, which, I was to understand later, was something she was contemplating when I found them. I had seen too many floating dead bodies not to know something already about the grim reality of the prevalence of family group suicides — I had sometimes towed bodies to the river banks where, more often than not, they remained for long periods. Such a fate would, I am sure, have been a real possibility had I not arrived on the scene in time. They had, it seemed, walked for countless hours hoping to cross the river and eventually to link up with relatives — and with them perhaps salvation.

I was so moved by their woeful condition, particularly the little boy and girl, that I decided to make some effort to reduce their misery by getting them and their belongings into the boat for a quick journey to the other side of the river. There was little else I could do, much as I would have liked, even if inconsistent with my military orders and duties. What little I did, however, in getting them across the river was appreciated and rewarded in a way which cannot be properly put into words since it involved matters not easily described — emotion, reward, sacrifice, value. The emotion was in the gratitude of the mother and two children, the reward was an apple which the poor woman dug out of a small food box which contained nothing more than a few crusts and two apples.

In the circumstances the apple gift represented supreme sacrifice and value if one considered, as I did, the law of relativity. I was touched deeply by the gesture.

But the final and real tragedy of it all, indeed, was when, having taken the apple absent-mindedly, I moved to pass it on to the child hidden among the clutter on the pram. I looked down closely — for the first time — to see a pair of staring eyes, and was shocked to find the cold stiff body of a two year old baby. The child had obviously been dead for some time. I blurted out 'Das Kind ist tot', but the woman, I remember, looked at me for several moments in an unexpectedly calm and resigned way and nodded her head. She then placed her hands and those of her two struggling little survivors onto the handlebar of the pram, and off they went to disappear into the night.

My solitary vigil over the next few hours did nothing for me to forget the tragic incident and I wondered why the God

Almighty, who seemed to have looked after me so well, had let those poor creatures down so badly. 'Suffer little children to come unto me' was not very acceptable in my book of reason. I could have some understanding in the matter of suffering, punishment and a Day of Judgement for those who had been around long enough to have some stain of guilt or blame, but to me it could only be abomination, obscenity and outrage that little children should suffer, or somehow be punished, for their innocence.

I suppose that I was never more than averagely religious, having views and thoughts perhaps more simplistic than the confused teachings, gospels, dogmas, etc., of the established Christian Church. For me the civilized world was a three dimensional affair of scientific, aesthetic and theological perspectives. I believed that they were and are the three fundamental and critical aspects of life, and that for me to be a stable and rational human being I should endeavour to be three persons in one — scientist, priest and artist, all on equal basis. I believed that my view of the morning sun should be slanted in three different ways (1) towards seeing it as a mass of energy and heat, (2) towards seeing it as a wonderful work of God, (3) towards seeing it as simply beautiful. It could only make sense if the balance was right.

Indeed, it seemed to me that the world, one's existence and even life's purpose were all about balance. In everything I knew there was so much difference, variation and contrast — big/small, light/dark, quick/fast, hot/cold, ugly/beautiful, good/evil, etc., (almost *ad infinitum*) that surely a philosophy that focused on the importance of balance was the right one.

So with this kind of philosophical direction how could I, even though angrily upset by the tragic incident, shake my fist at the God Almighty? The answer was surely that in the Creator's order of things there could be no peace without war, no joy without sorrow and no life without death. Perhaps here, too, was a lesson that man has somehow and somewhere to look for and find a balanced perspective.

20

With The Occupation Troops —
Occupied With Loving

Among the Allied troops of Occupation, in early post-war Germany, there were few who were not intent in redressing the balance with trying to make up for their wartime deprivations, particularly in females and sex. With a hefty proportion of the German male population permanently removed by the misfortunes of war there was plenty of scope and opportunity for them to do so. It was a time when resistance was low for the Frauen and Fräuleins, a time of desperate shortages for them when liaison and association with Allied troops might be of considerable social and material benefit. So the Allied soldier had little or no problem in pressing home his advantage in more ways than one, often converting those wartime deprivations to his peacetime depravities.

But it takes two to tango, as they say, except that here the number of twos were much more than two. Immorality and vice became the fungus which mushroomed on the pulverized heap of chaos that was post-war Germany. It was a time when most soldiers of occupation indulged themselves to the full, since it was all to easy to tempt, cajole, trick and often ruthlessly enforce those who were so disadvantaged. There were few barrack rooms where the conversation was not dominated by talk of female conquest, seduction, intercourse, cohabitation and every other aspect of sex. Elysian field days, indeed, for many a uniformed sex maniac, some of whom could be heard boasting of the triple conquest of grandmother, mother and daughter in a single session.

There was of course the other side of the coin, which was that not a few of our hitherto decent minded and well-behaved soldiers were corrupted by the many traps and pitfalls set before them by a defeated, demoralized and debased land of people. In any case the continental standard of morality was always held to be considerably lower than that of the British, and it was not possible to know on a broader scale who was corrupting whom. Anyway, in such a situation, who could blame whom? England or any other country would fall very quickly into the same kind of despair, immorality and degradation given the same circumstances of its people, as for example not knowing where the next meal was coming from; bereft, insecure and overrun by war-hardened, victorious troops with comparative plenty.

Against this kind of background I could hardly claim to be without my own catalogue of loving and lusting experiences. So, besides the encounters already mentioned in earlier chapters, there were others which together add up to what, supposedly, might be considered a bountiful supply of beautiful females over what was a relatively short period of time.

I think it was one of my early visits to Brussels — shortly after its liberation — which caused some change in my thinking and attitude towards women generally. Up to that time I had never encountered prostitutes, and I remember how shocked I was to discover that women in such numbers could be so readily and cheaply purchased for sex. It was a time when Brussels seemed crammed with such women, to be met with just about everywhere I went in that Belgian capital city — a veritable human flesh market where females old, young, ugly and beautiful bidded for favour and profit with their bodies. But despite the fact that so many of them were lovely by any standard, I was never inclined towards that kind of service. I did however have encounters of a different kind in Brussels, which I am sure were more interesting and exciting. Perhaps two of them are worthy of mention since they are part of the beginning of the present chapter which must of biographical and historical necessity be directed towards activities of this kind, for it seemed to me that the early post-war service of Allied troops of Occupation was involved in little else. It was a time maybe when most of the British contingent were suffering more from sexual exhaustion than from post-war weariness for any other cause.

My first visit to Brussels was made within hours of its

liberation, with a second visit some days later. On this latter occasion myself and a pal were lucky to have some time off between spells of duty and we sought to make the best of it by seeing the sights and maybe enjoying the delights of that fine city.

It was late afternoon when we left an hotel where the female staff — including Madam proprietress herself — had entertained us greatly with their games, horseplay and efforts to strip us of our clothes. It was only the promise of an early return visit which allowed us to be free of further embarrassing familiarities amounting almost to indecent assaults on our persons. Such a high-class establishment with such delightfully disgusting low class behaviour.

Our return, however, was much quicker than planned because as we got outside we found ourselves being pushed and ushered back into the same building by a very posh party indeed. All were in evening dress, two being handsomely elegant gentlemen accompanied by four lovely ladies. It was a party in a mood for celebration, seemingly all set for a good night out. They made it plain by linking arms with my friend and I that they wanted us to enjoy the evening with them.

It was difficult to reject the humour and spirit of a party looking as if they had stepped straight out of a Hollywood musical. I was fascinated by the women, who appeared to be actresses or models, and it was clear that the two maturely handsome gentlemen were of some standing, with wealth and influence, perhaps, to have such a bevy of beauty in close attendance.

Back in the hotel the evening lights were on as we were met by a rather more prim and proper staff who directed our hosts into a private room where a table had been laid out as for a banquet, obviously a reserved and familiar setting for those who were to be our new acquaintances.

I found myself seated between the two choicest women imaginable; the air laden with delicate fragrance of sweet perfume; the sparkle of jewellery, good food and plenty of excellent wine — all contributing to make our normally primitive and savage life in the field very remote indeed. Brussels, as a city, seemed little damaged by the war and for those of us who had come from Normandy it was very much a kind of oasis in the desert. Even so, this kind of company and setting was something special, which was rather more understandable when I learned later that one of the two gentleman of the party was — as per interpretation — the High Sheriff of Brussels. The other gentleman spoke excellent English, having spent many years in England pre-war as a director of a company producing electrical goods — which may have contributed so well to the *Bon ami* spirit of the evening. It was he who, after introducing me to the lovely ladies sitting beside me, quietly told me that they were two of Belgium's noted beauties and great artistes. I saw the beauty side of the matter as self-evident and beyond question, but I was too polite to ask what was meant by 'artistes.' Whatever other talent they may have had I was soon to discover that they were consummate perfectionists when it came to the art of making love.

What happened was that the two luscious ladies I had got along with so well during the evening took umbrage at something said by the 'sheriff' of the party who had rather overloaded himself with drink. The wine was surprisingly heady stuff and I was unable to resist the invitation and plea of my evening's close companions to go with them when they got up to leave the rest of the party. I wished to be on their side while my soldier pal was on the side of those who were staying. I was, anyway, tempted to go along with them when I was taken aside and told that I would be given a nice time for the rest of the evening with good music, dancing, etc., at their shared nearby luxury apartment.

True to their word and by way of gratitude for the few packets of cigarettes I had given them, I was treated to a fantastically enjoyable time which included a tipsy and hilarious bubble bath together and a threesome 'rough and tumble' in a luxurious bed. Being made love to by an outstanding pair of Belgian beauties and 'artistes' must thereafter, I suppose, have played a part in reducing or removing much of my sexual morality and innocence!

But I was again to suffer a little more erosion of my already somewhat dissipated moral fortitude on my next visit to Brussels, made some time later when things had changed greatly in a relatively short space of time. Because of the favourable progression of the war with its approaching inevitable end, the ordinary soldier's welfare was a matter much more in evidence than hitherto. Rest centres and hostels for short periods of leave were quickly established in Brussels as a place guaranteed to put the pep back into any war-weary soldier.

So together with another of my military friends I applied for a seventy-two hour pass, and indicated an arrangement to stay at a private address rather than one of an official centre, which often had long waiting lists. It was well worth fibbing about even if no prior arrangement was made to stay at a private address. To get away for a spot of freedom for a few days, even if it meant sleeping rough in a Brussels' park, was indeed well worthwhile, provided military officialdom knew nothing about it of course!

It so happened, however, that a couple of days before our furlough was due to start, my leave partner was hospitalized, leaving me with the dilemma of whether I should proceed alone. This I eventually did while pondering the problem of no arranged accommodation and no adequate funds to make good the situation. It was a problem I was turning over in my mind as I made the train journey to Brussels. I wondered whether I should be bold enough or lucky enough to rediscover delights already experienced in the city. Perhaps I was rather dreamily and smilingly reminiscing as I gazed into the face of an Army sergeant who sat opposite me in the coach of the train. He spoke to me in a friendly way, opening up a conversation for the short time before he left the train for some early destination. At some point in our conversation I mentioned the fact that I had neglected to make a proper reservation and that I hoped such neglect would be little or no problem. Before departing the train he gave me a quickly scrawled note of introduction which he said could be useful to me in such a situation. He quickly explained that the introductory note would, if I wished, see me well received by some hospitable Belgians, at an address in Brussels, whose acquaintance he had made earlier.

His hasty departure allowed no further information, and I cannot say that I was, just then, much taken by the idea of pushing myself on anybody in such a way. If I had been put more in the picture about the kind of people involved it might not have been so bad, perhaps. I certainly had no wish to spend such scant and precious time toeing the line in some strict household — made worse maybe by my being under obligation!

But in the city later, with no friend and little money, I was to find myself kicking my heels as the day wore on. I looked at the sergeant's piece of paper at least a dozen times before being forced to conclude that following up the suggestion might not be such a bad idea after all. I really had nothing to lose except my destitution!

So chin up, chest out, off I went in search of that which I preferred to think of more as a challenge than necessity. I walked for a good half hour and several times asked for instructions before I arrived at the door of the address shown on my piece of paper. It was a nice house, with a friendly warm look about it somehow, which encouraged me to lose no time in ringing the doorbell. I waited anxiously with an expectation and picture of a middle-aged, balding little Belgian appearing at the door, but instead I found myself confronted with a kind of picture that for several moments had me open-mouthed, wide-eyed and stammering. Before me was an extremely attractive female whose charm, just then perhaps, was enhanced by the revealing kimono-type housecoat or robe she was wearing. She was, I guessed, about four years older than myself.

It took me no time at all to recognize and appreciate that I had, indeed, been well blessed by the chance encounter which had brought me to the place. Inside I was soon put at ease by the young woman and her mother who lived together in the beautifully furnished house. Both spoke English and seemed genuinely happy to do whatever they could for me. I was totally honest about my situation and I explained all — which could hardly be otherwise considering the kind of people they were and the treatment I received to make me really feel at home.

I soon learned that, amazingly, the daughter was, or had been, married to a British sportsman but had somehow become separated from him by the outbreak of war. She had lost touch with him — presumably because of war barriers — but had somehow held on to the idea that he was a soldier in the Far East if he was still alive.

I was to discover, also, that both mother and daughter were stage performers in variety shows, the daughter performing some kind of song and dance act whilst creating funny caricature pictures from a random selection of bits of assorted papers. It seemed that the mother's variety show performance involved her pet poodle-like dog (mongrel) and a peculiar counting frame on which the trained animal could show its talent as a canny calculating canine. I gathered that mother and daughter had separate engagements, sometimes performing for British and American troops — which was how the sergeant had made their brief acquaintance, as I understood.

I had no idea of how the lovely daughter performed on stage, but I soon found out that she was quite a star performer in bed.

It happened that after a convivial first evening together I was given a fine room for myself and also a great big bed to sleep in. I slept well and contented at finding such unexpected comfort, certainly not daring to dream that morning would bring the pleasure to compliment the comfort.

When morning did come, I could hardly be expected to object to the young lady's uninhibited visit to my bedroom with a well-laden breakfast tray, or to disapprove at the enticing way she sat near me in her nightdress as I breakfasted in bed. It was soon clear that she was love-starved, eager and most impatient to get into the bed with me before I could properly see off the food so deliciously prepared.

I was to remember that particular Saturday morning rather well, not only for the bedroom capers with a beautiful, kind and loving lady, but also for an outing with her to a gathering of show business people — a kind of variety club or union meeting where, at some big hotel, I was introduced to some weird and wonderful people.

Among the many who turned out in good number — most, no doubt, mindful and optimistic for the better days to come with the fresh-blowing winds of change — were two brothers for whom I was very sorry. They had tears in their eyes as they explained to me that a third brother had just recently lost a leg when knocked down and run over by an American army vehicle. He was, I was told, the most talented of the three brothers, who had at some time earlier performed as a trapeze and balancing act troupe with Bertram Mills' circus.

A sad tale, indeed, but otherwise I enjoyed my outing

immensely and I could well understand afterwards what they mean when they say that 'there's no business like show business.'

My leave in the circumstances was too short by far. I had for a few days been in a different world altogether and with the ending of such comfort and pleasure, nothing but heartache when the time came to depart. I was never to see the charming Belgian mother and daughter again.

It may be said then that such sexual encounters and experiences were of the kind to set a soldier like me firmly on the side of love, and rather amenable to anything similar that might come my way. It was anyway, at that particular time, nice to imagine a new kind of love-peace door opening as the old war-hate door was closing. A time really for nature to put things to rights again with life, creation and reproduction, after so much death, destruction and decimation.

Perhaps it was God and Nature that had set my instinct and impulse working in this direction and saw to it that I had nothing to complain about in respect of sex opportunity and indulgence.

That I was not without my fair share may be gathered from a few more accounts of such experiences, which are rendered merely as bits of personal military history and as salacious variations on a soldier's favourite theme.

It was somewhere in the Ruhr-land of Germany where I made and enjoyed the intimate acquaintance of two young German sisters. Hostilities had ceased a few months earlier, with the Ruhr area suffering all the problems and hardships associated with the early post-war period. Because of the main problem, for a great many Germans, of survival, most of the boy/girl relationships — particularly British/German — were perhaps more of convenience and necessity than of love and romance. It was perhaps the thought and knowledge that the Germans were, by their desperate situation, compelled to make use of Occupation troops for material gain which introduced more lust than love into the associations and proceedings.

I met the sisters, aged eighteen and sixteen, who shyly approached me on one fine day in the hope of exchanging photographic equipment for anything in the way of food, coffee, cigarettes, etc. The girls were lovely creatures who, like so many others, were driven to part with personal possessions and property mainly for food. The camera on offer was a good one and belonged to the eldest sister who, up to the collapse of her country, was a trained professional photographer who had her own studio, as I was to learn later. She was, in effect, parting with her normal means of livelihood.

I explained as best I could considering the language problem — few Germans spoke English in those days and even less Britishers spoke German — that I was interested in the equipment and that I could produce the goods later in the day if given the address for delivery. The truth of the matter was that I hit the right note with the two lovely sisters and that I was much more interested in their physical property than their photo equipment.

The 'frat-ban', so rigidly imposed in those days by military authority and discipline, was always a deterrent factor for most soldiers in such situations. But for me, the chance of getting on intimate terms with the beautiful sisters was well worth the risks involved.

It happened then that I soon found myself at the home of the girls and was well received, particularly, I suppose, because of the coffee, tea, cigarettes and items of foodstuffs I took along with me. But I really was in favour with the girls when I gave the goods as a gift which generously allowed the elder sister to keep possession of her treasured camera etc. The parents of the girls were surprisingly elderly, considering the youthfulness of their daughters, and with them, also, I found favour enough to allow me plenty of scope for pursuing my more selfish objectives.

In the days that followed — a total of a couple of weeks or so — I spent a great deal of time with the delightful Mädchens, with many an evening full of fun and games, often playing around on the floor like children except that it usually ended in uninhibited love-making.

The old chap, *Herr Papa*, I felt sure was well aware of what I was up to with his pretty daughters, but seemed happy enough to keep himself and *Frau Mutti* out of the way if kept well supplied with my English cigarettes. We had then our privacy for all kinds of fun and games, some of which included taking nude photographs of each other in highly artistic, if sometimes naughty, poses.

For me, however, a night to remember was our very last night together which involved a delightfully charming third party. I had, as I recall, made my visit to the house later than usual in the evening to find only the elder of the two sisters at home. I was informed that the younger sister had gone to visit a friend and would return later.

Both girls were, as already mentioned, extremely pretty but they differed greatly in personality and character. For example, the older sister was always ready, willing, passionate and serious with sex. Usually she was the prime mover in our love-making as she signalled, encouraged and initiated the mounting procedure by preparing herself, in her own special way, on the couch or the floor and by saying '*Vorsicht — keine babi*.' Then she would engage herself in such a way as to make it difficult for me to be careful.

Her sister, in contrast, was a tomboyish, tantalizing and teasing young female who took nothing at all seriously, having at different times given me several hours of maddening frustration before succeeding eventually in breaching her virginity.

On this particular occasion, although the girls were unaware of the situation, I was spending my last evening at their home before soon having to move to a new and distant location. Both parents were away for a couple of days visiting relatives and arrangements had already been made for me to stay the night.

It was kind of strange, in the early part of the evening, not having the usual lively and seductive twosome for company, but I had no cause for complaint at the service given to me by the onesome — nor she at having my own undivided attention for a change. The usual happened, except that our love session was perhaps more passionate and satisfying because the place was unusually peaceful and quiet.

It was a few hours later, just as we began to wonder about the late return of the younger girl, that the knock on the door was heard. The sister had arrived but most unexpectedly, was accompanied by another strikingly lovely girl of about the same age. She was a newcomer who soon fascinated me with a bubbling smiling face, perfectly adorned with sparkling teeth and enchanting dimples. It was a face so obviously full of mischievous fun. It appeared that the prevailing late-night curfew, so severely imposed on the Germans by the British powers of Occupation, had somehow unkindly intervened to prevent her getting to her own home. She was therefore to share the house with us until early morning end of curfew. She seemed to be quite lighthearted — even cheerful — about it all and I was soon to find myself the subject of attention amid bouts of laughter, giggling and whisperings with the three pretty Mädchens.

Some of the hilarity was explained when something was said in German about 'the stall being left open and the bull ready to run loose.' It was then that I realized I was still somewhat undone and not properly dressed as a result of my love-making earlier. A little embarrassing, if amusing, perhaps but it helped towards a familiarity which hardly discouraged a friendlier relationship with the charmingly attractive newcomer. Indeed she was soon to say something that offered me all the encouragement I needed to press home the advantage. It happened when I gallantly offered up my bed to the new girl and choosing instead to make do on the settee. The problem was that the bedroom used by the parents was locked up for the period of their absence, leaving only three small bedrooms with three single beds.

The result was that I soon found myself in the favourable position of being tucked up in my makeshift bed by three pairs of soft caressing hands as their lovely manipulators murmured words of sympathy for my having to suffer the hardship of an improvised bed. The new girl laughingly apologized for being the cause of my inconvenience and jokingly suggested that I should, if I was cold and uncomfortable during the night, go to her to put matters right. A joking matter, maybe, but one that seriously had me drooling at the real prospect as I watched her move through the bedroom door.

I was uneasy and perhaps a little too excited to settle down readily for sleep. I knew also that early next day I would be leaving, almost certainly, never to see the delightful girls again. I therefore resolved to make the most of my last few hours with them. It was a situation which offered the rare chance of making love to three different young beauties in one night. Just two more to go!

I was quite thrilled at the thought of such a night of conquest, and I soon found my way quietly into the bedroom and bed of the younger sister whom I knew would be childishly happy to oblige as usual. I was not disappointed. It was clearly meant to be a night of nights for me because again I enjoyed myself to the full with the second of the night's lovely creatures. She was truly a creature who could, if anyone could, cause me to burst a blood vessel or two in mad, mad moments of desire and passion. I wonder that I didn't do so on this lusty last occasion!

I returned to my settee-bed totally spent by my decidedly greedy efforts to make the most of the young girl's delightful body for what I knew to be a final occasion. But it then became a point in time when at least a few hours sleep was called for in order to re-energize the somewhat denuded virility of a young soldier who was, nonetheless, still anxious to bow out with a final worthy performance. Instinct told me that if I could make the grade, I would be well received and appreciated by the certain person I had in mind for the grand finale.

But even with the best seductive will in the world, it so happened that it was not the exciting throb of sexual desire that caused me, some hours later, to awaken and leave my bed. It was something even more biologically compulsive that had me scuttling past the bedroom for a quick visit to the john. It was early morning and all was quiet until I heard a gentle cough as I passed the slightly open bedroom door of the new girl. It was then that I was reminded of my intention and earlier thoughts concerning a kind of super stud status. I was encouraged by a second gentle cough from the bedroom, made as if the occupant was awake and well aware that I was close to her bedroom door. I had taken to the girl very much and her attraction was enough to get me moving boldly through the bedroom door to realize the third of my loving encounters as imagined earlier. I crept into the bedroom without reservation to find the object of my desire awake and sitting up as if awaiting my visitation with a deal of expectation. She held a finger to her mouth to motion and murmur a 'sh-sh-sh' as I squeezed close to her on the small bed.

Together we were hand in hand and in joyous mood as we left the house a few hours later. I was happy and proud of an occasion and performance that was not only a gratification of my own desires but also pleasing satisfactions for my delightful partners. They, like myself, had seen enough of wartime to appreciate that there were much better things in life. Sadly I was never to see the girls again.

But there were more amorous adventures to come, some of which were to be more memorable than others. There was, for example, that with the young — almost nymphomaniac — daughter of a German church minister. Another involving two sophisticated but sexy daughters of a German professor, whose present to me of a valuable gold watch was an additional bonus. Also the case of a young homeless girl I comfortably set up in a 'requisitioned' garden summer house that became an ideal love nest. The time also with a shy, trembling, lovely young virgin being made love to on an ancient monument in a quiet churchyard. Also a day and night spent tramping and loving with a slim graceful girl, dressed so elegantly in a complete Tyrolean outfit which fascinated me as much as her elfin-like face, who had come from somewhere in Bavaria to search for relatives unsuccessfully.

There was also, I remember, a particularly strange and memorable encounter which was the result of some audacity or downright cheek on my part, hardly characteristic despite a certain boldness which may seem apparent in the foregoing catalogue of female conquests. It started simply when I gazed one afternoon out of the window of my temporary military quarters, which was a house in a street of German houses. Across the road I could see a German girl in the company of what obviously were two young male acquaintances who seemed to do a lot of shouting and some waving at the girl for some reason. But as they stood in a group for some time, I became more attracted by the beautiful body of the girl, who really did have the curves, lines, grace and vitality etc., to raise the pulse and temperature of any full-blooded male. It was, indeed, a classic female form that soon had me steaming up the glass of the window through which I was focusing on the scintillating image. As if hypnotized by the subject of my gaze and drawn by the sensual movement of graceful limbs, I soon moved to a position of being more than mere observer as I wandered across the street in an attempt — by way of being also rather nosey — to communicate somehow with the lovely Mädchen.

It was a bold move which was again to prove that a faint heart never won a fair lady. The two young Germans were, in age, little more than youths who, like most of their kind during those submissive days, found it hard to compete with victorious, better provided Allied soldiers. They soon pushed off leaving me a clear field with the girl for more direct communication which, when I think about it, was little more than a gesture or two by way of issuing a 'you and me' signal. The message and response appeared favourable and I remember following, or being led by, the girl along a ten minute stretch of roadway until we came to her place of residence. Hardly a word had been spoken or sound uttered on the way.

With such little communication between us, I was a little shamefaced and uneasy about what to expect. All I knew up to that point was the uncertainty of whether I had gone along with her or whether she went along with me. I had observed a natural reserve, a strong intelligent character and refinement about her that was in keeping with her stylishly smart appearance — so much so, indeed, that I felt a bit of a fool for having so crudely introduced myself in the first place. I knew so little about her, her thoughts and feelings, that I was apprehensive as to what was to happen next as she rang the doorbell of the building we had arrived at. It could be that somewhere in the background big brother, or husband even, had the wrong kind of treat in store for me.

The bell was answered and the door opened by a stern-faced old Frau who also had nothing to say as we entered to climb a good flight of stairs. I discovered, much to my surprise, that in the upper part of the building she had her own flat. It struck me as being an exceptionally tidy and cosy place for a young single girl, if single she was. I was, however, still at a loss in knowing if, how and when a more positive reception was in the offing for me. I sat myself down on a sofa while the young lady in question disappeared into another room.

I was left alone for what for me was a fidgety long time. I thought I heard the sound of a running water tap and wondered for a moment or two whether she had chosen to ignore me by washing dishes or clothes perhaps. I was puzzled but not without a feeling that, despite a lack of verbal communication between us, we had something going for us in the way of unspoken language of love or sexual attraction.

I waited patiently and was surprisingly rewarded by the glowing appearance of the lovely mysterious girl whose temporary absence was apparently due to having taken a bath for our mutual benefit. She stood in front of me in a bathrobe, which was loose and open, to reveal much of what was perfect in the way of female flesh and figure. I had observed that as well as thus far having said or uttered little or nothing she smiled not at all. She was, I guessed, a serious kind of person, a result of the war, perhaps, as with many Germans who, for so long, had so little to laugh and cheer about. She appeared before me as if it was her duty to do so and as if awaiting the nod of my approval. In her hands she had two cushions which I was soon to discover were to be carefully patted and placed in a position for lift and support for our love-making. There could be no mistaking my own burning desire to get to grips with the business now almost in hand. I watched thrilled and fascinated as she settled herself slowly and deliberately on the cushions so that her body was arched and ready for the engagement — not this time of the combatant military strategic kind, but which was soon a very active one.

She was too lovely and perfect to be anything other than totally satisfying, and I was left in no doubt that her own passionate needs matched my own. It was certainly a time to remember when the action did all the talking. I departed in the early hours of the morning. I couldn't have asked for more by way of body communication but I was still puzzled by the absence of words of conversation from somebody who surely was one of the loveliest girls I could ever have hoped to spend the night with. At best all I had managed from her in my attempted conversations was a slight nod or shake of the head perhaps.

As I went on my way I reflected on what a strangely silent, calm but very willing person I found her to be. It was then, for the first time, that the thought crossed my mind that perhaps she had been unable to talk for the reason that she was a born mute or maybe made speechless in some way by the war. The more I pondered the matter the more likely it seemed to me to be the case, and that she had preferred not to reveal the fact. I turned over our last moments together, about her final parting gesture to me when I wanted to express my feelings somehow before departing. What she did then was to put her fingers of one hand over her own mouth, and fingers of her other hand over my mouth. It was a gesture I took to mean that there should be nothing said or told and that she was happier with the unspoken word — particularly so perhaps because of the language problem. But as I made my way back to my quarters it struck me that I had probably got it wrong and that she was in fact conveying the message, at the very last moment, that verbal communication was not possible.

I was never to see the girl again because of another move of mine to another area, which quickly followed. It was, however, altogether a puzzle which was to keep me guessing for some time to come.

And so I move on to another interesting account of what was to be my final fling with the ladies in the occupied postwar land of Germany. It was a land where the disastrous war had left behind the big piles and little heaps of chaos, which only relative time and effort could possibly even out. Indeed, from my own point of view, sometime toward the end of 1946, a surprisingly good amount of recovery was apparent in many areas, particularly around the less devastated rural parts. The Germans — never short of fighting spirit — could themselves be credited with almost superhuman effort in attempting quickly to haul themselves out of the awful mire they had been so misguidedly led into. But they could really only succeed by receiving immensely generous support and cooperation in every way from the British/American victor nations. It may truly be said that never was a more kindly, helping hand shown by a conqueror to a defeated enemy. It was all a massive rescue operation which far exceeded anything the Germans had any reasonable right to expect.

There were those Germans who greatly appreciated what was being done for them and their nation's recovery, while there were others of the breed who were not in any way grateful. Some Germans regarded us as enemies still — understandable perhaps considering the battles and hardships of war experienced by many. It was, however, fairly certain that the Germans in the British and American Occupation Zones had considerably less to complain about than their brethren in the zone occupied by the Russians who, though, could hardly be condemned or criticized for a policy and practice of 'an eye for an eye.'

And it was, in a peculiar sort of way, thanks to the Russians and their harsh treatment of the Germans that allowed me to make the acquaintance of a truly remarkable person who might best be described as 'the choicest female and lady superior of them all.'

I was to know her by her first name as Erika — her Polish-sounding surname being almost unpronounceable and easily forgettable — and her story to me shortly after we had met was one I could not have doubted for a moment, simply because she was in every possible way the 'genuine article', in appearance, manner and talk, even speaking near perfect English which in those early days was quite exceptional for any German. Erika had the charm, grace, beauty, wit and style of one accustomed to moving in the very best of circles. Indeed, I was to discover later, much by chance, that she was at one time rather well-known as a Berlin top socialite, being the only daughter of wealthy and influential parents during those better days of the German Reich. Her father was, or had been (probably deceased since he appeared to be no longer in the picture), a general in the former German Military High Command, which may have had some part to play in her apparent hatred of the Russians and her liking for the British.

She was in Berlin when the Russians captured and entered the capital city, and she was therefore a witness and victim of the horrors and traumas of the time. Part of her incredible story was that she had escaped for her life from Berlin after having shot her way out of a near rape ordeal at the hands of two Russian Army officers in a a Berlin hotel. She had, it seemed, shot and killed one of the Russians with his own pistol and severely wounded the other. She then managed by marvellous ways and means to escape to the British Zone where, by another of those strange little twists of fate, I was to find her trying to keep a low profile in a small village near the town of Gutersloh.

I first met Erika on an evening when I visited a *gasthaus* which was run by a German landlord and his wife who were both well disposed towards us British soldiers. Their friendliness might, of course, have been because of the business potential presented by our military unit quarters in a nearby school building. I remember that the *gasthaus* was linked to a large barn-like outbuilding which was used jointly or separately by the villagers and ourselves for occasional dances, concerts, etc. I had been to the *gasthaus* on only a couple of previous occasions and I was not too familiar with the place. I was no great boozer, and the German beer anyway in those days was not the kind of brew to be taken in good measure by a Britisher if he were sensible.

As I entered the *gasthaus* on this particular occasion, I was greeted and called upon to join someone I knew from my unit who sat at a table in the company of two German females. One of the girls I faintly recognized as his regular girl-friend, and the other being a stranger — a strikingly beautiful one who was an immaculate platinum blonde. I sat down under the impression that the three were well acquainted, whereas in fact as I was to gather later, the blonde sitting at the table had merely exchanged a few casual words with the other two just before I came on the scene. I was soon chatting away, more so perhaps in the direction of the blonde, whose beauty and personality soon had me under her spell with very little effort on her part.

Later I was fortunate enough to find myself alone at the table with her and although I reckoned I had done rather well in having an hour or so of such wonderful company, I was to do even better when I volunteered to walk her back home and was surprisingly accepted.

Her place of residence was at a nearby small hotel, which took us but a few minutes to reach. But here again I was fortunate at furthering my acquaintance with the lovely lady by being allowed to continue my eager conversation with her in her small but pleasant hotel room.

She was no more than a year or so older than myself and, as described earlier, already quite a woman of the world. with whom a discussion on any subject was interesting, or an education even. Being then something of an idealist and philosopher myself, we talked a great deal on many subjects until at last I took my leave in the early hours of the morning.

My behaviour with her in the meantime had, one might say, been most gentlemanly in that I had made no moves whatsoever, nor had any thoughts concerning sexual advances. Somehow I had been happy and content just to be in her company and enjoy her personality, intellect and good looks. She was anyway much too refined or sedate a person to be viewed as a likely piece of easy conquest. In truth she was the nearest thing to a beautiful young countess I could have imagined. I could also well imagine her abhorrence and resistance to abuse by the Russians.

My own conduct in the circumstances must have been right since it earned me an invitation to return next evening for another get-together at the same place.

It seemed that I had, to some extent, gained her confidence and trust, and I gathered that she had more or less hidden herself away for some time — in her fear of being caught up for the Berlin shootings — and that her night out when I met her was a kind of rare occasion.

I was therefore uncertain whether it was simply company she was after, whether she felt an association with a Britisher might help her defensively in some way or whether she had truly taken a liking to me as a person. My wartime experience of fighting to defeat the Germans had, I suppose, given me a psychological advantage, attitude and option of showing kindness and mercy to those humble and submissive Germans, or a vicious harshness to those who were haughty and arrogant. In Erika I found a person who was much too aristocratic to be humble and submissive, with an air of German élitism which would be hard to feign or disguise. Yet it was also clear that her style and class was that of a gentlewoman — intelligent, kind and extremely lovely!

I was most eager and anxious to meet her again but, because she was such a superior person, I had my doubts about her own eagerness. I was therefore truly delighted to find myself being warmly and sincerely greeted by the charming Erika herself when I arrived for my second evening at the small hotel room.

It was not long before I was settled in for another series of talks and an exchange of views which all helped towards getting to know each other better. We were both, it seemed, idealists and romantics who sought the sanctuary and sanctity of a much better world. For Erika, too, it was the opportunity to express herself in the English language, for her a foreign language in which she excelled, although she had never once been to England. It was clear that she was interested in all things British and here our topic ranged from the sublime to the ridiculous. (Things British, to the unfamiliarized foreigners of those days, appeared all so often to be sublime or ridiculous.)

The hours passed quickly, and again it was well past midnight when I made my departure. Again it had been another evening of pleasant conversation only, with no romantic interludes. When we parted for the night it was with the formal and customary German handshake, not the usual boy/girl goodnight kiss. It may have been that I was inhibited or sexually reserved somehow because of my knowledge of Erika's Berlin experience, or maybe because of my respect for someone who was that bit older than myself. Perhaps also I might have been subconsciously aware of the possible danger of finishing up like one of the Russian officers!

But, even so, I was very consciously happy in the knowledge that I was to meet her again next evening. We had arranged a somewhat cosier set-up for ourselves for our next meeting in that I would provide something special in the way of food, with Erika — through her association with the hotel — being able to produce something special in the way of drink.

The little treat I had in mind for the occasion was a delicious two-tiered party cake which I could obtain, with a little deception, from one of the voluntary service organizations (YMCA/WVS/Church Army — I cannot remember which) recently established somewhere in the RAF encamped area of Gutersloh Airfield which was not so far away. I had earlier discovered that a friendly word with the manageress regarding a 'demob celebration party with the lads' would, after a short while of preparation, bring forth the package of gorgeous confectionery, to be paid for in easily available DMs.

So my next evening with Erika was again a most pleasant one, with the coffee, cake and Steinhager adding much to the enjoyment of the passing hours together. We talked a great deal as usual, with Erika at one point remarking on how she thought that my speech — with its distinctly Welsh accent — had some kind of hypnotic effect on her. I countered by saying I believed it was more a case of me being under the spell of her voice because of its own fascinating and charming accent. The evening, however, had sped by and because of the late hour, was again time to depart. I had behaved as a perfect gentleman in the company of a perfect lady and was completely satisfied that all was at it should be.

I made my way to the door of Erika's room, the outside of which would take me down the stairs and out on to the street via a side door exit. I could let myself out easily without disturbing anyone, as I had done so on my previous departures from the place. This time, however, I had the problem of being unable to open the door to the outside of Erika's room. Erika herself stood watching in thoughtful silence as I tried several times to open the door. I genuinely believed something was mechanically wrong with the catch and was about to make a shoulder lunge at it when I was stopped from doing so by my companion of the evening who came across to gently take hold of my hand. She looked searchingly into my eyes for a moment or two and explained that the door was locked from the outside and could not be opened again until seven o'clock in the morning. I thought it was some kind of joke, and as I rattled at the door again I was quite astonished when she whispered the suggestion that the situation was surely not so bad that I should make a fuss and noise about it. She confessed that she had earlier given instructions to the landlady for the doors — previously left open for me — to be locked on this occasion.

It was a surprise, something I had not expected from Erika, since there never had been the slightest indication that such was her inclination. I recall that my reaction was one of disappointment at seeing the aura of Erika's perfection fading a little. Perhaps I had put her on too high a pedestal. Perhaps also it was that in the course of the evening I had sipped too much of the potent Steinhager and was not quite up to the task which I then faced?

I remember that my attitude over the matter was one of displeasure and grumpiness. I watched almost with strange indifference as Erika undressed herself and got into the bed I was expected to share with her. I had never been backward in coming forward when faced with an appetizing and attractive bit of sex. Here, however, was the choicest and most appetizing gift of all, apparently being spurned as I sat alongside the bed, still dressed and unwilling. Perhaps I was somehow subconsciously upset that I had not in this case taken the initiative — a kind of questioning of male ego and hunter instinct!

I watched, unintentionally cruel as it must have been, Erika's nude postures on the bed as she encouraged me to join her. I had certainly not imbibed that much of the Steinhager to have made me drunk and incapable, but it must, I suppose, have had some part to play in my coolness as I watched almost impassively as she sat, curled or stretched herself on the bed. Her postures and poses, her beautiful face, hair, body — with its soft feminine curves and gleaming fair skin — were pictures to make her a model in a million, yet I remained unmoved and grumpy for some time.

She succeeded eventually in coaxing me to get undressed, but I was uncharacteristically shy about it because of the way she watched and waited. I would only do so with the light turned off. I had, anyway, little choice in the matter of where to sleep, as the double bed took up much of the room.

My attitude that night was for me strange, inexplicable and quite unforgiveable, because when I did climb into bed it was not to make love to Erika but to turn away from her, despite her frenzied display of almost uncontrollable passion and frustration.

The mind of man often plays him strange tricks, with mine just then playing a strange game on both of us. As I resisted Erika's desperate and angry efforts to get me to cooperate, I thought how ridiculously peculiar it was that here was the person who, having shot her way out of a rape attempt by the Russians, was herself now attempting almost to rape me — angry and passionate enough to shoot me for not making love to her! Maybe my subconscious harboured some kind of resentment, for was it not so long ago that the Russians were our friends and allies? Propaganda, after all, sometimes has a deep and lasting effect. As for Erika who resisted on the one hand and insisted on the other, was it not surely a matter of the difference between choice and compulsion — which may have been a little of my trouble too.

For the next few hours I was drowsily and perhaps heartlessly aware of Erika's sighs and tears of disappointment as she tried unsuccessfully to get me to respond to her passionate overtures of love.

I awoke later in the morning after some hours of sound

sleep, and, as I became more consciously aware of the peacefully sleeping figure of the lovely creature close to me, I was saddened by thoughts of my rotten behaviour earlier and was puzzled by it. In contrast, I had suddenly become a different person whose feelings for the girl were those of overwhelming passion and desire. I moved closer with hopes of a forgiving cuddle and a response to my own urgent call for love . . .

Considering the way I humbled and humiliated a very proud and sophisticated young lady, I really deserved no favours whatsoever, or certainly much, much less than the amount of genuine love and affection I had and was to get over the next several weeks. My association with her continued to be as close and desirable as I could have hoped for, particularly so when it soon became obvious that she could have the pick of any one of many officers in the area after her acceptance of a good offer of employment with the military. Her selection and position as superintendent of German labour and employment with local military units had much to do with her ability to speak excellent English and to liaise between the military authority and civil labour attachments. For a German female in those days it was quite a prestigious position, but despite her change of life-style Erika's feelings and attachment to me did not change. We continued to spend a great deal of time with each other, with Erika having a particular fondness for long walks and talks together. That it helped her towards a better knowledge of the English language and English way of life had, I suppose, some part to play in it, but it was also because Erika was a true lover of nature.

It was, as I remember, on one of our walks together when an occasion arose when it became my turn to fire a pistol in a post-war moment of anger, but unlike Erika — and fortunately for me — I did not kill anyone. It started one day when we encountered a degree of hostility as we went arm in arm past a block of houses which were 'end-on' to the lane down which we leisurely strolled. Erika claimed she was aware of it on an earlier occasion as we passed by the same place, but she had then chosen to ignore it and mention nothing to me. This time, however, was an occasion when my hearing and my German was not so bad that I could not understand the words of abuse, hisses and catcalls that came to us from the direction of the houses. I was angry and quite prepared to search around for the guilty party, but was stopped from doing so by Erika. She claimed that the hostility was directed towards her, and probably had something to do with her job and her collaboration with the British. She expressed the view that such people would think and act differently if they, too, had some experience of life in the Russian Zone. She said I should ignore them.

As we went on our way I couldn't help thinking that the sight of a strikingly beautiful Germanic platinum blonde, strolling arm in arm with a British soldier, was one that could easily provoke and make jealous many a German who felt cheated in some way by a war that went against them. I made a mental note of the place, however, and resolved that if it happened again I would most certainly do something about it. It was, after all, the British flag that was flying high now!

The incident was quite forgotten until some time later when, again on one of our walks, we found ourselves along the same road approaching the same spot. The situation was that the block of houses and the road were at right angles, so that the occupants of any one of the three or four houses could see us approaching until we passed at the end of the block. It was the point where we might expect a similar dose as before of the venom from the hissing worms or snakes when on the blind side.

This time, however, I was ready and waiting, and with little thought for Erika's concern or unconcern in the matter, I had already made up my mind what to do. I certainly had the means to do something about it, which was the secret little weapon well-concealed in the inside pocket of my battledress jacket. It was a small flat hand-gun which I had carried around with me for quite a long time, having obtained it through a wartime barter deal (although the war had ended — and with stern prohibitive regulations — there was still the temptation for ex-warriors to carry around the personal weapons obtained as spoils of war). I carried mine because it was easy to conceal, unlike the Luger or army pistol whose bulk could be a packet of trouble if spotted by the experienced eye of an army disciplinarian.

My gun was a deadly little short range killer with a fully

loaded magazine of five bullets. It was not so effective over thirty yards or so, but it was useful perhaps in at least scaring the Hell out of somebody who might not afterwards be so bold with insult and abuse!

There was no mistaking the sinister sounds and nasty noises when they came — almost exactly as before except that this time a couple of loud reports issued from my gun as I aimed to the right of an upper open window of the second nearest house where I spotted the slight, quick movement of the curtains and someone's disappearing head. My shots were followed by a distinct yell coming from the direction of the window. I stood and waited, hoping perhaps for some evidence of fear or submission from within — the sight even of a white flag. A skirmish of some kind was unlikely because such people are usually cowards who avoid the risk of open confrontation. Nothing happened.

Erika, when I caught up with her, was upset and quite cross with me for my pistol action. She previously had no idea that I carried a gun around with me and she was obviously worried because of her own 'gun-slinging past.'

I had no such reservation as did Erika, an hour or so later, about making our return journey along the same route, and although there was an alternative way back I was curious to know the effect of my retaliatory exchange. Going back to the place was the one way to find out. Anyway we Britishers did not win the war, nor should we win the peace, by turning away scared!

We were, however, both a little apprehensive as we neared the place, with myself having hopes that I should not be forced to expend the last three of the five bullets that had for so long been my close companions.

What happened next was something that was to give me a good deal of satisfaction, and for Erika no doubt much less anxiety. Our steps had just about taken us in line with the building when a Frau appeared in front of us waving a white handkerchief. She was wailing and bleating as she threw herself at our feet to clutch pathetically at Erika's clothing, apparently in the act of begging for mercy. I watched as she wailed, howled and babbled away in German, which Erika was able to translate for me. I understood that the woman was apologizing on behalf of herself and her husband, who, I gathered, had his ear clipped by my bullet, was lying doggo and afraid of a similar fate for his other ear. The grovelling Frau bleated out her excuses whilst promising that they would never do such a thing again — so would we please forgive and forget and not shoot any more, etc.

I was pleased to let the matter rest with a final warning — an idle threat of course — that I would bring up a field gun if I got wind of anything like it again from them. I somehow felt sure that the threat was unlikely to be challenged by the miserable cowardly pair!

I must confess, however, to being more than a little surprised to learn that my shot had been *that* close . . . !

My time with Erika and my stay in the area was a period and experience that suited me perfectly for the necessary psychological transition from wartime to peacetime. It is not at all easy for any soldier suddenly to cast off the aggression, fears, rudeness and crudeness etc., after a long spell in the field of battle. Although the war had been ended for a year or so, much of the condition and atmosphere of war still persisted, a good deal of it being still in the minds of people.

But a little of Erika's sophistication began to rub off, for I soon found myself sharing some of her taste in classical art and music, particularly music which for her and most other Germans was very much Beethoven. After all, how could they or why should they feel defeated, humiliated, criticized etc., when they had such a composer whose name and music gave pride, solace and comfort — always the musical spirit and refuge? Lose a war or two, maybe, but nobody, but no one, but nothing could ever take away their Beethoven from them, a treasure supreme that could never be lost!

Germany has never lacked music, musicians or music lovers, and it was therefore to be expected that the 'first signs of life' from war-stricken Germany were the groups who had somehow 'got their strings together again' for a gradual revival of fine bands and orchestras, as for example their Berlin Philharmonic.

And it was, I am sure, this orchestra, or some part of it struggling to reorganize and re-emerge during the early post-war period, that gave an evening concert performance at a place to where I was taken by my Beethoven-mad girl-friend. Erika I well knew to be a person full of surprises, but even so

I was hardly prepared for the surprise of the evening when something happened which was also to prove some of the truth of Erika's Berlin experience. (I write about it because it was one of the two incidents concerning music and art I was to remember as matters worth remembering.) The concert hall was full and crowded, with Erika and myself being seated somewhere in the middle of one of a good few rows from the front. Our faces were just two in a sea of faces, and it therefore astonished me when, during an interlude, Erika was spotted and greeted like a long lost friend by none other than the orchestra's conductor himself.

It was clearly a meeting after long absence of two people who must have been closely acquainted during earlier days in Berlin. From the snatches of conversation I listened to during the interlude, and later after the performance, I gathered that Erika some time in the past had been involved in the music world as a radio presenter, announcer or commentator of some kind. Somehow I was not entirely surprised, although Erika had told me nothing of that part of her life. She was not very forthcoming either when I questioned her later, and I could only put it down to a reluctance to bring too much to the surface because of the Russian incident or episode.

The evening was one that was strange and unforgettable, perhaps not only because of the unexpected coming together of two such personalities, but also because of the atmosphere, audience and music. Altogether it seemed to me, as a kind of outsider or observer, to be a mixture of escapism on the part of an audience suffering post-war degradation, humiliation and weariness, with a musical expression of defiance and exaltation on the part of the orchestra through the composer. Beethoven for salvation, deliverance and Heaven! A religious substitute, perhaps, for the God who seemed to have let them down badly with so much destruction and death.

Equally strange and mysterious was another experience, a short time later, concerning an artist and his painting, which was also to leave a lasting impression. This time an image of a painter and a picture to be stamped almost indelibly on my mind's eye as with the orchestra and music earlier on my mind's ear!

It was through a conversation and chance remark by Erika concerning a portrait pencil sketch, watercolour or oil painting — by which I might be remembered by her — that led to her telling me that someone, somewhere not too far away, might be just the artist with the competence perhaps to oblige with a portrait of reasonable likeness. The reward of a pound or two of coffee or tea would in such hard times tempt any German to give his utmost in any performance of skill and labour. A time, country and situation for bargaining and exploitation, to be sure, when love, music, art, etc. — those non-material things of life — were cheaply available to innumerable exploiters in the armies of Occupation.

Erika gave me the name and address of the artist and said that I should mention her name for the fellow to oblige. She claimed he would remember something she had done for him in the past by way of a good deed. Erika said also that she wanted something of the artist's work, which she had earlier seen and admired. A portrait of me would be the very thing!

I set off, as I remember, for a region within the Ruhr area totally unknown to me. I had some notion of finding someone of an ex-art teacher type who might deliver the goods after a couple of hours or so of a sitting session. That I should be so lucky was not the case, however, and I had great difficulty in finding the fellow whose studio habitat was something of a hovel. After considerable enquiry and search I found both amongst the rubble of war-demolished buildings and streets. I knew Erika was knowledgeable, well-informed and knew strange people, but here I was puzzled as to how on earth she was acquainted with this extreme poverty end of the scale. For poverty it really was that I found when I was admitted into the pathetic dwelling of the two pathetic persons I found living there. The couple were a middle-aged 'Darby and Joan' pair who shuffled around arm in arm in their dingy abode consisting of two rooms which had the daylight reduced because of the partly boarded up glassless windows.

The male half of the pair was a tall gaunt figure who talked slowly and stammeringly in what were mostly mixed syllables of German and English. Surprisingly — perhaps because he did speak so slowly and deliberately and because of my own imitative contribution to the dialogue — we both managed to understand most of the utterances that passed between us.

I was soon to find out that the other half of the pair was an ailing woman, whose illness perhaps was some of the reason why she clung so tightly to the arm of her better (?) half. But it seemed more likely, from what I was able to piece together in our talks, that their clinging together, in a weird kind of arm in arm stance or shuffle, had more to do with a long-standing justifiable fear of separation owing to the persecution of both of them because the woman was a Jewess.

That they had suffered considerable hounding because of the Nazi doctrine of anti-Semitism was all too evident in what I heard and saw; but yet there was no trace of bitterness or hatred apparent in the couple who had been so victimized. Indeed, it would appear that so thorough had been the persecution, brainwashing and hounding that they seemed apologetic even, almost resigned to humiliation and adversity because of their 'sin and guilt' of a mixed marriage (German/Jew) through falling in love. But I had no doubt that bonded together in such a way gave them an indifference to worldly possessions and personalities, and I had the feeling that they would have simply huddled together in a corner, uncommunicative and apprehensive, had I not at the outset gained their confidence by mentioning the name of Erika. I knew that she had been of assistance to them in some way in the past but I was never given the details of the circumstances.

When I explained the reason for my visit, I soon realized that any hope I had of a quick oil painting portrait of myself was a vain one, in more ways than one. Although the old maestro was happy enough to oblige, perhaps as much for Erika's sake as for the promised tea and coffee, it was explained to me that several sittings would be necessary, involving visits over a number of days. He was obviously no dashing dabbler in the painting medium, but rather a painstakingly thorough artist who could only paint with thought, feeling and the blood of his soul. I could see he was a kind of artistic genius who could only work according to his own time, pace and inspiration.

I soon discovered that of the only two rooms in the place, the larger one was the cluttered studio containing pots, paints, brushes, trestles and easels which took up most of the room. A very large canvas on one of the easels was partly hidden by a dust cover. It appealed to my curiosity and I requested that he show me the unfinished work, which I understood was the painting currently taking up most of his time. The canvas on its easel reached up to the ceiling and I was quite shocked and staggered when the old fellow duly obliged to reveal the most amazing picture I had ever seen. My visual senses received a truly astounding impression of grotesque shapes and figures in a horrific crucifixion scene. I remember gazing at the nearly finished picture with a mixture of astonishment, awe, admiration, pity and revulsion. The picture, as it stood on its easel to reach up and touch the ceiling, created a kind of optical illusion of catching motion in the still representation of the uprising cross, to show the startling foreshortened projecting head of Christ with tortured face and upturned eyes.

I remember vividly the short squat Hebrew figures struggling with props, ropes, etc., to raise the cross and the pinned body of Jesus into the upright position. The painting was for me the ultimate in oil and canvas depiction of human cruelty, suffering, tragedy and drama. For me, too, it was artwork of frightening realism, imagination and skill. Such a picture and its artist creator were to keep me thinking for a long time as to whether both would emerge from their obscurity to gain acclaim for the artist and a museum place for the painting. Indeed I was to ponder the question long afterwards — still do — as to 'Where oh where is the painting now?'

Hopes of a portrait however were not realized because I was unable, due to a change in circumstance, to make any further visit to the place.

In the meantime my days with Erika were fast running out, and I had not the heart to tell her of an impending military transfer which would be the definite parting of our ways. Also, with the post-war disbandment of armies and demobilization of troops, my own time was fast approaching when I would have to say 'Goodbye' to Germany and the Germans. Our military codes and orders at that time strongly disfavoured the marriage of a British soldier to a German 'Alien', and in any case the top priority and anxiety of any soldier then was his demob from army service. Recent life and death battles and the harsh conditions of war made every weary warrior dream, above all, of his release from the military ranks and disciplines.

Conditions for love and marriage were therefore not

normal — with many a German girl 'left holding the baby.' Such a literal tragic situation may or may not have been Erika's, but our final parting when it came was not without its pangs of sadness and regret.

Erika knew nothing of my impending move, and I remember that we had a slight tiff just a few days before it was due to happen. The cause of our little difference was some jealousy on my part which showed itself in the objection I made when Erika was invited to some major's farewell party at an officers' mess. I had wanted her to spend that particular evening with me instead, but she felt that because of her job she was under an obligation to attend. I was unreasonably hurt at not having my own way in the matter, and I found it to be a timely and good enough reason to fall out with her for the definite break that was about to happen anyway. I refused to see Erika for the few days remaining since there appeared no point or comfort in settling such a difference just before being parted forever. I reckoned that it was all for the best and that — like those other lovely creatures in my life — I should have to get her quickly out of my mind.

But Erika had her own special little way of getting through to me which was to get a letter to me through a female member of the cookhouse staff who delivered it on a plate with my dinner. I was loathe to read or accept the letter, but was unable to return it to anyone willing to accept. My permanent move from the place was less than twenty-four hours away and I was therefore tempted to tear up the unopened envelope. Instead I crushed it angrily into the pocket of my denim trousers, where it was to remain ignored, unread and forgotten for many days to come.

Eventually, however, when hundreds of miles away at my new and final location, to await repatriation and demob, I happened to turn out the contents of my trouser pocket and discovered the letter, by now at least a couple of weeks old. I opened the letter but soon wished I had not done so because of the sadness, guilt and hopelessness I felt as I read and re-read the lines Erika had written to me.

First she apologized for going to the party against my wishes — she left early it seemed — and hoped that I was not still cross. She then expressed all the love and affection I could have hoped for in writing from anyone, and finally she concluded by saying that she was almost sure that she was expecting a baby — mine! She would, she said, like to see me as soon as possible, hoping that I too would be delighted at such a marvellous likely event . . .

Again, like the peculiar artist and his picture, I was to find myself long afterwards — still do — asking the same question 'Where oh where are they now?'

21

Journey's End — And A Time To Go

I thought the day would never come, but finally the time had arrived. I was to be demobbed from a tented camp which had not long been set up on the hillside overlooking the ancient town of Hamelin, on the River Weser. The ghost of the legendary Pied Piper himself would be around, perhaps, to see me off!

Earlier I had seen the unit move up the hillside, to cut down the wire fences of a desolate area and field — the beginnings of a long-term permanent camp and training area for successive countless REs in Germany. My unit, too, was a comparatively new one, my old wartime field Coy, RE, being disbanded shortly after VJ Day. (I remember all too well the dropping of the first atom bombs on Japan, because at that time I was one of a reformed and re-equipped group of Assault Engineers who were held in a state of readiness, at an airport, for action against the Japanese. Our flight, for the forty-eight hours or so, was delayed, postponed and eventually cancelled because of the impact of the atom bombs on the war with Japan. The bombs, therefore, whilst unmercifully killing many Japanese, were merciful in preventing a planned departure and fate which could have killed me and a great number of British soldiers besides.)

My own demob date coincided with that of OC unit, who was truly the most peculiar officer I had encountered in the whole of my army service. Perhaps my earlier limited experience of OCs had spoiled me somewhat in having had for so long a marvellous OC whose leadership and example, on and off the field of battle, was such as to be totally outstanding. My former OC must — considering the dangerous and lengthy wartime action which involved us both — have had some good part to play in helping me to survive

246

the war. A different Major OC, at a very late stage in my army life, was sure, therefore, to be a different 'kettle of fish' as, indeed, it turned out to be!

I never did know whether the peculiar OC was a Britisher. I understood that much of his earlier life and service had been spent in South Africa, or Rhodesia, in command of native soldiers, which could perhaps explain some of his eccentricities. He seemed to be well above average age for a Major OC.

He was a short little man with a bristling sandy-grey moustache, a fierce-looking pock-marked face with a blue-veined bulbous red nose, above which was a monocle. In appearance he was the perfect comic-opera-monocled-colonel type, except for the ridiculous shortness of his stature. He had a very deep tone of voice and a very deliberate way of speaking, his 'ugh — mm — I see — ah — ah — !' being the deepest, slowest and most deliberate imaginable. His was a truly remarkable voice which gave out the bass reverberating sound of a foghorn which seemed to come right up from the ground floor — which was hardly surprising, really, considering his sound box was not far above it! His voice may have been compensation for his size, for he was able to project it to put fear into the heart of any soldier serving under him. Altogether an unfriendly character and a savage disciplinarian! Among the more unfortunate lower ranks he was known secretly as 'Nickolai the Ridiculai' because of the sound-play on his name. It was also because of a habit he had of playing ridiculous practical jokes and tricks which were anything but funny to anyone else — his retaliation, perhaps, to other people's attitudes and jokes about his own dotty character and appearance!

Usually it was the young inexperienced soldiers who would be fooled and fouled by him, as, for example, the young L/Cpl who told me of the time when he was 'told' to report with great urgency to the 'mad Major.'

Upon reporting, the young NCO was first told to report back a second time with the best vehicle and driver he could immediately find within the unit. The Major explained that he had especially chosen him for a deadly mission and critical task, the success of which was vital to King and country. He was sure he had picked the right man for the job and was therefore giving him all the authority and command to see that the operation was properly carried out, etc.

So, with the truck and driver sorted out, the L/Cpl was soon back to see the Major for orders and instructions concerning the deadly mission. The Major held out a brick-sized package which was neatly wrapped, tied and labelled. It was stamped 'HANDLE WITH EXTREME CARE — Personal and Confidential' and addressed to a particular staff officer at a Divisional HQ located some sixty or so miles away.

The Major instructed that the package was to be delivered as soon as possible to the address and person indicated. It was a package to be protected and guarded at all costs, not to be opened, bumped, lost, damaged etc. The NCO was to carry it personally, and in such a way that it was not to tilt this way or that so as to remain level and safe as possible.

The conscientious young soldier apparently took the task at hand most seriously and was soon on his sixty-mile errand, nervously clutching but holding steady, the precious parcel on his lap. Every bend and pothole in the road were anxieties and balancing acts that made the L/Cpl wish the Major had not held him in such high regard, but picked on someone else for the job instead.

The package was a mysterious item and so clearly very important. The young soldier could only wonder what it might be and pondered on its many possibilities. The REs — according to his brief knowledge of military history — had, after all, been often involved in mysterious and important military work, equipment, weapons, development, etc. For example, was it not the REs who played the founding rôle of the RAF, the submarine service, the Tank Regiment, the Signals Regiment and the REME? Could be, perhaps, that the package he held was some kind of development in the new age of nuclear warfare, such as a fuse, a trigger device, initiating mechanism, detonator or such like for an atom bomb? Better maybe to know nothing about the package — but by God what a relief it would be to get rid of it!

The NCO experienced what must have been the worst journey of his life, all the way worrying and concentrating like mad, one eye on the 'deadly cargo' and the other eye on the road in anticipation of the bumps and turns of the vehicle.

The journey finally came to an end with the weary soldier

desperately anxious to contact the officer who would relieve him of a duty and mission which had put years on his young life in just a few hours. To this end he was taken along the long corridors of power at the Div HQ, where at last he came face to face with the staff officer concerned, who was sitting at his desk. He was a cheerful officer who acknowledged the young soldier's salute and delivery with a friendly wave of his hand and some kind words of thanks for the trouble taken.

The L/Cpl watched first with apprehension then with fascination and finally with stunned incredulity as the officer in front of him hurriedly tore open the parcel to expose nothing more mysterious or sinister than a pack of officers' mess invitation cards for a Regimental 'do' within the Division. 'Just the job!' said the officer, having examined the cards. 'Tell your OC I shall be ringing him to thank him personally. Dismiss, Corporal!'

And so another dupe was added to the Mad Major's long list of those who had been 'had' in similar and other ways.

I relate the above incident as an example of the different kind of military company and character I had at the end of my services. Hardly the heroic types of my earlier days — but then, of course, the testing days of war were over, and with them the spirit and camaraderie that only war and battle can produce and engender.

It was the day of my demob, with everything about the unit and OC 'nut' adding a delicious flavour to the eagerness and pleasure I felt at soon being off and away on a one-way journey to dear old Blighty and my native Wales.

Both the Major and myself would finally depart the tented camp around the same time in the early afternoon on scheduled demobees transport. But thanks to the Major the morning was not to be one wasted in idleness, or doing the handshaking rounds, and the saying of goodbyes to old pals, etc. Instead he had taken it upon himself to deal with the case of two young soldiers — green arrivals from the UK — who were jointly charged with a petty military offence. The Major could so easily have let the matter rest in the capable hands of his Captain 2 I/C, who was anyway OC (or acting) designate, but decided not to do so.

I had, for the few days prior to my release, been given a clerical task in the unit Orderly Room (tent) and it was myself who set up a table, chair and 'bibles' for the disciplinary hearing of the case. In the process of doing so I overheard a conversation between the two officers. The 2 I/C, it seemed, already had the exonerating explanations of the two young soldiers, and he wished to drop the charge against them. The Major on the other hand, was all for discipline for discipline's sake, insisting that it was the 'spice' of a young soldier's life, a bit of pushing around, a charge of two now and again with some CB or 'Jankers' thrown in, were all part of good military training for young soldiers; but for the veteran soldier, of course, like... (I heard my own name mentioned) it was different, people like (me) had come to the end of a very long road, having gone through the war, and warranted different respect and treatment, and whereas the road for one had ended, it was for the others just starting, with perhaps a new and more deadly war not far along the way. The Russians, after all, could start something any day, and the Middle East was hotting up, and so the new intakes of British soldiers should be properly trained, hardened and disciplined. There should be no 'end of war psychology' for them!

I reckoned that there could be some logic in the old fellow's 'madness' after all. But I had my doubts a short time later — just an hour or two before the final departure of both of us — when I was the detailed 'silent witness' at the disciplinary hearing of the two unfortunate accused offenders.

The case against them — riding three in a vehicle cab contrary to Army rules and regulations, etc. — was clearly a poor one since there was every justification, considering the circumstances, for doing so. The Major had no option but to dismiss the case against them. But he was not to be outdone, however, for he almost immediately demanded that they be brought back to face the new charges he instructed the CSM to make out against them i.e. contrary to good conduct and military discipline etc. being unkempt on parade — one whose haircut was not up to the Major's liking and the other whose morning shave was also not up to the Major's satisfaction. Both soldiers were found guilty and each given fourteen days CB, confined to barracks.

The matter is of interest, perhaps, if only for the very good reason of recalling what was to be my final act of regimental duty of Army service, which was replacing the table, chair and the Army's two 'bibles' — Manual of Military Law and King's Rules and Regulations. Altogether strange — when I later came to think about it — that fate, or the 'somebody up there' who pushed the buttons on my behalf, decided that my last act of duty before setting off for 'home sweet home' was to shelve and set aside the most authoritative symbols and embodiments of Army power — the MML and KRRs which together are the 'joint masters' of all serving soldiers! A most appropriate sign and confirmation that I was freed from military bondage and commitment!

And so my joyous ride to the Celestial City of Civvy Street began. It was a journey to be made in three stages, the first being at a transit camp in Germany, another at a transit camp at the 'Hook of Holland' before embarking for the UK, and finally the actual demob depot in the UK for the necessary procedures and issues for civilian life — clothes, documents etc.

I departed on the first stage of my demob journey with all the mixed thoughts, feelings and emotions of one whose mind and heart were too full of the pains and ecstasies experienced for so long as a serving soldier. Or was it perhaps not such a long time, August '41 to December '46? Perhaps the real truth of the time was in the events and experiences which —

'Crowd Eternity into an hour
Or stretch an hour into Eternity.'

Knowing as I moved away that an amazing chapter in my life was at its close was, I suppose, a reason for looking back on it and hosting a flood of memories. Such memories as I then had were of a sort worthy and unworthy of remembrance, those to be easily forgotten later or those later to be easily brought to mind. Some have already been recalled and recounted within these pages, while others of incidents and images, equally memorable, will be untold because of the limit of time and space, or detailed in another volume. Memories, for example, of our 'Corridor' run towards Nijmagen and Arnhem; tasks and experiences in the Ardennes, The Battle of the Bulge; of seeing a train bomb-damaged, crippled and struggling to move out from the war-wrecked station of München Gladbach, being so overloaded with refugees that young children were pushed and falling from the roofs, buffers and broken windows of the train; of ashen faces of cold and starving kiddies pressed flat against windows to watch 'Tommies' enjoy their own treat (at the time) of a wad and a cuppa within the shelter and warmth of an SA or CA canteen; of watching a German family preparing their own treat of ersatz coffee — the brew of roasted ground acorns sweetened with the pulp-juice of sugar beet; of spending a day with a friendly German family whose offerings for meal times could not extend beyond fried apple for breakfast, stewed apple for dinner and roast apple for tea thanks to the garden trees and season's bounty; of seeing a couple of German Army prisoners of war, an Aryan-type and a Mongol-type, fight nearly to the death after having a tin of bully beef and a blanket thrown over into their barbed wire pen; of witnessing the release of prisoners, some who had been taken at Crete, from the Stalag at Fallingboxtel; of seeing the Belsen Concentration Camp soon after it was freed; of seeing homeless people, deprived and despairing but still turning up for Sunday church spotlessly clean and determined to 'keep up with the Schmidts.'

With many such memories I should be sorry in many ways to be leaving Germany and the Germans. My own particular war with them had been as fair as a war could be, and now, towards the very end of it all, I was more inclined to shake hands than spit. No nation of people could have given more or suffered more in the way of patriotism — even if misguided!

The first stage of my journey was completed, and involved a very brief stay at a barracks well-placed and organized as a reception station for personnel in transit for demob. There were certainly enough orders and instructions about the place, not this time about military training and efficiency as a soldier, but rather about demilitarization and how to be a good civilian. One poster plastered around the place had me a bit worried in the way it visually screamed out about handing in all personal weapons. 'Surrender your weapons now — Demob at risk — is it worth the risk?, etc.' I was worried because of the little pistol I still carried around with me inside my jacket, also the pair of admiral's dirks carried in my kitbag, both gun and dirks referred to in earlier chapters. I had carried them around with me for too long to part with them too easily. In any case one of the dirks was at the top of my kitbag with the other awkwardly placed at the bottom.

It seemed altogether unfair that such items should have been classed in the same category as bayonets, swords, pistols. In modern warfare such items could surely only be for ceremonial and decorative purposes. A fine pair of souvenirs, to be sure, but were they really worth the risk of jeopardizing my release date?

But despite a good deal of concern in the matter I was still in possession of my weapons when I arrived at stage two, being the port of embarkation for the UK, the Hook of Holland. Here I found even more insistent and threatening posters about weapons, ammunition and explosives. It was made quite clear that the penalties were severe for any serviceman caught smuggling such items into the UK. But, of course, it made good sense when one considered the matter fully. Civilian life might not be so peacefully attractive after all if World War Two ex-servicemen were allowed a discretion in the matter. The problem, it seemed to me, was the little time and teaching in preliminaries for resettlement and adjustment of such aggressive military characters for civilian life – how to get the military training and war experience out of their systems. For some, perhaps, only the passage of time would be the answer, and for others, maybe impossible and never!

I decided that my pistol and dirks would have to go. My time to embark the ship for Harwich and the UK was drawing near and, because of my reluctance earlier to part with the weapons, I was rather late and hard-pressed to ditch them somewhere. But at last, and almost with tears in my eyes as I thought about their inglorious end, I reached up high to drop them into the cistern flushpan of a ramshackle toilet hut I found close by. Hardly the kind of wall decoration I earlier had in mind for the gleaming admiral's ceremonial dress dirks!

But who knows that perhaps a similar inglorious end was also the admiral's who once wore them so proudly.

For me, though, the end of my time in the Service was much less inglorious – at least the Army testimonial I got was nothing to be ashamed of and was (is) as follows:

'...has served in the REs for the past five years during which time he has proved himself to be a hard-working and gallant soldier.

He has been mentioned in Despatches and also awarded a certificate from the Commander-in-Chief for gallantry in the field during the European Campaign. He is honest, sober and has a cheerful personality.' (The above assessment given on his release 11.12.46) Serial No. 8319 AFB108D

As for my little bronze oak leaf (MID) not mentioned in earlier chapters, well... I honestly have no idea what it was for!

95